# State-Corporate Crime and the Commodification of Victimhood

T0298718

This book highlights the continuing impunity enjoyed by corporations for large-scale crimes and in particular the crime of toxic waste dumping in Ivory Coast in 2006. It provides an account of the crime and outlines contributory reasons for the impunity both under the law and from a criminological point of view. Furthermore, the book reveals the retrogressive role of civil society organisations (CSOs) in Ivory Coast, contrary to expectations made of 'non-governmental' organisations (NGOs) and CSOs.

This book reveals that in the case of this particular example of state-corporate crime, civil society as an agency of censure and sanction actually played a distinctly retrogressive role. Here, in fact, state and state-corporate crime facilitates corruption within the civil society sphere through a process referred to in the book as the 'commodification of victimhood' and, as a result, ensures that impunity is virtually guaranteed for the corporation and the Ivorian government. This book also examines the failure of international and domestic legal measures to sanction the perpetrators alongside civil society's shortcomings and ultimately advocates a more cautionary approach to civil society's potential to label, censure and sanction large-scale state-corporate crime.

This book will help readers understand the difficulties in sanctioning such crime as well as promoting the theoretical framework of state crime, the understanding of which could lead to the alleviation of human suffering at the hands of deviant states and corporations.

**Thomas MacManus** is a Research Fellow and concentrates on the crimes of the powerful. He is based at the International State Crime Initiative (ISCI, statecrime.org) in the Department of Law at Queen Mary University of London (www.law.qmul.ac.uk/). He is admitted as an attorney-at-law (New York) and solicitor (Ireland). He is an editor in chief of *State Crime Journal*, and joint editor of *Amicus Journal: Assisting Lawyers for Justice on Death Row*. He is a director of the Colombia Caravana (www.colombiancaravana.org.uk/).

## Crimes of the Powerful
Edited by Gregg Barak
*Eastern Michigan University, United States*
Penny Green
*Queen Mary University of London, UK*
Tony Ward
*Northumbria University, UK*

**Crimes of the Powerful** encompasses the harmful, injurious, and victimizing behaviors perpetrated by privately or publicly operated businesses, corporations, and organizations as well as the state mediated administrative, legalistic, and political responses to these crimes.

The series draws attention to the commonalities of the theories, practices, and controls of the crimes of the powerful. It focuses on the overlapping spheres and inter-related worlds of a wide array of existing and recently developing areas of social, historical, and behavioral inquiry into the wrongdoings of multinational organizations, nation-states, stateless regimes, illegal networks, financialization, globalization, and securitization.

These examinations of the crimes of the powerful straddle a variety of related disciplines and areas of academic interest, including studies in criminology and criminal justice; law and human rights; conflict, peace, and security; and economic change, environmental decay, and global sustainability.

# State-Corporate Crime and the Commodification of Victimhood

## The Toxic Legacy of Trafigura's Ship of Death

Thomas MacManus

Routledge
Taylor & Francis Group

LONDON AND NEW YORK

First published 2018
by Routledge

2 Park Square, Milton Park, Abingdon, Oxfordshire OX14 4RN
52 Vanderbilt Avenue, New York, NY 10017

*Routledge is an imprint of the Taylor & Francis Group, an informa business*

First issued in paperback 2020

*British Library Cataloguing-in-Publication Data*
A catalogue record for this book is available from the British
Library

*Library of Congress Cataloging-in-Publication Data*
A catalog record has been requested for this book

ISBN: 978-0-8153-8153-2 (hbk)
ISBN: 978-0-367-48210-7 (pbk)

Typeset in Bembo
by Apex CoVantage, LLC

Have you built your ship of death, O have you?

O build your ship of death, for you will need it.

*Extract from* The Ship of Death *by D. H. Lawrence (1933)*

Perhaps it was inevitable that the main media focus during [the *Probo Koala*] affair was on the allegations of harm from the waste. For the company's management, though, it was a struggle for survival, and one that it came through. Trafigura had continued support throughout from its extensive network of banks.

*Extract from trafigura.com (2015)*

# Contents

# Maps

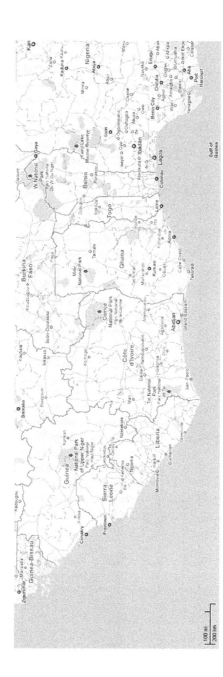

Map 0FM.1 West Africa

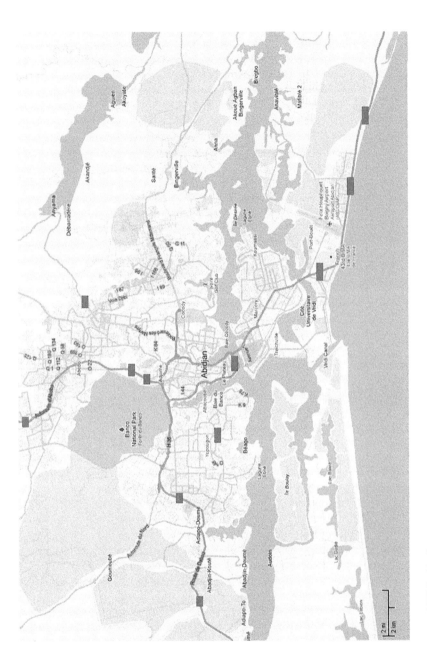

*Map 0FM.2* Abidjan

Map data: Google

# Acknowledgements

This book could not have been completed without the help and support of Kris Lasslett and Tony Ward, my Ivorian guide Adjé, the Law School at King's College London, and my PhD cohort at Melbourne House. This book was only made possible by the continuing support of my PhD supervisor, Penny Green. And a special thanks to my wonderful family, especially my wife, Celina.

# List of acronyms

## Ivory Coast non-governmental organisations (NGOs)

| | |
|---|---|
| AI CI | Amnesty Intentional Côte d'Ivoire |
| APDH | Action pour la Protection des Droits de l'Homme |
| CEFCI | Centre Feminin pour la Democratie et les Droits Humains en Côte d'Ivoire |
| Club UA | Club Union Africaine Côte d'Ivoire |
| FIDHOP | La Fondation Ivoirienne pour les Droits de l'Homme et la Vie Politique |
| LIDHO | Ligue Ivoirienne des Droits de l'Homme |
| MIDH | Mouvement Ivoirien des Droits Humains |
| OFACI | Organisation des Femmes Actives de Côte d'Ivoire |
| RAIDH | Regroupement des Acteurs Ivoiriens des Driots Humains |
| WANEP | West African Network for Peacebuilding Côte d'Ivoire |

## Ivory Coast victims' organisations

| | |
|---|---|
| CNVDT | Coordination Nationale des Victimes des Déchets Toxiques de Côte d'Ivoire |
| FAVIDET | Fédération des Associations de Victimes de Déchets Toxiques de Côte d'Ivoire |
| FENAVIDET | Fédération Nationale des Victimes des Déchets Toxiques de Côte d'Ivoire |
| RENADVIDET | Réseau National pour la Défense des Droits des Victimes des Déchets Toxiques |
| UVDTAB | Union des Victimes des Déchets Toxiques d'Abidjan et Banlieue |
| VUCAH | Victime Unies contre les Catastrophes Humaines |

# Chapter 1

# Introduction
## Applying a criminological framework

On the night of Saturday, 19 August 2006, more than one hundred gallons of toxic waste were dumped in various sites around the coastal city of Abidjan, Ivory Coast. The next morning local residents awoke to a foul, overpowering stench, and many people quickly developed serious health problems. The source of the noxious smell and associated illnesses was initially unknown, and panic soon spread throughout the city. Rumours started to circulate that a large ship had brought waste to the city, and that this was the source of the sickness. This 'ship of death' – as it was to become known locally – departed a few days later with the assistance of the port authorities, leaving sixteen people dead and potentially hundreds of thousands poisoned.

The offending tanker ship, the *Probo Koala*, had been chartered by Trafigura – an enormous transnational commodities trader. The waste was the by-product of a widely banned chemical process, known as 'caustic washing', undertaken by Trafigura on board the *Probo Koala* and designed to produce low-grade marketable oil from a cheaper, practically unsellable oil product. The caustic washing process is banned in the European Union (EU), the United States and Singapore because of the hazardous nature of the waste produced. The company appears to have been well aware of this fact, as revealed by leaked emails between the Trafigura CEO and some of his subordinate commodities traders in London. Trafigura had previously tried to offload the toxic by-product in Amsterdam and Lagos but was unsuccessful. Frustrated by a lack of low-cost solutions to its waste problem, the corporation ultimately engaged a small-time, fledgling Ivorian company called *Société Tommy* ('Tommy') to 'get rid of' the waste in Abidjan.

You may not have heard some of the details of this crime. Since the dumping, the corporation has deployed a wide range of measures to deny, neutralise and cover up any evidence pointing towards its involvement in the poisoning. This strategy has been largely successful, and to date Trafigura has encountered no significant sanctions for its actions. However, attempts have been made, with varying degrees of success, to extract compensatory damages from the corporation.

In 2007, in a surprise move, the Ivorian government imprisoned two Trafigura executives, "until the firm agreed, without admitting liability, to pay US$200m for a clean-up" (Leigh 2009a). This settlement was duly paid and on its legally dubious terms thereafter immunised Trafigura and its agents from any criminal prosecution by the Ivorian state (TCE 2009). The clean-up was never completed (Tiembre et al. 2009), and a sizable portion of the settlement money has reportedly since been squandered. Twelve hours after the payment was made, three Trafigura officials were freed from prison (Associated Press 2008). The lack of due legal process and the subsequent release of the captives almost immediately after payment of a 'ransom' suggest that the detention of the Trafigura executives by the Ivorian state was more like a high-level shake-down than a legitimate form of legal sanction. Although two directors were detained, no representatives from Trafigura were ever tried for the crime in Ivory Coast (Coulibaly 2008), and Ivorian prosecutors focused only on those who were not afforded the protection of the corporation or the state.

Salomon Ugborugbo, the Nigerian director of Tommy, was arrested in Ivory Coast shortly after the incident, and in October 2008 he received a twenty-year sentence for 'poisoning'. The prosecution had asked for a life sentence. Ivorian shipping agent Desire Kouao received a five-year sentence for 'complicity' in relation to the same charge (Coulibaly 2008). They were the only two people sentenced for the dumping by the Ivorian courts (NBC 2008; Leigh 2009b; Greenpeace 2010). Five customs officials, the Abidjan port's military commander and its maritime director were acquitted (NBC 2008). The Ivorian criminal justice system did not seek to attach criminal liability for the dumping beyond the prosecution of these individuals.

Traditionally, criminal law concerns itself only with individuals as perpetrators – but some domestic legal systems have embraced a concept of organisational liability for corporate crime; in Europe the company faced legal challenges from multiple sources.

In the Netherlands the *Probo Koala*'s Ukrainian captain, Sergiy Chertov, received a five-month suspended sentence and €25,000 fine for his role in violations of Dutch and EU law.[1] Trafigura was fined €1 million by the Dutch court in July 2010[2] for breaching Dutch criminal law (in relation to environmental crime), EU waste export environmental laws and concealing the nature of the waste. A case against Claude Dauphin (Trafigura's CEO at the time of the dumping and who has since died in 2015) launched in May 2007 was dropped late in 2012 by the Dutch prosecution team in exchange for a €67,000 fine (van Wingerde 2015).

In the UK about 30,000 victims of the dumping sued Trafigura in a civil case known as *Motto & Ors v Trafigura*, the largest personal injury claim ever filed with England and Wales Courts (Dunt 2009). However, in September 2009, Trafigura reached an out-of-court settlement agreement which included payment to victims and their families of about USD$1,000 each (Leigh 2009c; Moore 2009). This settlement precluded any legal sanction for wrongdoing being applied to Trafigura by ensuring that the facts of the dumping were not considered by a law court and therefore not exposed to public scrutiny. Furthermore, it included a joint statement by both sides denying the liability of Trafigura for the dumping as well as including a confidentiality agreement which swears the claimants' UK lawyers to secrecy.

It is clear then that the company enjoyed a high degree of impunity. A UN investigation confirmed that the dumping caused the death of sixteen people and injuries to thousands of others (UNHRC 2009), but the crime did not attract any significant legal, or other, sanction in the UK (from where the dumping was directed), Ivory Coast (where the dumping took place) nor under any other jurisdiction that was involved along the way. The British Crown Prosecution Service (CPS) passed the buck to the UK Environment Agency who refused to investigate the crime due to "limited experience of complex investigations" compounded by a lack of "appropriately skilled and experienced staff". Furthermore, the Environmental Agency's cost-benefit analysis recommended against pursuing the issue due to fears that Trafigura would probably throw money and aggressive lawyers at the problem and "take any and every procedural opportunity to challenge steps taken in a further investigation", which would push the agency beyond its financial means (Ball and Davies 2015). This was a kowtow by a British government institution to the raw cash power of Trafigura.

The level of impunity enjoyed by Trafigura, given the seriousness of the crime and the resultant harm, is curious and raises some fundamental questions relating not only to the behaviour of the corporation but also to the role of the Ivory Coast state in facilitating Trafigura's deviant practise, the failure of international and domestic criminal law, and the lacklustre response of global and local civil society as a social audience.

To attempt to understand the processes through which a well-publicised crime by a powerful corporation attracts impunity, I employ here criminological theory. Whereas the law is useful at interpreting and enforcing social norms, through the enactment of laws in parliament based upon some consideration of public will and the meting out punishment in courts, most criminal law systems are not adapted to deal with crimes that are organisational in nature (Alvesalo and Whyte 2007; Hillyard and Tombs 2007). International criminal law applies in practise only to individuals.[3] Similarly human rights law is generally not the concern of corporations. This is despite the efforts of the United Nations (UN) and its special rapporteur, John Ruggie, who has strongly urged corporations to voluntarily 'respect' human rights.[4]

The deficiency in domestic and international law may not simply be an oversight or mere technicality. Critical criminologists have long focused on "the power of privileged segments of society to define crime, and to support enforcement of laws in accord with their particular interests" (Friedrichs and Schwartz 2007: 4). In a global economy where states vie to attract corporate investment, it would be counter-productive to enforce a strong regulatory regime that may deter the big players. Thus criminal justice systems have an inherent tendency to avoid the prosecution of powerful organisations for corporate and state-corporate crimes. Criminology does not suffer the same aversion to thinking along organisational lines, and Kauzlarich and Kramer (1998) argue that organisations can and should be considered as actors capable of 'deviancy' for the purposes of a criminological enquiry.

Now, 'deviance' is a theoretically loaded term, and the framework of symbolic interactionism which underpins the concept[5] will not be revisited here. Instead, following Green and Ward's (2004) and Ward's (2004) formulation of deviance as *a breach of a social norm or standard of behaviour that is accepted by a social audience*, this monograph seeks to survey how human rights organisations can act as a labelling and sanctioning social audience. Borrowing again from Green and Ward's (2004) and Ward's (2004) formulation of deviance, impunity is defined here as a failure to apply significant sanctions (i.e., significant from the point of view of the criminal actor) to violations of norms that are accepted as a standard of behaviour by a social audience. The relevant standards, or norms, are predominantly legal rules, like international and domestic criminal, human rights and environmental law, but the norms of social morality as interpreted by domestic and international human rights and 'green' (or environmental) organisations are also duly considered. Human rights and environmental NGOs are concerned with accepted standards of behaviour and are disposed to both expose and apply sanctions to violators. The sanctions that these NGOs may apply include the pursuit of criminal and civil legal punishments and widespread censure through open letters, press releases, campaigns and reports that may damage the corporation's domestic and international reputation and thereby impact net profit.

The determining elements of crime, according to Henry (2006), are that someone has been harmed, there is social agreement that they have been harmed and there is an 'official societal' response (2006: 76). Corporate crime, at the most general level, is committed by a corporation (or individuals acting on behalf of the corporation) in furtherance of the organisation's goals[6] (Erman and Lundman 1978; Coffee 1980). Tombs and Whyte adopt a more precise and legally framed definition: "illegal acts or omissions, punishable by the state under administrative, civil or criminal law, which are the result of deliberate decision-making or culpable negligence within a formal organisation" (2006: 74). The main criminological study of corporations comes under the overlapping subject headings of corporate crime and state-corporate crime.

Since the pioneering work of Ronald Kramer, Ray Michalowski and David Kauzlarich, corporate criminality has increasingly been linked to the state. In criminology terms the behaviour of Trafigura and the states that helped it along the way can be understood as a 'state-corporate crime'. State-corporate crime is defined as deviant acts (or omissions) that cause human rights violations as a result of a mutually reinforcing interaction between (1) policies and/or practises in pursuit of the goals of one or more institutions of political governance and

(2) policies and/or practises in pursuit of the goals of one or more institutions of economic production and distribution (Kramer et al. 2002, as modified by Green and Ward 2004). This book is primarily concerned with state-corporate crime and reveals the significance of the state's interaction with the corporation in facilitating the crime and in ensuring impunity for the corporate perpetrator at a domestic legal level. The state-corporate crime paradigm, as opposed to criminal law definitions, allows for the study of actions that are neither legislated for nor enforced by legal systems and instead relies on the concept of deviance.

Green and Ward's (2004) modification of Kramer et al.'s (2002) definition of state-corporate crime requires a deviant act that violates human rights as a result of an interaction between states and corporations. The presence or absence of a deviant label does not, in itself, impact on the nature of the act (Sykes 1978) as "deviance is *not* a quality of the act ... but rather a consequence of the application by others of rules and sanctions to an 'offender'" (Becker 1963: 9). However, the circumstances surrounding the act are not wholly independent of the reaction. Downes and Rock argue:

> It is not simply the presence of deviance but its quality, scale and location which typically shape a reply ... It is only when it is inexplicable, disordering, harmful or threatening that a gross reaction can take place.
>
> (Downes and Rock 2003: 187)

It might be expected that the dumping in Ivory Coast would prompt a 'gross reaction' from social audiences (such as NGOs). It was initially inexplicable, caused death, serious injury and widespread environmental damage, and led to panic but is to this day somewhat shrouded in mystery.

It is precisely the nature of the reaction, or lack thereof, that this book seeks to explore. The continuing impunity enjoyed by Trafigura and the Ivorian state since the dumping is evidenced by the distinct lack of legal reaction or censure from the Ivorian state, foreign states or the international community. Furthermore, local organisations sought to exploit victim-survivors, which compounded their injures. This book aims to shed light on this phenomenon by studying the complex mechanisms and institutions through which impunity was both nurtured and propagated. The roles of corporation, implicated states and civil society are thus at the centre of an analysis which has at its core the anatomy of the dumping incident – from the organisational decisions that led to it through to the multiple consequences which reverberated from it.

Research of this nature is not without its difficulties. There were, of course, the anticipated barriers of corporate and state secrecy and the obfuscations of power which all empirical scholars of state crime and corporate crime encounter (Tombs and Whyte 2002). Why would a corporation, whose actions have been deemed criminal or deviant, allow researchers access to its personnel and its documentation of internal communications? The same question may be asked of states, which are "likely to be even more tightly sealed from outside scrutiny where the aim is to investigate actual or possible illegality" (Tombs and Whyte 2002). Leaked internal documents and emails between Trafigura employees (including the CEO, traders, subsidiaries and the captain of the chartered *Probo Koala*) allowed for greater insight into the crime than would normally be expected.

Access to civil society is generally an easier task, and a field trip to Ivory Coast was particularly illuminating. My fieldwork was also to throw up unanticipated cultural challenges related to misapprehension, trust and deception. In my first week in the country, at a checkpoint on Pont General de Gualle, I was given the choice of a trip to the local police station or a 20,000 Francs (de la Communauté Financière Africaine [CFA]) fine (about €30) by an armed, uniformed young man. I took the 'fine' and put it down to field trip expenses.

To triangulate fieldwork data it was necessary to consult a variety of corroborating sources, and these included official documentation in the form of official and unofficial reports, journalistic accounts, Internet-based resources, internal organisational artefacts, supplementary interviews, leaked data and personal observations.

## Chapter outline

Chapter 2 examines the origin of Trafigura, the corporation, and details the dumping incident. The dumping precipitated further crimes, and the state of Ivory Coast acted as a nexus between the market, organised crime and civil society sectors. The corporate criminal dumping could not have been committed without the tacit approval and collaboration of state actors. The victims created by the state-corporate crime of dumping are further exploited as a result of state-organised crime, again facilitated by the Ivorian state. Chapter 2 also introduces the role of denial in Trafigura's criminal trajectory. Three forms of denial are identified, operating at both the individual and organisational level of corporate, state and organised malfeasance. Drawing on Cohen's elucidation of denial in state crimes, the chapter examines denial of history, denial of fact, and the employment of "excuses, justifications, rationalisations or neutralisations" (Cohen 1993: 110). Denial and cover-up are frequently indicative of deviant behaviour (Green and Ward 2004) but do not, in themselves, equate to deviance. Denial can, however, be engaged in to avoid exposure of acts to an audience to avoid or 'neutralise' the effects of a deviant label. And Green and Ward (2004) argue that "deviant behaviour is not only that which other people so label, but that which the actors conceal because of their anticipation of how a social audience would label it if it became known" (Green and Ward 2004: 20).

Chapter 3 will look at possible explanations for the staggering impunity enjoyed by Trafigura and the Ivorian state due to failures of law enforcement and asks whether civil society could act as an effective censuring and sanctioning mechanism for crime in lieu of ineffective state systems. Criminal legal systems deploy various tactics to avoid the prosecution of corporate harms, and critical criminologists have focused on the power of privileged segments of society to frustrate any meaningful application of criminal law to state-corporate crime. The dumping of toxic waste in Ivory Coast provides an illuminating case study of the potential and limitations of civil society's role in the censure and sanction of state and state-corporate crime, and the last section of this chapter explores the potential of civil society as a mechanism for sanctions against powerful offenders.

Chapter 4 looks more closely at a theoretical framework for understanding civil society and details the modest successes and catastrophic failures of Ivorian and global civil society in relation to the toxic waste dumping incident.

Chapter 5 reveals some surprising findings of this study: the emergence of 'victims' organisations as organised crime networks. The victims' organisations which flourished in the wake of the toxic dumping turned out to be in the business of producing victimhood for a fee. This chapter looks at the genesis and development of these victims' organisations and argues that these would-be 'champions of the people' are in fact criminal organisations engaged in the 'commodifiction of victimhood'.

Chapter 6 explores the value of Cohen's (1993) three forms of state crime denial in understanding the criminal nature of events and relationships associated with Trafigura's toxic waste dumping. The chapter examines the attempt by mainstream British media to censure Trafigura and a 30,000-claimant personal injury case filed against the corporation in London. Both attempts at censure or sanction reveal the formidable power of a corporation engaged in denial and the 'barriers of denial' enshrined in the UK legal system.

Chapter 7 (Conclusion) argues that this criminological case study contributes to the empirical literature on state and state-corporate crime and should be added to a growing library of scholarship in the field. The chapter explains how this book modestly develops our understanding of the means by which powerful entities are able to avoid censure and punishment and suggests new directions of research for criminology. The chapter warns that one must take a more cautionary approach to civil society's capacity to label, censure and sanction than that suggested by Green and Ward (2004).

## Notes

1 See District Court of Amsterdam, case number LJN BN 2068 (Trafigura Employee), http://jure.nl/bn2068.
2 See District Court of Amsterdam, case number LJN BN 2149 (Trafigura), http://jure.nl/bn2149.
3 Rome Statute of the International Criminal Court, 17 July 1998.
4 Report of the Special Representative of the Secretary General on the issue of human rights and transnational corporations and other business enterprises, 21 March 2011 (A/HRC/17/31).
5 See Charon, J. M. (2007) *Symbolic Interactionism: An Introduction, an Interpretation, Integration*, Upper Saddle River: Pearson Prentice Hall and Meltzer, B. N., Petras, J. W. and Reynolds, L. T. (1975) *Symbolic Interactionism: Genesis, Varieties, and Criticism*, Boston: Routledge and Kegan Paul.
6 White collar crime, on the other hand, is committed by an individual (usually to the detriment of his or her employer corporation) in furtherance of personal goals.

# Chapter 2

# State-corporate crime
## Origins of the 'ship of death'

In the Spring of 2006, a consignment of coker naphtha, a 'heavy' oil with a high sulphur content produced as a by-product of some refinery operations, was transported through the United States from the Mexican Cadereyta refinery and was loaded onto a Trafigura-chartered, Panama-registered ship, the *Probo Koala*. On board this ship, the coker naphtha was mixed with caustic soda in a rudimentary refining process which produced a hazardous by-product. Once the 'caustic washing' was completed, the toxic waste was pumped into 'slop' tanks designed to store excess oil and water. The cleaned oil was then blended with other oil products to make it marketable. The destination of the cheap oil product was Estonia, and on its way there the *Probo Koala* stopped to refuel at Amsterdam. According to Dutch judicial records the company attempted to dispose of the toxic waste while docked in Amsterdam by passing it off as standard ship's slops. The Dutch port rejected the waste (Böhler 2009). This rejection, and the subsequent reloading of waste onto the *Probo Koala*, was contrary to EU rules designed to restrict the export of toxic waste and to curtail any possibility of dumping in countries with weak regulatory regimes. Trafigura made further attempts to arrange for the waste to be unloaded elsewhere (including Tunisia and Nigeria) before finally deciding to berth, unload and dump 550 cubic metres of the waste in Abidjan, Ivory Coast. Trafigura's choice of disposal method was at all times dictated by the search for a cheap way to offload or outsource the waste, and the consequences of the dumping is indicative of what happens when "criminal profiteers seek low-cost solutions" (Knauer et al. 2006: 2).

The dumping was a complex event, spanning half the globe and involving multiple political and economic organisations. The results were catastrophic. Achim Steiner, director of United Nations Environment Programme (UNEP), argues that the dumping was "a particularly painful example of how illegal waste disposal causes human suffering" (quoted in Knauer et al. 2006: 2).

This chapter offers a detailed narrative of how the Trafigura corporation reportedly created lethal toxic waste by processing a cheap oil product from Mexico and, with the support of key sections of the Ivorian state, offloaded that waste in Abidjan, Ivory Coast in August 2006. Much of what we know about the dumping arises from the documentation and exposure provided by civil society actors and is catalogued here to illuminate the criminal collusion between Trafigura and the Ivorian state. The chapter will track the decision-making by Trafigura agents and will follow the waste's path from off the coast of Gibraltar and Malta (where caustic washing took place aboard the *Probo Koala*) to sites around Abidjan, Ivory Coast.

There was direct collusion between Trafigura and elements of Ivory Coast state apparatus, both of which were pursuing deviant organisational goals, and the impunity which follows from this relationship, which effectively stifles regulatory control and formal sanction, forms the core of the elaborate anatomy of the overarching crime.

It will also be demonstrated in this chapter that Trafigura employees used 'implicatory denial' (Cohen 1993) to organise the dumping in the face of warning signs that the results may be potentially damaging to the health of the local population.

What follows is the story of the toxic waste, from its source underground in Mexico to its victims in Ivory Coast, and the organisational decisions made along the way. Using internal, leaked emails from Trafigura, it is possible to piece together the decision-making process of the corporation in relation to the waste and its disposal. Using official government reports and statements made by Ivorian government representatives and others, it is also possible to demonstrate how the waste was allowed to be dumped without the requisite regard to the consequences on the local population. But before embarking on an examination of the series of interconnected events that led to the criminal dumping, we begin with a detailed examination of the Trafigura corporation.

## Origins of Trafigura

Jenkins and Braithwaite identified two recurring themes in the empirical literature on corporate crime. First, the worst corporate crimes result from pressure from senior management: "organizations, like fish, rot from the head down" (Jenkins and Braithwaite 1993: 221); second, "it is greed or the profit motive that is responsible for corporate crime" (Jenkins and Braithwaite 1993: 222). The accusation of greed is relatively uncontroversial (although by no means universally accepted), and most companies would agree that their primary goal is that of profit maximisation (Hirshleifer et al. 2005). The related argument, however, that the worst corporate crimes are a direct result of a corporation's normative value system and the subsequent pressure brought to bear on employees by management, offers a more fine-grained path for analysis. The major shareholder-owners of Trafigura were heavily involved in the day-to-day running of the corporation[1] and were personally involved in the state-corporate crime of toxic waste dumping. The founding partners notably (and rather unfortunately phrased in this context) "took out their own trash", and Claude Dauphin was the 'uncontested leader' who, to many Trafigura staff, "became an inspirational mentor, even a father figure" (Trafigura undated).

Pressure from senior management can induce criminal behaviour (Jenkins and Braithwaite 1993), and corporate culture is often created and directed by senior management. It is to the chief executive officer (CEO) and founders of a company that lower echelon staff will look for corporate behavioural norms. Some of the emails analysed in this study display an obsequious tone by Trafigura staff when addressing the CEO. Trafigura's organisational culture and approach to 'doing things' may have been dictated by the corporate family from which it was born.

Trafigura is a corporation that evolved from a group of companies set up and controlled by Marc Rich in 1993 (Leigh 2009b; Ammann 2009). It was founded by Claude Dauphin and Eric de Turckheim, both former colleagues of Rich (Milmo and Adetunji 2009). Rich launched rival Glencore, the world's largest commodities trader (Pidd et al. 2011), under his own name in 1974, and he is credited by some commentators with the development of a spot market for crude oil (Onstad et al. 2011). In 1983 Rich was indicted by Rudolph Giuliani[2] for breaching sanctions against Iran and tax evasion.[3] He was also involved in deals that breached sanctions against South Africa (Milmo and Adetunji 2009) and has admitted bribing officials in Nigeria and working with Mossad[4] (Ammann 2009). Rich evaded capture for nineteen years, living as a fugitive of justice, and in 2001 he was pardoned by the outgoing U.S. President, Bill Clinton, on his last day of office (Leigh 2009b; Milmo and Adetunji 2009; US DoJ 2001). Clinton (2001) outlined his eight 'legal and foreign policy' reasons for the pardon in an op-ed article in the *New York Times* listing various lawyers and academics that agreed with him – and stressed an 'important' reason as being:

> Many present and former high-ranking Israeli officials of both major political parties and leaders of Jewish communities in America and Europe urged the pardon of Mr Rich because of his contributions and services to Israeli charitable causes, to the Mossad's efforts to rescue and evacuate Jews from hostile countries, and to the peace process through sponsorship of education and health programs in Gaza and the West Bank.
>
> (Clinton 2001)

This preferential treatment by the US president points to the powerful connections enjoyed by Rich. Senior Israeli politicians, Ehud Barak and Shimon Peres were among those who lobbied for his pardon (Ammann 2009). Trafigura is in direct competition with Glencore, but as former executives in his successful empire, Dauphin and de Turckheim experienced and learned from Rich's way of doing business. Trafigura, like Glencore, has links to powerful figures, most notably Thomas Galbraith, former Conservative leader in the House of Lords, UK, who was a director at Trafigura (and specifically at the Galena Asset

Management, a commodities hedge fund) until he decided to step down in readiness for the 2010 UK general election (Leigh and Evans 2009). Galbraith rejoined Trafigura in April 2013 as a member of the supervisory board of Trafigura (Beheer BV) and as a non-executive director of Galena Asset Management (Farchy and Blas 2013; Trafigura 2013). Galbraith had reportedly recommended Peter Fraser (aka Lord Fraser) to do an 'independent' study into Trafigura's actions and as such was personally involved in the public relations campaigning that followed the dumping (detailed in Chapter 6). Fraser's final report never materialised before his death in 2013.

## Trafigura's corporate structure

Trafigura is a large, privately held or 'close' international corporation. A close company does not have the same reporting obligations as one that is publicly traded company[5] as its shares are not available to members of the public. Public limited companies are subject to stricter reporting regimes as government regulations seek to protect the interests of the public shareholders by ensuring that information on corporate activities is readily available. Close companies are inherently more secretive. Although this form of corporation is popular, profits can be limited as they lack the advantage of being able to publicly raise capital by floating on a stock exchange. To give a comparison of the economic size of these types of firms, the largest 223 privately held firms in the United States earn about US$1.4 trillion in revenues per annum (average of 2009 and 2010) (DeCarlo et al. 2010). The top seven publicly owned firms in the United States earned about US$1.4 trillion in revenues in 2010 (Fortune 500 2010). Privately held companies may have limited abilities to raise capital publicly, but these limitations are mitigated by their board's ability to maintain control of the corporation – as there is no risk of a hostile takeover, for example – and to keep its activities and standard operating procedures (SOPs) secret.

The term 'Trafigura' is used here to describe the corporate entity that includes a large group of incorporated bodies. In the UK, Trafigura Ltd[6] was incorporated in 1992 and was formerly known as Merongroom Ltd and thereafter Raw Material Services Ltd. Trafigura Derivatives Ltd[7] was incorporated in 1998 and was formerly known as Trafigura Brokers Ltd. Trafigura Energy Ltd[8] was incorporated in 2001, and Galena Asset Management Ltd[9] was incorporated in 2003 for business related to security broking and fund management and was formerly known as Trafigura Asset Management Ltd. All the foregoing UK-based corporate vehicles had listed their registered office as Portman House, 2 Portman Street, London W1H 6DU, UK, at the time of the dumping in August 2006 (Companies House 2010). Other main corporate units include Farringford NV[10] and Farringford Beheer NV,[11] widely believed to be Trafigura's parent companies; both incorporated in September 1992 and registered in Curaçao, the Netherlands, Antilles (Curaçao Commercial Register 2011); Trafigura Beheer BV (the Netherlands); Puma Energy Holdings

BV (the Netherlands); Trafigura AG (Switzerland); Trafigura Pte Ltd (Singapore); Trafigura Maritime Ventures Ltd (Greek Branch); Trafigura Canada General Partnership, and in Ivory Coast Trafigura has the 100 per cent owned subsidiary called Puma Energy (Trafigura 2010). There are innumerable further subsidiaries, holdings and memberships making the full organisational structure and functioning of Trafigura – and indeed of any large international corporation – highly complex, a complexity made more difficult in the case of private and secretive non-stock, exchange-listed corporations. Furthermore, in 2012, Trafigura began shifting its main operations' base – from London to Genève to Singapore – in an ongoing bid to avoid tax and scrutiny (Farge et al. 2012). Although this kind of tax avoidance may be strictly legal, civil society actors (see, e.g., UK Uncut, ukuncut.org.uk) are increasingly portraying the behaviour as deviant.

Harding (2007) defines an organisation based on three characteristics: "a clear structure, the existence of organizational goals which creates a sense of shared mission, and the substitutability of the individuals who work in them" (Harding 2007: 39). Trafigura does have a clear hierarchical structure despite its secrecy and the complexity of the relationships among its member units. It is run by executives of a small number of major parent companies and displays cohesive organisational goals across the corporate group (described as follows). When examining organisational crime, wholly owned subsidiaries should be considered as an integral part of the larger group as they are merely subunits of the whole – even though they may be incorporated as a separate legal entity. Subsidiaries owe their existence to, take direction from and strongly tend towards the organisational goals of the parent company.

Despite being frequently misrepresented as Dutch, Curaçaon, British, Swiss or, more recently, Singaporean; Trafigura is in fact a truly international and stateless corporation which operates across borders with a physical presence in at least forty-four countries (Trafigura 2010). At all salient times, for the purposes of the events described in this monograph, Trafigura's "operations were essentially run from London" (Leigh 2009b). But this may oversimplify the issue of corporate direction and overlooks the difficulty of how we define the *where* for a company's centre of operations. International corporations may purposefully not be tied to any one base and can close down, move and set up offices wherever they see fit, at any time and without difficulty, to take advantage of disparate domestic criminal, civil and tax legal systems. For example, in early 2011, Galena Asset Management (a major Trafigura subsidiary) moved to Switzerland to take advantage of lower tax rates (Leigh 2010). The main operations of the corporation followed to Switzerland and subsequently moved to Singapore (Farge et al. 2012). But the question of *where* a company is based is essentially a problem of legal construction as most domestic or nation-state legal systems require a physical presence before they can exercise jurisdiction over 'legal persons'.[12] A criminological inquiry does not suffer from the same limitation, nor are criminologists constrained by the identity of the legal jurisdiction in which corporations may be operating. Our concern is with establishing organisational deviance and the resultant violations of human rights, wherever they may occur.

In considering the interrelationship between Trafigura and the Ivorian state, it is important to briefly examine the balance of power between them. The oil trading market is very lucrative, and on any given day about 1 billion barrels of oil change hands on the New York Mercantile Exchange, with a value of more than US$70 billion (Leigh 2009b). Trafigura is one of the world's top three largest independent oil traders, along with Vitol and Glencore (Davis 2008; Tan 2010), and made a US$440 million profit in 2008 (Leigh 2009b), a US$1 billion profit in 2009 (Blas and Sakoui 2010) and had an annual turnover in 2008 and 2009 of more than US$70 billion (Leigh 2009b; Milmo and Adetunji 2009). This turnover dwarfs Ivory Coast's average GDP in the 2000s of US$25 billion (OECD 2011; UN 2011). The corporation charters about one hundred tankers and controls tank farms around the world, where fuel can be blended (Leigh 2009b), and claims to trade more than 2 million barrels daily, with access to 30 million barrels of storage facilities employing 2,000 people across the group (Trafigura 2010). Galena Asset Management alone is claimed to have assets of US$1 billion (Trafigura 2010). Trafigura's 2014 annual report[13] reveals revenue of US$133 billion in 2013 and US$127.6 billion in 2014, gross profit of US$2.9 billion in 2013 and US$2 billion in 2014, net profit of US$2.2 billion in 2013 and US$1.1 billion in 2014, with three-quarters of revenue from oil and petroleum products. This puts the relative financial power of the two organisations into stark perspective – Trafigura can routinely turnover the equivalent of Ivory Coast's annual GDP in about four months. However, financial might is not the only way to measure power – the Ivorian state retained the authority to permit or otherwise the dumping of toxic waste on its territory. This included the power to issue corporate licences to the companies involved and authorise access to the state-run ports. Beyond the competence of any corporation, the exercise of this state power was an essential element of the criminal dumping.

As a private company Trafigura's accounts are not routinely made available to the public, and when they are they are difficult to verify. There was a 'rare glimpse' into the corporation's 2009 figures when Trafigura issued its first Eurobond in 2010, requiring the organisation to reveal details that it had previously guarded closely (Blas and Sakoui 2010). This limited insight prompted the *Financial Times* to declare that "global traders enjoy a more profitable model than previously thought" (Blas and Sakoui 2010). The form of the model is unclear, but the founder-CEO owned approximately 20 per cent of the corporation, with the rest controlled by some 500 senior employees (Blas and Sakoui 2010). Therefore, any profits made by Trafigura directly correlate to the CEO's personal fortune. In such cases motivational catalysts for action overlap at the individual and organisational levels of analysis; in other words the individual CEO and organisational corporate goals merge. A lack of transparency and cooperation with any regulatory authorities means that there is very little information available to allow any analysis of Trafigura's other reported incidences of deviant behaviour. However, with the dumping in Ivory Coast in August 2006, there have been numerous reports and documentation – some of which have been leaked[14] – that allow for an insight into the mechanisms of such a large-scale crime.

The analysis that follows explores the motivations for and opportunities available to Trafigura for criminal activity and examines in detail the creation of the waste and its subsequent dumping. It relies on a range of primary documentation, including the Minton report (compiled on instructions from Trafigura's solicitors and leaked by WikiLeaks and the *Guardian* newspaper), the report of the Hulshof Commission,[15] United Nations reports, the reports of the International Commission of Inquiry and National Commission of Inquiry (both based in Ivory Coast), internal emails of Trafigura and the internal letters of criminal investigators.

We first look at how oil from Mexico became waste in Ivory Coast.

## From Mexico to Ivory Coast

Petróleos Mexicanos (Pemex) is a parastatal company formed in 1938, when the Mexican state forcefully commandeered and nationalised the assets of UK and US oil companies. In 2005 and 2006 and for almost sixty years prior, Pemex was the only company allowed to explore, produce, refine and sell oil and its derivatives in Mexico (Bogan 2009). By 2006 Pemex's revenue had peaked, and the company claimed to be "the biggest enterprise in Mexico" (Pemex 2011).

Up to 2006 the Mexican government received around 40 per cent of its total budget from Pemex, and the company was accurately referred to as the country's 'golden goose'. However, a decline in daily oil production since 2004[16] (Rodriguez 2010), despite a buoyant world market where oil was trading up to US$100 per barrel, led to national debt of more than US$50 billion (Caruso-Cabrera 2011). Pemex's decline coupled with the pressure of poor performance led Mexico's Congress to change industry rules in 2008, allowing Pemex to hire private and foreign companies to explore and produce oil (Bogan 2009).

PMI Comercio Internacional, SA de CV (PMI) is the commercial arm of Pemex and exports crude oil and related products, including coker naphtha (PMI 2007) – a by-product of the refinery process. Its stated mission is, inter alia, "[t]o maximize the value of petroleum exports" (PMI 2007). This mission, an organisational goal in criminology terms, was important not only to the company but to the Mexican state, and Pemex was under considerable political pressure to generate profit at an institutional level, compounding internal managerial pressure at the corporate level. An alignment of two levels of 'motivational catalysts' (Kauzlarich and Kramer 1998) for criminal action provided a strong driver for goal attainment, each of which on their own could be a significant factor in the deviancy to follow (Jenkins and Braithwaite 1993).

In 2002 Pemex overhauled and refurbished its refinery at Cadereyta, Mexico. In an internal letter from Holland and Knight, lawyers for PMI, to a US Environmental Protection Agency (EPA)[17] criminal investigation agent, it was revealed that at this time, Pemex "began refining heavier crude oil slate 47/53 Isthmus/Maya ratio",[18] which produced large quantities of coker naphtha as a by-product. The letter also contained an explanation for the export of coker naphtha to the US by PMI: "[c]oker gasoline is normally reprocessed at the refinery through the use of a reactor to remove sulphur and silica. However, the Cadereyta revamping project did not consider the construction of such a reactor" (mainly due to budget reasons).[19] According to research conducted by the BBC's legal team, coker naphtha rarely comes onto the open market as it is usually refined on-site,[20] and the exclusion of such facilities at Cadereyta was an unusual decision. The coker naphtha had, since early 2003, been stored anywhere the company could find space, in "crude oil tanks, gas oil tanks and gasoline tanks within the refinery".[21] After thirty months of accumulation, full capacity at the refinery was reached, and Pemex made the decision to offer the unrefined oil for sale on the market.[22] This decision was founded on basic economics – storage capacity had run out, and to continue production, at any level, storage needed to be cleared quickly. The urgency will have devalued the contents of the storage, thus leading to PMI showing prices that were very attractive to Trafigura, which purchased at a "very low cost".[23]

The commodity needed to be trucked to a suitable point of sale because the relevant Mexican and US pipelines only accepted 'finished' or refined product. PMI transported around 84,000 tonnes of coker naphtha on trucks to the Port of Brownsville, a deepwater seaport in Texas, United States, and a terminus of the Gulf Intracoastal Waterway, located about thirteen kilometres from the US-Mexico border on the Rio Grande, where Trafigura accepted delivery.[24]

Three loads of coker naphtha of approximately 28,000 tonnes[25] each were loaded onto three ships at Brownsville[26] *Mt Seapurha*,[27] *Mt Moselle*[28] and *Mt Seavinha*.[29] The cargos were transferred to the *Mt Probo Koala* on 11 April, 19 May and 18 June, respectively (Minton 2006a). The *Probo Koala*[30] is a 'bulk cargo transporter' or oil tanker and was first chartered by Trafigura in 2004. It sails under a Panamanian flag[31] (Eze 2008) or 'flag of convenience', a devise used to circumnavigate regulations.

By 2006 around 16 per cent of the world's fleet of oil tankers were recorded in Panama's open registry, and about 55 per cent of all oil tankers were registered in the ten major open and international registries.[32] Ships on the high seas are only subject to the authority of the state whose flag they fly,[33] and some commentators have argued that vessels sailing under flags of convenience have become almost "synonymous with environmental hazards . . . [as] [o]pen registries do not sign on to marine safety and environmental treaties and have also been said to be apathetic toward enforcement of international law" (Duruigbo 2001: 115, 116). Even when the open registry states sign international treaties, they "appear reluctant to enforce standards against their ships"

(Lowe 1975: 108). The main reason for oil-shipping multinational corporations to adopt flags of convenience is simply the maximisation of profit (Payne 1980) – sailing under these flags ensures that corporations need not bear the cost of complying with international standards (Emeka 2001). Furthermore, open registry states have no incentive to adopt or enforce standards that may send a lucrative business elsewhere. Panama receives 5 per cent of its national budget from fees charged for the registry and in Liberia (Panama's main open registry competitor); the ship registry earns one-sixth of the country's total revenue (DeSombre 2008). The use by Trafigura of a ship registered in Panama allowed it to increase profits while avoiding the costs of complying with international environmental norms.

The *Probo Koala* had, according to the UN investigation, two slop tanks for the storage of "cargo residues, tank purging water and hydrocarbon mixtures" (UNHRC 2009: 7). The waste produced by caustic washing at sea was stored in these tanks. The sulphur content of the unrefined coker naphtha needed to be reduced to make it saleable, and the method of caustic washing decided upon was that of caustic soda ($NaOH$, one-third aqueous) combined with the ARI-100 EXL catalyst (cobalt phthalocyanine sulphonate). The tanks were allowed to circulate for one day on the high seas and then allowed to settle. It may have been the first instance of the industrial process of caustic washing at sea (District Court of Amsterdam 2010: paras 5.4, 8.3.2.8 and 13.3.4). The caustic solution, the extracted sulphur and the bottom layer of the naphtha were pumped into the slop tanks to ensure removal of all the undesirable by-products (Day 2010). The process reduced the sulphur content of the naphtha by half, and it was then used as a blend stock to make gasoline. The slops were reported as containing 150 cubic metres of $NaOH$, 370 cubic metres of treated naphtha and free water, and twenty-four kilogrammes of ARI-100 EXL catalyst – capable of causing serious, potentially fatal health problems (Minton 2006a: 7).

Internal emails among a group of ten Trafigura personnel – including the CEO and London-based traders – released simultaneously by the *Guardian* (Guardian 2009) and WikiLeaks (WikiLeaks 2009) reveal the decision-making process that led to the waste travelling from Europe to its dumping in Ivory Coast. Greenpeace France argued that the emails show that Trafigura's management were fully aware that the waste was dangerous but decided, nonehtheless, to send it to Africa so that it could be disposed of cheaply (Greenpeace 2011). At the outset, on 27 December 2005, the emails made reference to the profit that could be realised by the deal: "This is as cheap as anyone can imagine and should make serious dollars", wrote a Trafigura trader.[34]

However, the corporation quickly became aware of the problems associated with the caustic washing of such cheap oil, and this fact was acknowledged internally in December 2005: "US/Singapore and European terminals no longer allow the use of caustics soda washes since local environmental agencies do not allow disposal of the toxic caustic after treatment."[35] According to an email from a London-based trader (Guardian 2009), the solution was to employ a 'floating' location for the caustic washing, but the problem of treatment and outsourcing of the waste remained: "find a chemical carrier and treat cargo on vessel outside US (but we still need to find a company that will take the waste)".[36]

The first attempt to offload the waste involved engaging a Baltic region caustic supplier to take away the unwanted toxic material after the caustic washing[37] and revealed a careless disregard for legality, "the Caustic supplier disposes the slurry in Fujairah (not sure if in a legal way!)".[38] And at one point, early on in the exchange, a trader based in London displays ignorance of the process involved in washing the coker naphtha: "This is not very hazardous in the overall scheme of things, a bit of caustic in some water with trace gasoline,"[39] but further investigation by employees of the corporation revealed that the options for the disposal of waste from this type of process are very limited: "There is only one specialist disposal in rotterdam [sic] they charge $250/kg but not allowed to drive across EU borders etc."[40] At this stage the corporation was plainly aware that the caustic washing process was illegal in some states because of the toxic nature of the waste produced, but management was determined to continue the operation.

Punch, in a study of cases of corporate wrongdoing, argues that "some managers, in order to control their markets and environments (and for a broad spectrum of other motives), will consciously and forcefully employ almost any means – devious, foul, or downright illegal – to achieve their aims" (1996: 1). This was apparently the approach taken by Trafigura.

By late December 27 an email was sent to the Trafigura CEO from a Trafigura trader praising his innovative intervention in the issue of the unwanted waste and promising more cheap oil: "FYI – following your lateral thought about cleaning the PMI origin high Mercaptan Sulphur material and paying a disposal company to process the waste away. We will make it happen. PMI showing us more barrels for Super Cheap now."[41] The CEO's idea was pushed to others, along with a reminder of the profits available: "Claude owns a waste disposal company and wants us to be creative. Graham has worries that it will all turn black. Me and leon want it cos each cargo should make 7m!!"[42] The motivation provided by this high profit margin is a goal of capital accumulation which is often, as argued by Green and Ward, a "highly criminogenic force" (2004).

The situation by the end of 2005 was summarised by a chemist based in Trafigura's London office (Milmo 2010) on 28 December:

> I have approached all our storage terminals with the possibility of Caustic washing and only Vopak Fujairah and Tankmed La Skhirra our [sic] willing to entertain the idea, and currently perform this operation at FRCL (Fajairah) only. This operation is no longer allowed in EU/US and Singapore. Caustic washes are banned by most countries due to the hazardous nature of the waste (mercaptans, phenols, smell) and suppliers of caustic are

unwilling to dispose of the waste since there are not many facilities remaining in the market. There is a company in Rotterdam that burns such waste in a high stack chimney and charges are approx $200/kg and could have up to 1000kgs of sludge after a treatment operation. Under EU law you no longer allowed to transport such waste across EU borders.[43]

This email clearly shows that in 2005 Trafigura was fully aware that the waste produced by the caustic washing process was hazardous. The staff member who wrote this email was instrumental in attempting to pass off the waste as slops in Amsterdam. More important to note is that the CEO of Trafigura was carbon copied on this email.

By the end of December 2005, Trafigura staff had described further attempts to dispose of the waste with the caustic supplier in Estonia, but the supplier wanted to test it first, and this deal appears to have fallen through after the waste was tested.[44] The same issues were to recur in Amsterdam (discussed as follows). The authorities at La Skhirra, Tunisia, were also considering disposal at that time, and Trafigura was engaged in negotiations with them.[45] But as both these options fell through, Trafigura was forced to consider 'creative' alternatives for both the washing and the waste disposal.

La Skhirra finally agreed for the coker naphtha to be de-sulphurised at the Tunisian port, but on the second attempt the process led to offensive fumes "which caused great distress to the local workers and population".[46] From 1 February to 10 March 2006, the company was forced to look into alternate possibilities for caustic washing. A large, cheap old ship – "costed at $15,000 [about €12,000] per day"[47] and big enough to treat 40,000 cubic metres – was considered a good option as there was a distinct possibility that the washing process would erode a ship's seals, leading to the vessel's sinking. The specific decision to use an ageing ship for a process that may precipitate that ship's sinking displays a disregard on the part of Trafigura, both for the crew of the ship as well as the oceanic environment. Another scheme involved converting a small crude unit at Statia Terminals (Caribbean) into a Merox unit (i.e., mercaptan oxidation, a chemical process for the removal of mercaptans) "to treat the 1500 PPM mercaptains in the coker naphtha".[48] This option would take up to four months with an estimated cost of about US$1 million to put in place. Such a capital outlay was not considered viable unless Trafigura could guarantee a long-term supply of the coker naphtha, which appeared uncertain in December 2007 according to an internal Trafigura email in which staff enquired as to how long they expect PMI to have availability.[49]

On 10 March, there was a tentative mention of dumping in an email between the head of Trafigura's gasoline traders in London and US-based staff: "I don't know how we dispose of the slops and I don't imply we would dump them, but for sure there must be some way to pay someone to take them."[50] This email was interesting from the point of view of the denial of the subsequent crime. It seems that emphasis was being shifted by the email's author from dumping to paying someone to take it away, absolving the company of responsibility. The statement was a kind of implicatory denial in which the phrase 'taking the waste away' simply replaces the term 'dumping' (Cohen 1993).

The *Probo Koala* was built in 1989 by a Greek company (Helsingin Sanomat 2006), old enough to assuage traders' worries of losses in the event of the ship sinking. Additionally it was authorised to transport liquid sodium hydroxide – the caustic soda to be used to remove mercaptans (sulphur-containing organic compounds) from the coker naphtha (UNHRC 2009). At some point prior to April 2006, a decision was made to drop anchor off the coast of Gibraltar as a makeshift, floating (Milmo 2009b) processing plant. Trafigura informed the subsequent UN investigation that "gasoline blend stocks were transferred to the Probo Koala in the Mediterranean between April and June 2006. The blend stocks were treated with caustic soda in order to reduce the level of mercaptans" (UNHRC 2009: 7). Trafigura sold the cleaned or 'sweetened' naphtha for a reported profit of UK£4 million (about €6 million) per cargo (Milmo 2009b) with total profits of US$19 million (about €15 million) and then had to deal with the waste contained in the slop tanks, which the corporation falsely reported to the UN investigation as "a mixture of water, blend stock and caustic soda" (UNHRC 2009: 8). Without a clear and legal solution for waste disposal, the corporation turned to subversive means, and the following message sent to the captain of the *Probo Koala* showed a clear intention on the part of Trafigura to hide the nature of the waste: "pls ensure that any remains of caustic soda in the tanks' interface are pumped into the slop tank to the best of your ability and kindly *do not, repeat do not disclose the presence of the material to anyone* at La Skhira and merely declare it as tank washings"[51] (emphasis added). This is 'literal denial' of the toxic nature of the waste and is clear evidence of the awareness with which the company operated in relation to its criminal behaviour (Cohen 1993). The corporation clearly felt it had something to hide.

In late April 2006, communications over the issue of the waste material display a more desperate tone and emails now bore the subject line "PMI Shit":[52]

> we are coming up with some problems regarding treating/disposing of the PMI naphtha out of Brownsville. We are now limited to caustic washing on a ship. La Skhirra where we were washing/discharging will not let us discharge this material anymore, so the ship we're using for washing is now converted to floating storage. We also still haven't tackled how we will dispose of the washings on board the vessel washing the cargo.[53]

In late June the possibility of offloading the waste in Amsterdam was considered, and an email was sent by Trafigura's London chemist to Amsterdam Port Services (APS) seeking to dispose of the material as 'slops' (Day 2010):

> We would like to dispose between 200–250 cbmsos [sic] gasoline Slops Majority is Water, Gasoline, Caustic Soda). This is currently stored in the

slop tank of our vessel, *Mt Probo Koala* we would sil [sic] to the port of amsterdam [sic] and discharge.[54]

It is important to note here that while declaring the waste to Dutch authorities as gas and caustic soda, Trafigura was at this stage well aware that the material in question was not in fact what is commonly known as 'slops' – wastewater from the ship. This obfuscation of the truth forms part of a pattern of denial employed by Trafigura. Furthermore, the company was also aware that only Rotterdam, and not Amsterdam, had the facilities to treat and dispose of this particular type of waste.[55/56]

APS produced quotes for the offload and treatment of the waste to which Trafigura agreed, stating, "we would like to proceed with this offer",[57] giving an estimated arrival at Amsterdam of 30th June 2006.[58]

The *Probo Koala* – en route to Paldiski, Estonia – docked in Amsterdam at the predetermined time with the stated intention of refuelling and purging its slop tanks. On the night of 2 July 2006, APS collected some material from the *Probo Koala*'s slop tanks and, noticing a strong smell, took a sample, "which revealed a significantly higher chemical oxygen demand than it was permitted and able to process on its premises, in addition to a high quantity of mercaptans, which was causing the foul stench" (UNHRC 2009: 8). An employee of APS stated that it was "the worst stench we have ever experienced here" (Eze 2008: 352).

Based on the toxicity of this material, APS then gave Trafigura a revised cost estimate – up from €20 to €900 per cubic metre, totalling up from about €10,000 to about €500,000 (Day 2010) – for treatment at Rotterdam (Eze 2008: 352). Trafigura rejected this quote outright. It posed a significant threat to profit margins, and the company ordered that the waste be reloaded onto the *Probo Koala* (UNHRC 2009; Eze 2008): "we have instructed the slop barge to re-deliver the slop washings back to the vessel in subject due to the high cost of delivery and processing at Amsterdam".[59] The avoidance of a sensible, viable solution to the waste issue because of this reduction in profit showed the lengths the corporation was willing to go to to maximise profit – as Jenkins and Braithwaite argued was a key indicator of the likelihood of corporate criminality (1993).

The Hulshof Commission reported that this reloading of waste back onto the ship was against environmental regulations, but Amsterdam's environmental department was apparently unaware of this and failed to report the matter to the Amsterdam port authority (Hulshof Commission 2006). APS and the city of Amsterdam have now been successfully prosecuted by Dutch authorities for this failure (Amnesty International and Greenpeace 2012). On 5 July 2006, the *Probo Koala* sailed for Paldiski, but Amsterdam port officials had sent an urgent message to port authorities in Paldiski, warning of a "suspicious cargo" (Eze 2008: 352), and the *Probo Koala* was unable to offload the waste there either (Knauer et al. 2006; Eze 2008). At Paldiski Trafigura offloaded 3,300 tonnes of gasoline and loaded 26,000 tonnes of unleaded gasoline bound for Lomé,

Togo and Lagos, Nigeria, before setting sail on 13 July (Eze 2008; UNHRC 2009). As noted Trafigura again tried to offload waste in Paldiski, leading to an investigation by the Estonian police. There were also attempts to offload in Nigeria, but according to Trafigura, "the slops were not discharged in Nigeria as it was clear that there were insufficient facilities in place to receive them" (BBC 2009c). This is a curious claim in light of the eventual use of Abidjan, unlikely to be considered to have superior facilities to Nigeria.

As outlined at the beginning of this chapter, the criminal dumping of toxic waste in Ivory Coast was not limited to Trafigura and its subsidiaries and agents. The Ivorian state's role is crucial in understanding the mechanics of what has to be understood as a state-corporate crime. Other European and African states rejected the waste. The waste was, for example, repelled from the states of Estonia and Nigeria before arriving in Ivory Coast, where it was apparently welcomed. Trafigura avoided dumping in Nigerian waters because, as stated in an email of 10 August, to do so would have had "potential implications on us";[60] likely meaning that the effects of the waste on the environment or the local population could be negatively imputed to Trafigura. When it became clear that the company receiving the waste was not happy to take delivery in international waters, Trafigura stated that "[i]n this instance due to the nature of the slops on board I would prefer the slop to be discharged in a different port other than Lagos if possible".[61] Trafigura was concerned that dumping in Nigeria's largest city would more likely be traced back to the company. Trafigura's CEO then reportedly suggested that they try to smuggle the waste into Nigeria: "I spoke to [Trafigura's CEO] . . . go to Lome [sic], charter a barge and bring it back to Nigeria for Daddo [Marine Services] under a different name."[62] Nigeria is Africa's largest oil producer and one of the world's largest oil producers,[63] and the company would not want to sully its relationship with the Nigerian state nor subject its activities to an experienced Nigerian civil society; the Nigeria oil industry has already "received considerable attention in academic literature or from human rights organisations" (Green and Ward 2004: 30). Nigeria was also sensitive to potential ramifications of such an issue because of a scandal over deadly toxic waste dumped at Koko in 1987. A less commercially important and more vulnerable state, Togo, was chosen as the next target for the waste, and an email dated 15 August asked, "[S]ee if they can arrange for a barge to pick up the slops, preferably offshore Lome or as far as possible offshore Nigeria and within international waters".[64] Trafigura stated a preference for the freedom provided by the legal regime applied to international waters, again indicating a clear awareness that its actions could be labelled deviant. International waters were the preferred location for the transfer of waste because there the domestic laws of Nigeria would not apply. The corporation was clearly aware that what they were doing was likely to be illegal under Nigerian law.

An email from Comoditex[65] to the captain of the *Probo Koala* dated 15 August stated, "[T]hey will only be able to arrange for a barge to de-slop in

Nigerian waters . . . He will also ensure that we get proper paperwork for receipt of slops."[66] The next day, 16 August, an email made clear that if the waste was to be offloaded by Daddo Maritime Services, then Trafigura must receive documentation to show that the cargo had been cleared:

> Understand and share your concerns about doing this in Nigerian waters. If we can not manage to convince Daddo to do it outside Nigeria then please make sure that Daddo understand that we do not want any issues and proper clearances should be obtain [sic] in order to avoid any implications for Trafigura or the vessel.[67]

Trafigura's CEO, however, expressed concerns about the possible traceability of such an operation, and it was aborted later that day: "Dude, pls call CD [Trafigura's CEO]. I spoke to him yesterday and he said no to any such operation in Nigeria."[68] After unloading its gasoline cargo at Lomé and Lagos, the *Probo Koala* sailed to Ivory Coast. Because the tanker did not have a cargo, and none was scheduled to be picked up, its journey to Ivory Coast could only have been to unload the toxic waste. The company would have been (or ought to have been) well aware that the facilities in Ivory Coast would be no better and more likely less sophisticated than those in Nigeria.

On 17 August, an employee of Trafigura emailed the head of Puma Energy a local Trafigura subsidiary, stating that "we would like to discharge approx 528 CBM of . . . a mix of Gasoline with caustic Soda and high concentration of Mercaptan Sulphur". The email, referring to the waste as 'slops', stated that the waste should be "disposed properly to avoid any environmental concerns or problems with authorities".[69] Puma Energy then telephoned WAIBS, Trafigura's local shipping agent, who gave them a number for a 'two-bit' (Day 2010) company called 'Société Tommy' (Tommy) – the organisation that was ultimately contracted to receive the waste. The next day, 18 August, the same Trafigura employee telephoned the head of shipping services for WAIBS to ask him, "if it was possible for a ship, before passing through the Port of Abidjan, to include in its port costs the costs of discharging the slops in case of emergency".[70] WAIBS agreed that this was possible and had been done in the past. WAIBS then informed two shipping agents of the specifics of this telephone conversation. Later that day one of those agents informed Salomon Ugborugbo, director of Tommy, of the impending arrival of the *Probo Koala* and told him to make arrangements for the discharge of 'slops'. During the afternoon of 18 August, the shipping agent introduced Ugborugbo to Puma Energy at Puma Energy's request. Puma asked Tommy to make an offer which, when produced, took the following form:[71]

> Given the high concentration of Mercaptan Sulphur and the strong smell of these products, a chemist, after reading your two emails, has advised us

to dump the waste in an area outside of the city, called Akouédo, equipped in an adequate manner for receiving these kinds of chemical products. In order to avoid any risk of environmental accidents being imputed to Puma Energy, the ship or to you, the Tommy company assumes all responsibility and assures you that a good job will be done. The necessary documents will be given to the ship following the operation.

   Marpol slops: 30 $ US per m3
   Chemical slops: 35 $ US per m3

The terms of this handwritten 'quote' suggested that Tommy was an unprofessional operation, despite stating that they would 'do a good job' while assuring Puma Energy that any environmental accidents would not be imputed back to them. This view was validated by the National Inquiry in 2006, which argued that Tommy had neither "the competence nor the technical or human means to treat the waste from the Probo Koala".[72] The inability of Tommy to deal with this toxic waste was a fact that Trafigura would have been or ought to have been aware of. Furthermore, the offered price of about US$35 per cubic metre was significantly less than the Dutch quote, and this should have put Trafigura on notice that further due diligence and an investigation of Tommy's capabilities was necessary. The Marpol Convention at 11(d) enumerates a list of waste-receiving facilities in each state and includes details of their capacity. Ivory Coast is not listed as possessing any suitable facilities, and the National Inquiry stated that this fact was acknowledged by the CEO of Trafigura and the West African director of Trafigura.[73/74] Tommy is believed by some commentators to be a vehicle set up by Ugborugbo solely for the purposes of this transaction and "had just been established in July" (Eze 2008: 352).[75] Some commentators maintain that Simone Gbagbo, the Ivorian 'first lady', was involved in the incorporation of this company, and Gonto reports that he was arrested and charged with 'offences against the head of state' for writing a newspaper article that suggested as much (Reporters Without Borders 2006).

   On 18 August an advisor to Puma Energy telephoned the Abidjan port commander, Bombo Dagni Marcel ('Bombo'), to ask if he knew the head of Tommy, Ugborugbo. The port commander invited Ugborugbo to his office, verified the existence of Tommy's documentation and thereafter reassured the Puma Energy advisor as to the 'conformity' of them. This appears to be the extent of Trafigura's due diligence of the suitability of Tommy to carry out the specialised operation. That same day a message from Trafigura – which refers to 'dumping' in the subject line – asked WAIBS to coordinate with Tommy and set out the following details of an operation to eliminate 528 cubic metres of "wastewater":[76]

   Would you kindly confirm that you are able to make the arrangements for the collection and removal of the wastewater and to provide suitable documentation from the slop removal company about compliance with local regulations by environmental administration and customs on disposal of the wastewaters.[77]

After months of seeking alternatives, the scene was now set for offloading of the toxic waste at Abidjan Port.

## Notes

1  See EMAIL From: JMN; To: CD [CEO]; Sent: Tue Dec 27 2005 23:24; Subject: Re: More High Sulphur from PMI).
2  Acting as US federal prosecutor.
3  United States District Court, Southern District of New York, United States v Marc Rich (and others), Indictment S 83 Cr. 579 (SWK), available at www.thesmokinggun. com/file/pardon-me-marc-rich-indictment, accessed November 2011.
4  Mossad, Israel's secret service, has been repeatedly accused of operating outside the law, from the illegal transfer of Adolf Eichmann from Argentina in 1960 to the assassination in Dubai of Mahmoud al-Mabhouh (a leader of Hamas) in 2010.
5  Under UK law (Companies Act 2006) this would include directors' and secretaries' names and some financial information about the company.
6  UK company number 02737924.
7  UK company number 03621790.
8  UK company number 04160239.
9  UK company number 04657028, FSA (UK) registration number 223696.
10  Curaçao company number 61251.
11  Curaçao company number 61175.
12  Legal personhood is a legal fiction whereby corporate entities are treated by law as if they were real people.
13  Available at www.trafigura.com/media/1990/2014-trafigura-annual-report.pdf.
14  Reports have been received from international press correspondents based in Abidjan and international NGO staff in the United Kingdom. The sources wish to remain anonymous.
15  A report prepared at the request of the deputy mayor of Health, Environment, Human Resources, Public Space of the city of Amsterdam and the alderman of Finance, Economic Affairs and the ports of the city of Amsterdam.
16  Down from 3.8 million barrels per day to 3.25 million by 2006, and to 2.5 million by 2010. In 2006 output declined by more than 13 per cent (Malkin 2007), and in 2009 output fell at its fastest rate since 1942 (Martinez and Rodriguez 2009).
17  A special agent of the US EPA investigating PMI Trading and Coker Naphtha.
18  Letter of Holland and Knight, McLean, Virginia, United States, to Criminal Investigations Division of the EPA, Boston, Massachusetts, United States, dated 14 December 2006.
19  Ibid.
20  Claim No. HQ 09X02050; Trafigura Limited (Claimant) and British Broadcasting Corporation (Defendant); Defence (of 11/09/2009) against claim issued on 15 May 2009 in the High Court of Justice, Queens Bench Division, drafted by Andrew Caldecott QC and Jane Phillips and signed by Stephen Mitchell, head of Multimedia Programmes at the BBC (available at http://wikileaks.org/file/bbc-trafigura.pdf or mirror.wikileaks. info/leak/bbc-trafigura.pdf, accessed 16/02/2010), page 6.
21  Letter of Holland and Knight, McLean, Virginia, United States, to Criminal Investigations Division of the EPA, Boston, Massachusetts, United States, dated 14 December 2006.
22  Ibid.

23 Quoted in Claim No. HQ 09X02050; Trafigura Limited (Claimant) and British Broadcasting Corporation (Defendant); Defence (of 11/09/2009) against claim issued on 15 May 2009 in the High Court of Justice, Queens Bench Division, drafted by Andrew Caldecott QC and Jane Phillips and signed by Stephen Mitchell, head of Multimedia Programmes at the BBC (available at http://wikileaks.org/file/bbc-trafigura.pdf, or mirror.wikileaks.info/leak/bbc-trafigura.pdf, both accessed 16/02/2010), page 5, paragraph 4.2.

24 Letter of Holland and Knight, McLean, Virginia, United States, to Criminal Investigations Division of the EPA, Boston, Massachusetts, United States, dated 14 December 2006.

25 A tonne is a term sometimes used in shipping and is equivalent to 1,000 kilogrammes (kg).

26 Claim No. HQ 09X02050; Trafigura Limited (Claimant) and British Broadcasting Corporation (Defendant); Defence (of 11/09/2009) against claim issued on 15 May 2009 in the High Court of Justice, Queens Bench Division, drafted by Andrew Caldecott QC and Jane Phillips and signed by Stephen Mitchell, head of Multimedia Programmes at the BBC (available at http://wikileaks.org/file/bbc-trafigura.pdf or mirror.wikileaks.info/leak/bbc-trafigura.pdf, accessed 16/02/2010), page 5, paragraph 4.2.

27 On 20 March 2006.

28 On 25 April 2006.

29 On 1 June 2006.

30 Renamed 'Gulf Jash' in 2011.

31 And owned by Greek shipping company, Prime Marine Management Inc.

32 Antigua and Barbuda, Bahamas, Bermuda, Cyprus, Isle of Man, Liberia, Malta, Marshall Islands, Panama, and Saint Vincent and Grenadines.

33 Case of the S.S. "Lotus" (France v. Turkey), 1927 P.C.U. (Ser. A) No. 10, at 25.

34 EMAIL From: JMN; To: LC, JT, FA, AH; CC: NA, JM, JL; Sent: Tue Dec 27 16:54:44 2005; Subject: Re: More High Sulphur from PMI.

35 EMAIL From: NA; To: JMN, LC, JT, FA, AH; CC: JM, JL; Sent: Tue Dec 27 2005 19:29; Subject: Re: More High Sulphur from PMI.

36 EMAIL From: NA; To: JT, JMN, LC, FA, AH; CC: JM, JL; Sent: Tue Dec 27 2005 19:31; Subject: Re: More High Sulphur from PMI.

37 EMAIL From: NA; To: JMN, LC, JT, FA, AH; CC: JM, JL; Sent: Tue Dec 27 2005 19:29; Subject: Re: More High Sulphur from PMI.

38 EMAIL From: NA; To: JMN, LC, JT, FA, AH; CC: JM, JL; Sent: Tue Dec 27 2005 22:42; Subject: Re: More High Sulphur from PMI.

39 EMAIL From: JMN; To: NA, LC, JT, FA, AH; CC: JM, JL; Sent: Tue Dec 27 2005 22:42; Subject: Re: More High Sulphur from PMI.

40 EMAIL From: NA; To: JMN, LC, JT, FA, AH; CC: JM, JL; Sent: Tue Dec 27 2005 22:42; Subject: Re: More High Sulphur from PMI.

41 EMAIL From: JMN; To: CD; Sent: Tue Dec 27 2005 23:24; Subject: Re: More High Sulphur from PMI.

42 EMAIL From: JMN; To: NA; Sent: Tue Dec 27 2005 23:24; Subject: Re: More High Sulphur from PMI.

43 EMAIL From: NA; To: LC, JMN; CC: JL, JT, FA, AH, GS, CD; Sent: Tue Dec 28 2005 15:11; Subject: Re: More High Sulphur from PMI.

44 Ibid.

45 Ibid.

46 EMAIL From: White Consulting Group; To: NA; CC: TB; Sent: 24 March 2006 11:46; Subject: La Skhirra.

47 EMAIL From AH; To: LC; CC: PE, JJ, BS; Sent: Wed Feb 01 03:12:46 2006; Subject: Coker Naphtha – 1500 ppm Mercaptains.

48 Ibid.

49 EMAIL From: JMN; To: LC, JT, FA, AH; CC: NA, JM, JL; Sent: Tue Dec 27 16:54:44 2005; Subject: Re: More High Sulphur from PMI.

50 EMAIL From: LC; To: JL, TG; CC: JMN, NA; Sent: 10 March 2006 23:05; Subject: Caustic washing requirements.
51 EMAIL From: Cpt TheologsGamierakis (as agents for and on behalf of Trafigura); To: Probo Koala; CC: Prime Marine Management; Attn: Master Attn: Ops; April 15 2006.
52 EMAIL From: LC; To: JT; CC: JMN, JL, CD; Tue Apr 18 12:36:19 2006; Subject: PMI shit.
53 Ibid.
54 EMAIL From: NA; To APS; June 20 2006 10:43; Subject: Re: Gasoline Slops Disposal.
55 EMAIL From: NA; To: JMN, LC, JT, FA, AH; CC: JM, JL; Sent: Tue Dec 27 2005 22:42; Subject: Re: More High Sulphur from PMI.
56 EMAIL From: NA; To: LC, JMN; CC: JL, JT, FA, AH, GS, CD; Sent: Tue Dec 28 2005 15:11; Subject: Re: More High Sulphur from PMI.
57 EMAIL Van: NA; Verzonden: maandag 26 juni 2006 12:41; Aan: bert.wolf; CCAPS – BiankoVonk; Oderwerp: FW: offer Probo Koala.
58 Ibid.
59 EMAIL From: TG; To: Bulk Marine Services BV; CC: Trafigura Athens Operations; Subject: Probo Koala / Re-Delivery of Slop Washings.
60 Claim No. HQ 09X02050; Trafigura Limited (Claimant) and British Broadcasting Corporation (Defendant); Defence (of 11/09/2009) against claim issued on 15 May 2009 in the High Court of Justice, Queens Bench Division, drafted by Andrew Caldecott QC and Jane Phillips and signed by Stephen Mitchell, head of Multimedia Programmes at the BBC (available at http://wikileaks.org/file/bbc-trafigura.pdf or mirror.wikileaks. info/leak/bbc-trafigura.pdf, accessed 16/02/2010), page 15.
61 Ibid at page 15.
62 Ibid at page 16.
63 From www.bbc.co.uk/news/world-africa-13949550, accessed October 2011.
64 Claim No. HQ 09X02050, page 16.
65 A commodities trading firm headquartered in Dubai.
66 Claim No. HQ 09X02050; Trafigura Limited (Claimant) and British Broadcasting Corporation (Defendant); Defence (of 11/09/2009) against claim issued on 15 May 2009 in the High Court of Justice, Queens Bench Division, drafted by Andrew Caldecott QC and Jane Phillips and signed by Stephen Mitchell, head of Multimedia Programmes at the BBC (available at http://wikileaks.org/file/bbc-trafigura.pdf or mirror.wikileaks. info/leak/bbc-trafigura.pdf, accessed 16/02/2010), page 16.
67 Ibid at page 16.
68 Ibid at page 16.
69 Ibid.
70 Ibid.
71 Abidjan, 18 August 2006, To Jorge Marrero, Via Captain Kablan, Subject: Collection of Slops, quoted in the report of the National Commission of Inquiry on the Toxic Waste in the District of Abidjan, pages 24–25.
72 The report of the National Commission of Inquiry on the Toxic Waste in the District of Abidjan, page 51.
73 The report of the National Commission of Inquiry on the Toxic Waste in the District of Abidjan.
74 Eric de Turckheim, a Trafigura director, has also denied this stating on BBC *Newsnight* (on 16 August 2007) that the port at Abidjan "is a sophisticated port, fully equipped to handle such waste", available at www.youtube.com/watch?v=tQBS82kFQjE, accessed July 2013.
75 The report of the National Commission of Inquiry on the Toxic Waste in the District of Abidjan, page 51.

76  From: PS of Trafigura, To: DA of Waibs Shipping, Sent: 18 August 2006, Subject: 20951 Agency Appointment: Probo Koala – Dumping of Slop in Abidjan, quoted in the report of the National Commission of Inquiry on the Toxic Waste in the District of Abidjan, page 26.

77  The report of the National Commission of Inquiry on the Toxic Waste in the District of Abidjan, page 26.

# Chapter 3

# The *Probo Koala* arrives at Abidjan

With all the arrangements made, "the receipt of the toxic waste had its starting point with the authorisation for entry into port of the Probo Koala ship".[1] This authorisation was requested from the Port Abidjan Captaincy by WAIBS and was received by the transmissions agent of the port in the afternoon of 18 August, who noted the mention of 'wastewater'. At the same time Tommy attended the customs office and sought the assistance of customs officials in waste disposal operations. The head of this office put three agents at Tommy's disposal.

Tommy then went to the PETROCI landing stage office at around 4 p.m. to obtain a work permit for the collection of slops from the *Probo Koala*. This office contacted Puma Energy for confirmation of the ship's entry and of the planned operation. Puma Energy confirmed by telephone *Probo Koala*'s entry and the disposal of the slops. The port captain also confirmed the details. The team leader at Vridi-Gasoline customs also confirmed the disposal operation for the next morning.[2]

The *Probo Koala* arrived from unloading its main cargo in Nigeria at around 10 a.m. the next morning (Saturday, 19 August 2006) at the PETROCI wharf in the port of Abidjan.[3] The WAIBS agent was on the wharf to supervise the reception of the waste and stated that his role was to help "the ship's commander in his dealings with the port authorities".[4] WAIBS stated that the port services agents from the Administrations for Maritime, Health, Immigration, Pollution and for the Environment all boarded the ship.[5] How it was that none of these services was able to determine that the waste may have been harmful is dealt with next.

Tommy had visited the dump facility at Akuédo in the morning of 19 August to confirm that the waste would be dumped as had been arranged on 18 August with a Pisa-Impex employee. Tommy had paid 500,000 CFA francs (about €760) in fees to Pisa-Impex (AFP 2006), a private company that jointly manages rubbish with the Abidjan administration. The Pisa-Impex officer present on 19 August stated that his superior had been informed and a team had been put in place in case the dump closed before the operation had been completed, but this fact was denied by that superior when interviewed by the National Commission of Inquiry on the Toxic Waste in the District of Abidjan (the 'National Inquiry').[6]

The dumping started with the collection of material from the *Probo Koala* on Saturday, 19 August 2006, at about 1 p.m.[7] Tommy had hired around twelve tanker trucks with drivers and "offloaded the sulphurous sludge from the cargo vessel and deposited the waste at 18 locations around the . . . city" (UNHRC 2009) during the night of 19 August and into the morning of 20 August (Eze 2008). Three of the trucks belonged to a company, Les Camionneurs, the manager of which stated to the National Inquiry that these drivers had acted without the knowledge of the company.

The first tanker truck arrived at the dump at about 7 p.m. and left at about 8 p.m., after which the dump was closed by agents of the District of Abidjan – some three hours earlier than usual. An agent for the city of Abidjan based at the dump told the National Inquiry that although security was the official reason given for the closing of the dumpsite, this was actually a pretext to ensure staff avoided the odour emanating from the toxic waste. Despite the official closure of the dump, and an inability to weigh the trucks as a result, Pisa-Impex remained at the site until 3 a.m. to assist three further trucks with the dumping.[8] Pisa-Impex, which had originally agreed with Tommy to calculate the fee based on the total weight of the waste dumped, had to extrapolate the final price based on the weight of the first truck. Pisa-Impex representatives say that it was after these four loads of waste were dumped that they noticed an odour from the dumped material. A fifth truck arrived at around 6 a.m. but was immobilised by an Abidjan port spokesman (in charge of the environment) who took the keys and some parts from the truck. A senior member of staff of Pisa-Impex intervened and returned the key and parts to the driver, who dumped his cargo upon the departure of the Abidjan port spokesman. Although Tommy paid Pisa-Impex 500,000 CFA (about €760), according to a Pisa-Impex employee's personal receipt book, only 90,000 CFA (about €140) was paid into the Pisa-Impex bank account, the rest being distributed among Pisa-Impex employees.[9] This irregular accounting procedure cast a shadow of doubt on the integrity of the internal control systems at Pisa-Impex and implied poor corporate governance, at the very least, and corrupt practise at worst (Wu 2005).

By the dawning of the next day, toxic waste had been dumped at multiple sites all around Abidjan. With access to the city dump denied, drivers of the remaining truckloads of waste sought alternative sites across the city: "the other drivers panned out across the city and just dumped it wherever they could" (Day 2010).

Eze reports that "Tommy simply poured 528 tons of the waste at 17 public sites around Abidjan" (Eze 2008: 353). The waste is known to have contained "a mixture of petroleum distillates, hydrogen sulphide, mercaptans, phenolic compounds and sodium hydroxide" (WHO 2006). It is important to note that "[n]one of the dumping sites had proper facilities for the treatment of chemical waste" (UNHRC 2009) and waste was dumped "into vegetable fields, watercourses and outside a baby-food factory" (Goode 2010).

## Resultant health issues

According to the International Commission of Inquiry on the Discharge of Toxic Wastes, in the District of Abidjan (the 'International Inquiry') 15 people died, 69 were hospitalised and more than 108,000 medical consultations were sought as a result of the dumping.

The National Inquiry found:

> Since Sunday August 20, the nauseating odour emanating from this waste has spread considerably and polluted the surrounding atmosphere. Because of its high level of toxicity, the inhabitants of the contaminated areas had to at some points abandon their homes.[10]

As well as people abandoning their homes, "businesses forewent commercial earnings for a significant period of time following the contamination" (UNHRC 2009: 9).

The smell was described as "thick and suffocating", and Eze reports that in the surrounding area, "eyes were stinging, noses bleeding, stomachs, chests and ears were aching" (Eze 2008: 353). Within days thousands of people from populations local to the dumping areas started complaining of health issues and seeking medical treatment for symptoms that included "nosebleeds" and "nausea, headaches, vomiting, abdominal pains, skin reactions and a range of eye, ear, nose, throat, pulmonary and gastric problems" (WHO 2006; UNHRC 2009: 9). The World Health Organization (WHO) stated that these symptoms were "consistent with exposure to the chemicals known to be in the waste" (WHO 2006). Tests of the 'sludge' confirmed that it "contained mercaptans and hydrogen sulphide, a potent poison that, particularly in confined spaces, can cause blackouts, respiratory failure and death" (Eze 2008: 353). And the National Inquiry found that "people were affected with various illnesses requiring medical assistance and hospitalisations, whilst others, sadly, died".[11]

The University of Cocody (Abidjan) study included efforts to describe the epidemiologic profile of the people poisoned and to identify their symptoms:

> Of 4573 people surveyed, 4344 people, about 95%, were home during the toxic waste discharge. In all, 2369 (51.8%) had signs of poisoning. Sex, district of residence, and presence at home at the time of the discharge were all statistically related to poisoning.
>
> (Tiembre et al. 2009)

Of those surveyed who sought treatment (1,297–64.4%), the main signs of poisoning were respiratory problems, in particular a cough and thoracic pains; digestive complaints, diarrhea and abdominal distension; and cutaneous (pruritus) and neurological (headaches) issues (Tiembre et al. 2009). The study concluded that there was "persistence of the symptoms among many of those poisoned more than 4 months afterwards . . . [and] . . . although the sites have been partially cleaned: the long-term effects on population health remain alarming" (Tiembre et al. 2009). The suppressed Minton report, released by WikiLeaks, was commissioned by Trafigura immediately after the dumping. Based on the information provided to them by Trafigura, the report found:

> The most severe symptoms are likely to be experienced by those living and working at or near the dump sites who may come into direct contact with the liquid slops residues and high concentrates of gas. For these people, the possible consequences are burns to the skin, eyes and lungs, vomiting, diarrhea, loss of consciousness and death.
>
> (Minton 2006a)

The WHO and University of Cocody studies suggest that these 'possible consequences' were in fact a stark reality for inhabitants of the affected area. Furthermore, according to the UN report, "[s]uffocating odours originated from the dumping sites" (UNHRC 2009: 9) and

> [r]esidents in areas close to the dumping sites were directly exposed to the waste through skin contact and the breathing in of volatile substances. In addition, secondary exposure reportedly occurred through contact with surface water, groundwater and eventually through the consumption of food grown on or extracted from contaminated land and water.
>
> (UNHRC 2009: 9)

With regard to operations on the Mt *Probo Koala*, the Minton report concluded: "It is not unreasonable to surmise that there was a considerable quantity of mercaptide, sodium sulphate and sodium hydrosulphide dissolved in the aqueous phase of the slops, possibly far greater that found in the refinery produced caustic waste" (Minton 2006a: 4). Following the dumping of waste from the *Probo Koala*, the senior examining magistrate of the Fourth Chamber of the District Council of Abidjan ordered an investigation of its consequences by the Laboratoire de Toxicologie et Hygiène Agro-Industrielle, Abidjan. As part of its investigation, numerous solid and liquid samples were taken from the bodies of twelve deceased people by forensic scientists – including from the brain, the lungs, the heart, the liver, the kidneys, subcutaneous fat and the psoas muscle.[12]

In March 2007 samples of organs that were likely to have been affected by hydrogen sulphide ($H_2S$), that is, the lungs and the brain, were analysed.[13] The results ranged from 2.4 to 18.28 $H_2S$ in $\mu g/g$ of brain or of lungs, above the reported fatal poisoning rates of 0.8 to 0.92. At the High Court in the UK, the BBC argued that there "is no alternative credible source for the Hydrogen Sulphide other than the Probo Koala Waste".[14]

I collected testimony from victims across Abidjan, which confirms the devastating effect of the dumping:

> We live in the Deux Plateaux,[15] almost all my family has been contaminated. Now I carry the illness, my eyes hurt and are scratchy all the time and they are crying. My mother as well, she's always sick. We go the hospital, but we really don't know what she has. My older sister as well, actually all my house has been contaminated in general.[16]

Another victim from around the same area also complained of persisting symptoms four years after the dumping:

> Ever since that morning I have felt it. I have a headache that doesn't stop. Then I have a chronic cough, it calms down for a bit but then it comes back again. And then sometimes my body heats up. Sometimes when I walk a bit my whole body gets tired. Ever since that day, I haven't felt well.[17]

These testimonies, relayed to the author at the end of 2010, reveal how that the effects of the waste from the *Probo Koala* continued long after the ship left port on 22 August 2006.

## Deviance of the Trafigura corporation and its subsidiaries

Despite the reported evidence presented, Trafigura denied any connections among the company, the dumping and the resultant human suffering and instituted what has been described as a widespread cover-up operation. Greenpeace Nederland argued that it was "a scandal that to this day the company denies guilt and through law firms and PR agencies . . . cover up the facts" (Harjono 2009).

Trafigura's wholly owned subsidiary, Puma Energy, also played a significant role in the dumping. The assistant general administrator of Puma Energy told the National Inquiry that he was not involved in the "illicit transfer of toxic waste"[18] and reasoned that "Puma Energy CI's activities . . . did not have anything to do with Trafigura's commercial operations".[19] However, based on the testimony of WAIBS's shipping agents to the National Inquiry, "[the assistant general administrator of Puma Energy] took an active part in the phase of the illicit transfer of toxic waste which involved the Cote d'Ivoire".[20] Further, as noted, the assistant general administrator of Puma Energy was at the meeting with Tommy where he received a handwritten quote for the offloading of waste which he transmitted directly to Trafigura.[21] The National Inquiry stated that he "played a determining role in the operations of transferring and dumping the toxic waste in Abidjan".[22]

It seems clear, as Dimas argued, that "an illegal shipment of European toxic waste caused health and environmental havoc among the population" (Dimas

2006), and the health effects described are clear violations of the human rights of the local population. The pressure this incident placed on the health facilities also had foreseeable knock-on effects, crippling an already stretched service. The University of Cocody[23] study revealed that "highly toxic waste products" were dumped around Abidjan on the nights of 19 to 21 August and that "numerous cases of poisoning were reported to the health authorities, who were unprepared for such a problem" (Tiembre et al. 2009). It also showed that health centres were faced with double their normal workload in the weeks that followed, "such that regular consultations have all-but-ceased" (WHO 2006). In one day – 11 September 2006 – in the Cocody neighbourhood, more than 1,000 people visited the local teaching hospital, and the Yopougon teaching hospital and Akouédo Health Centre reported that six hundred and three hundred people (respectively) were attending daily, "including many children and young infants" (WHO 2006). The WHO report stated:

> The overwhelming numbers of people seeking medical attention because of this chemical waste are severely disrupting medical services and have resulted in shortages of medicines. This has put a double burden on the already weak health system of Cote d'Ivoire. This crisis has shown that the country does not have the capacity to deal with such an emergency.
>
> (WHO 2006)

The UN special rapporteur's investigation uncovered deviance, without naming it such, identifying problems with "specific elements of due diligence in relation to the dumping of the waste from the *Probo Koala* in Abidjan" (UNHRC 2009: 7). These problems related to the following:

(a) Full disclosure of and clarity on the composition of the *Probo Koala*'s slop tanks and destination for disposal prior to the unloading of the waste;
(b) Evaluation of port reception capacities and waste disposal facilities in terms of environmentally sound waste treatment prior to the unloading of the waste;
(c) Remedial action after the dumping of the waste.

(UNHRC 2009: 17)

The first two issues have each attracted a label of deviance by a variety of audiences. According to the Hulshof Commission (2006), the waste was described as a "mixture of tank washing, petrol and caustic soda", "oily tank washings and cargo residues", "watery cleaning liquids" and "waste from steam degreasing" (quoted in UNHRC 2009: 17). The UN report noted that upon arrival in Abidjan, Trafigura called the waste "chemical waste water" (UNHRC 2009: 17). The UN special rapporteur argued that this showed a lack of transparency: "the discretion with which different descriptions were used appears to be broad and not conducive to transparent decision-making on the treatment of potentially toxic waste" (UNHRC 2009: 17). The PMI product, as stated by Trafigura, "has 1500ppm Mercaptans, high Gums, H2S, Cu Corrosion and low oxidation stability",[24] and the Minton report adds: "the slop/residue waste discharged from the vessel is likely to have contained very high concentrations of noxious sulphur compounds" (Minton 2006a: 5). It is clear from both these sources as well as from the internal Trafigura emails analysed that the company did not consider that the slop tanks contained merely 'wastewater' and were denying the harmful potential of the cargo.

The second problem noted by the special rapporteur (UNHRC 2009) relates to Trafigura's investigation of the suitability of Abidjan port to receive this type of waste. Having been refused the possibility of treating the waste in Amsterdam, because of a lack of appropriate facilities, the special rapporteur argued that "the onus would be on Trafigura to show in what way the port of Abidjan would be equally or better equipped to process the waste" (UNHRC 2009: 17). The Basel Convention secretariat-mandated mission found that the Abidjan port was "not equipped with the necessary facilities for the offloading and treatment of wastes covered by the MARPOL Convention" (referred to in UNHRC 2009: 17). Further to the facilities at the port, the special rapporteur examined the companies that were available to take the waste and process it:

> At the time of the events, the port of Abidjan reportedly had only one experienced de-slopping service provider, the company Ivoirienne des Techniques des Energies (ITE) . . . [and] . . . the exercise of due diligence would seem to suggest that ITE was the only viable option in this particular case.
>
> (UNHRC 2009: 17)

These failures of due diligence were recognised in the internal emails of Trafigura. As early as 27 December 2005, staff admitted that they knew very little about the process and requested information listing "locations that allow caustic washing – if [name redacted] hadn't informed us we still wouldn't know about it – as I don't think we have scratched the surface of caustic washing yet".[25] And on the issue of finding an appropriate company to deal with the waste, Trafigura seemed to be aware that this too should require some level of due diligence, noting that "[w]e should also be talking to specialist Chemical clean up companies about the process of clean up afterwards if that is the rate determining step."[26] It is no surprise then that the UN special rapporteur found a lack of due diligence in the hiring of an inexperienced company in Abidjan to take on the waste:

> Tommy . . . was only created shortly prior to the arrival of the *Probo Koala* and had neither previous experience with waste treatment nor adequate facilities, equipment and expertise to treat waste. It is of concern to the

Special Rapporteur that these shortcomings do not appear to have been taken into consideration by Trafigura.

(UNHRC 2009)

The process of caustic washing is not new but has lost favour because of the hazardous waste it produces. It is banned in the US, European Union and Singapore for that reason. According to Atherton, "Refineries used to wash with caustic soda back in the bad old days but it's a really dirty old-fashioned process" (John Atherton, quoted in TCE 2009). There are only a limited number of refineries today (as listed in the Basel/MARPOL conventions) that process this 'very hazardous' waste, containing both sodium hydroxide and hydrogen sulphide (TCE 2009).

According to its International Chemical Safety Card (ICSC), sodium hydroxide causes burns when touched directly and burns the lungs when inhaled, and exposure can result in nausea, headaches and respiratory problems. The ICSC lists unconsciousness and death as possible effects of hydrogen sulphide.[27] The BBC claims to have seen an analysis by the Dutch authorities which reveals the toxic waste to be lethal. They quote John Hoskins from the Royal Society of Chemistry, who stated that it would "bring a major city to its knees" (Jones and MacKean 2009) and reported that the waste included "tons of phenols which can cause death by contact, tons of hydrogen sulphide, lethal if inhaled in high concentrations, and vast quantities of corrosive caustic soda and mercaptans" (Jones and MacKean 2009). As for the problem of 'remedial action' following the dumping (UNHRC 2009), it appears that no comprehensive clean-up was undertaken (Tiembre et al. 2009), and Trafigura denies that it has responsibility for any such operation.

The question of whether the actions by Trafigura amounted to organisational deviance requires an analysis extending beyond the findings of the special rapporteur's (UNHRC 2009) report: how has the dumping breach institutionalised rules? Have the company's "actions been labelled deviant by national and international civil society organisations"? Furthermore, have these organisations "attempted to institute sanctions" against the company? (Green and Ward 2004: 42). By answering these questions can we fully determine the extent of the criminality of Trafigura's actions.

## Abused institutionalised rules

The dumping of the toxic waste has been considered by many commentators to breach European and international rules designed to avoid harmful consequences for people and the environment (Cox 2010). The transgressions also include violations of criminal law and of human rights and environmental treaties.

The main legal, institutionalised rules come from international treaties, regional (African) treaties, European directives and local domestic law. Eze

(2008) argues that the incident in Abidjan "constitutes a litmus test for the existing international instruments, revealing their strengths and weaknesses" (Eze 2008: 351). In this case the results of the litmus test showed mainly weaknesses, and as argued by Dimas, "[s]uch highly toxic waste should have never left the European Union. European and international laws were broken" (Dimas 2006). The fact that the waste ended up on African soil exposes a severe weakness in a regulatory system in which European rules and procedures 'pushed' the waste away from Europe towards other, less developed continents.

According to a BBC legal team,[28] the waste produced by the onboard caustic washing fell within Regulation 3(1)(A) of Marpol[29] Annex II (as interpreted under Appendix 1 of Annex 2) and Regulation 5 of Marpol Annex II.[30] Regulation 5 requires the disposal of Regulation 3(1)(A) waste to a suitable reception facility, and no such facility was available in Abidjan. The BBC team further argued that the waste was covered by the Basel Convention[31] under Annex 1[32] as it had properties as listed in Annex III.[33/34] No notice of the importation of the presence of waste was given under Article 6 of the Basel Convention and was therefore illegal.[35] The National Inquiry argued that the waste should have received special treatment under Article 13.[36] The Basel Convention had been designed to prevent incidents such as the one under study here, specifically to prevent transfer of hazardous waste from developed to less developed countries, and the preamble to the treaty states that the signatories are "[c]oncerned about the problem of illegal transboundary traffic in hazardous wastes [and] the limited capabilities of the developing countries to manage hazardous wastes."[37]

Similarly no notice of the importation was given as required by Article 9 of the Bamako Convention[38] and was therefore illegal.[39] The case has also shown failures of the institutional and operational systems implemented by these international treaties and designed to prevent the dumping of toxic waste. For example, under the Basel regulations, the German authorities should have been notified of the ship's passage through its waters (Knauer et al. 2006).

The dumping would have been illegal in Europe under Council Directive 91/689/EEC on hazardous waste as amended by Commission Directive 94/31/EC[40] and Council Directive 99/31/EC of 26 April 1999 on the landfill of waste. Although these directives have no direct legal effect in Ivory Coast, they would be well-known to Trafigura, which has an extensive presence in Europe. The objectives of these directives to prevent harm would also be well-known to Trafigura executives, and any violation would be a clear breach of institutionalised rules.

Domestic, Ivory Coast Law S8–651 of 1988 prohibits the importation, deposit or storage of industrial toxic waste.[41] This law was clearly violated, and the mechanism by which the relevant authorities did not carry out their duties is examined next.

The export and movement of toxic waste around the world illegally is a "thriving business" and an "infamous trade" (Eze 2008: 351), and Dimas estimates that "up to half of the sea transports of hazardous materials could be illegal" (quoted in Helsingin Sanomat 2006). Eze argues that the incident demonstrated the "drastic lack of capacity of a large number of countries to manage waste in an environmentally sound manner" (Eze 2008: 351). The evidence suggests that opportunities to commit these types of organisational crimes are plentiful and that the legal enforcement of constraints and controls are wildly deficient.

To summarise, the reported criminal acts of Trafigura include illegal disposal of toxic waste, fraud, forgery, deception and concealment of evidence; that is, the forgery of documents; concealing the nature of the waste in Amsterdam, Lagos and Abidjan; attempts to dump toxic waste in Nigeria and the proposed use of a barge from Togo returning to Lagos under a different name; employing the services of Tommy when the company clearly had no experience in dealing with toxic waste and requesting false invoices from Tommy; and quickly departing the port to avoid exposure to censure or sanctions once the dumping had taken place.

## Crimes of Trafigura's subcontractors

Tommy (officially 'Compagnie Tommy SARL') registered its company statutes in Abidjan on 24 May 2006, and they contain the company's objectives,[42] which make no mention of waste management. The company's route into the waste management business was through a series of licences and authorisations by multiple subunits of the Ivorian state shortly before the arrival of *Probo Koala*. On 9 June, Tommy submitted an application for a maritime chandler[43] licence to the general director of Maritime and Port Affairs. On 23 June, Tommy's licence was approved and transmitted to the transport minister, who signed it on 12 July 2006. On 20 July, Tommy applied to the general director of the Port Autonome of Abidjan (PAA) for authorisation to collect and remove oil and waste from ships and on 9 August was granted the authorisation to be in practise in the Abidjan port by Bombo.[44] The National Inquiry felt that Tommy was an organisation specially incorporated to receive this Trafigura's load of toxic waste and argued:

> The speed with which Tommy's license and authorization to practise in the port was obtained is unsettling and appears to be a fraudulent collusion . . . [and] . . . the Tommy Company had all the appearances of a cover company created specifically for the circumstance . . . and . . . it is undeniable that Ugborugbo was the principal author of the toxic waste dumping in the Abidjan district.[45]

Before the clean-up operation ordered by CIAPOL on 23 August, Tommy – at the request of Pisa-Impex – poured ninety-six litres of cresyl-pure over the waste at Akuédo "in an attempt to dissipate the smell".[46] This was repeated on 24 and 25 August and can be viewed as an attempt to hide the waste, literally to cover it up. Once this operation had been completed, representatives of Puma Energy, WAIBS and Tommy met, and Puma Energy and Tommy were asked to provide a bill for 10 million CFA for work done and provide another one for 100 million CFA "in order to conform with international standards".[47] This fake invoice was an attempt to feign conformity with international norms and can be understood as an indicator of deviant behaviour.

Pisa-Impex was founded in the 1990s to lease construction plant equipment and is headquartered in Yopougon, a neighbourhood of Abidjan. In 1999 and 2002 the company was awarded the contract for the management of the Akuédo dump.[48] Without any sufficient controls or oversight put in place by the contract, Pisa-Impex was able to contract for private waste to be dumped at Akuédo and the National Inquiry found:

> the Pisa-Impex agents who manage the Akuedo dump were in grave violation of the public service conceding contract clauses and without any control from the Abidjan District. The Commission also notes that the company Pisa-Impex has no expertise to manage a dump like Akuedo.[49]

Tommy paid 500,000 CFA to an agent of Pisa-Impex who said he used half to repair a damaged truck and up to 200,000 CFA to each of the other two Pisa-Impex agents present that day.[50]

The relationships between Trafigura and its subsidiaries and subcontractors are clear. The oil trader used its local subsidiary and agents to find a solution to a problem that had been preoccupying them for months, and they colluded with corporate associates and subsidiaries to dump the waste.

The dumping of the toxic waste has been considered by many commentators to breach European and international rules, including violations of criminal law and of human rights and environmental treaties (see Cox 2010). The Hulshof Commission concluded that the reloading of waste back onto the *Probo Koala* in Amsterdam violated EU environmental regulations (Hulshof Commission 2006). Furthermore, the company should have been well aware that Ivory Coast lacked the facilities and expertise to treat the waste. The terms of the handwritten 'quote' provided by Tommy corroborate this, a view which was supported by the National Inquiry of 2006. The UN special rapporteur too found that there was a lack of due diligence in hiring Tommy. The National Inquiry found that Trafigura's wholly owned subsidiary, Puma Energy, took an active part in the illicit transfer of toxic waste[51] and that Puma Energy received the handwritten quote from Tommy and transmitted it directly to Trafigura.[52] The resultant detrimental health effects of the dumping have also been outlined by international civil society actors (Dimas 2006; WHO 2006). But what is it about the character of the Ivorian state that allowed the waste to be dumped on its territory when it had proved so difficult elsewhere? The following sections will examine the role of the Ivorian state in promoting a space for deviance to flourish.

## Notes

1  Ibid., page 28.
2  Ibid.
3  Ibid.
4  Ibid., page 29.
5  Ibid.
6  Ibid.
7  Ibid.
8  He had already informed his Pisa-Impex superior (GC).
9  The report of the National Commission of Inquiry on the Toxic Waste in the District of Abidjan.
10 Ibid.
11 Ibid.
12 Claim No. HQ 09X02050; Trafigura Limited (Claimant) and British Broadcasting Corporation (Defendant); Defence (of 11/09/2009) against claim issued on 15 May 2009 in the High Court of Justice, Queens Bench Division, drafted by Andrew Caldecott QC and Jane Phillips and signed by Stephen Mitchell, head of Multimedia Programmes at the BBC (available at http://wikileaks.org/file/bbc-trafigura.pdf or mirror.wikileaks.info/leak/bbc-trafigura.pdf, accessed 16/02/2010), page 29.
13 Ibid., page 30.
14 Ibid., page 30.
15 Suburb of Abidjan.
16 Interview, Abidjan, September 2010.
17 Interview, Abidjan, September 2010.
18 The report of the National Commission of Inquiry on the Toxic Waste in the District of Abidjan, page 48.
19 Ibid.
20 Ibid.
21 Abidjan, 18/08/2006, To Jorge Marrero, Via Captain Kablan, Subject: Collection of Slops.
22 The report of the National Commission of Inquiry on the Toxic Waste in the District of Abidjan, page 49.
23 Department of Public Health in Faculty of Medical Sciences in partnership with the Swiss Tropical Institute.
24 EMAIL From: NA; To: LC, JMN; CC: JL, JT, FA, AH, GS, CD; Sent: Tue Dec 28 2005 15:11; Subject: Re: More High Sulphur from PMI.
25 EMAIL B From: JMN; To: LC, JT, FA, AH; CC: NA, JM, JL; Sent: Tue Dec 27 2005 1:12pm; Subject: Re: More High Sulphur from PMI.
26 Ibid.
27 International Chemical Safety Cards (ICSCs), available at www.inchem.org/pages/icsc.html.
28 Acting in defence of a libel claim by Trafigura.
29 Marpol (73/78) is the International Convention for the Prevention of Pollution from Ships, 1973 as modified by the Protocol of 1978. 'Marpol' is short for 'marine pollution'.
30 Claim No. HQ 09X02050; Trafigura Limited (Claimant) and British Broadcasting Corporation (Defendant); Defence (of 11/09/2009) against claim issued on 15 May 2009 in the High Court of Justice, Queens Bench Division, drafted by Andrew Caldecott QC and Jane Phillips and signed by Stephen Mitchell, head of Multimedia Programmes at the BBC (available at http://wikileaks.org/file/bbc-trafigura.pdf or mirror.wikileaks.info/leak/bbc-trafigura.pdf, accessed 16/02/2010), page 25.
31 Ivory Coast signed the Basel Convention in 1994 and ratified it with Decree 94–327 of 9 June 1994.

32  For example, Y8 and/or Y11 of Annex 1 of the Basel Convention.

33  Code H6.1 and/or H11 and/or Annex VIII Code A3010.

34  Claim No. HQ 09X02050; Trafigura Limited (Claimant) and British Broadcasting Corporation (Defendant); Defence (of 11/09/2009) against claim issued on 15 May 2009 in the High Court of Justice, Queens Bench Division, drafted by Andrew Caldecott QC and Jane Phillips and signed by Stephen Mitchell, head of Multimedia Programmes at the BBC (available at http://wikileaks.org/file/bbc-trafigura.pdf or mirror.wikileaks.info/leak/bbc-trafigura.pdf, accessed 16/02/2010), page 25.

35  Ibid.

36  The report of the National Commission of Inquiry on the Toxic Waste in the District of Abidjan, page 43.

37  The Basel Convention on the Control of Transboundary Movements of Hazardous Wastes and Their Disposal, Preamble, page 4.

38  Ivory Coast ratified the Bamako Convention in 1994. The convention was negotiated by twelve nations of the Organization of African Unity, came into force in 1998 and was designed to address the failures of the Basel Convention.

39  Claim No. HQ 09X02050; Trafigura Limited (Claimant) and British Broadcasting Corporation (Defendant); Defence (of 11/09/2009) against claim issued on 15 May 2009 in the High Court of Justice, Queens Bench Division, drafted by Andrew Caldecott QC and Jane Phillips and signed by Stephen Mitchell, head of Multimedia Programmes at the BBC (available at http://wikileaks.org/file/bbc-trafigura.pdf or mirror.wikileaks.info/leak/bbc-trafigura.pdf, accessed 16/02/2010), page 25.

40  Repealed by Directive 2008/98/EC on waste, with effect from 12 December 2010.

41  Claim No. HQ 09X02050; Trafigura Limited (Claimant) and British Broadcasting Corporation (Defendant); Defence (of 11/09/2009) against claim issued on 15 May 2009 in the High Court of Justice, Queens Bench Division, drafted by Andrew Caldecott QC and Jane Phillips and signed by Stephen Mitchell, head of Multimedia Programmes at the BBC (available at http://wikileaks.org/file/bbc-trafigura.pdf or mirror.wikileaks.info/leak/bbc-trafigura.pdf, accessed 16/02/2010), page 25.

42  The refuelling and maintenance of ships; the provision of mechanical, electric, refrigerating and miscellaneous equipment; commercial performance, importation, exportation and commercialisation of various products; construction and restoration of buildings; and operation of all industrial and commercial buildings, according to the report of the National Commission of Inquiry on the Toxic Waste in the District of Abidjan.

43  A type of retailer that specialises in shipping supplies.

44  The report of the National Commission of Inquiry on the Toxic Waste in the District of Abidjan.

45  Ibid.

46  Ibid., page 38.

47  Ibid.

48  Ibid.

49  Ibid., page 70.

50  Ibid.

51  The report of the National Commission of Inquiry on the Toxic Waste in the District of Abidjan, page 49.

52  Abidjan, 18/08/2006, To Jorge Marrero, Via CaptnKablan, Subject: Collection of Slops.

# Chapter 4

# The development of the state of Ivory Coast

The criminogenic landscape of Ivory Coast could be viewed as a direct product of its post-colonial legacy. This section will chart the development of a 'model' capitalist state and its subsequent, resultant slide into a site of significant criminality. Although this case study is orientated around the toxic waste dumping crime, it should be noted that since the completion of my research, the Ivorian head of state has been transferred to the International Criminal Court in The Hague for international crimes allegedly committed during the fighting that followed the recent presidential elections. Gbagbo, who violently contested the election results faces four charges of crimes against humanity. . . . The trajectory of contemporary Ivorian state criminality can be traced back to the birth of the West African nation. This chapter focuses on the economic and political history of Ivory Coast and explores how the state became susceptible to large-scale, state-corporate crime.

The de facto capital of Ivory Coast (also known as Côte d'Ivoire) is Abidjan.[1] It is the largest city, site of the financial centre and government, and home to most foreign embassies. The flag of Ivory Coast, based on the French flag, displays three equal vertical bands of orange (on the hoist side), white, and green (similar the Irish flag but shorter and with the colours in reverse order). Orange symbolises the savannah in the North, green the forest in the South, and white symbolises peace and unity. In 2006 there were two state-owned television and radio stations, no private television stations and few private radio stations. The extent to which 'outside' (non-government-generated) information is available to the general public is restricted to those who can afford satellite channels and access to the Internet.

While in the past the coastal region – and potentially the whole territory – was sparsely populated (Fage 1980; Jones and Johnson 1980), today most of the population live along the coast, with the exception of Yamoussoukro, and 50 per cent of the total population live in urban areas.

In 2012 the population was estimated at about 20 million, 40 per cent of whom were less than fourteen years old. This population estimate is up from 18 million in 2010, and population growth was about 2.44 per cent (UN 2011). In comparison Africa had a population of about 965 million and a growth rate of about 2.46 per cent (UN 2011). Life expectancy (at birth) in Ivory Coast is fifty-six years, higher than the sub-Saharan Africa average of forty-six, and the median age is nineteen years. Some 75 per cent of the population are 'indigenous Ivorians', and an estimated 20 per cent of total population is migrant workers from Liberia, Burkina Faso (about 50 per cent) and Guinea. Of these migrant workers approximately 70 per cent are Muslim. Approximately 3 per cent of the permanent population is originally from further afield – including some 130,000 Lebanese and 14,000 French (1998 estimate). Lebanese migration to Ivory Coast had been ongoing in some form since the 1890s but really began in earnest during the prosperous 1920s (Bierwirth 1997; UN 2006).

The predominant ethnic groups arrived in Ivory Coast within the last 500 years: the Kru from Liberia and the Senoufo and Lobi from Burkina Faso and Mali around 1600. In the eighteenth and nineteenth centuries, respectively, two groups (the Agni, southeast; and the Baoulé, central) from the Akan family (from Ghana) and the Malinké (from Guinea) invaded and migrated into the territory. Most ethnic populations (outside the cities) are concentrated in regions that correspond to adjacent, bordering origin territories and the largest ethnic group in the country is the Baoulé, originating from Ghana (Zolberg 1967).

French is the official language, and there are an estimated sixty native dialects – of which Dioula is the most widely spoken; illiteracy stands at about 50 per cent, and the average length of schooling is six years (UN 2006). In 2008 it was estimated that approximately 40 per cent of the population was Muslim, 33 per cent was Christian, and around 12 per cent adhered to traditional belief systems.

It is believed that there were settlements in the region that is Ivory Coast today dating at least as far back as the Neolithic era (Chenorkian 1983), but European influence did not begin in earnest until the eighteenth century. Europeans flocked to Africa in the late eighteenth century, following Livingston's call to deliver the three Cs – commerce, Christianity and civilisation. However, the French may have had a different motivation. Following humiliation in the Franco-Prussian war, France's armies were seeking to restore some of their former prestige and sought an overarching fourth 'C' – conquest (Packenham 2003).

Ivory Coast is so called because ivory was the only commodity available with which to entice adventurous eighteenth-century Europeans to trade (Fage 1980) and 'coast' because that was all that was apparent and relevant from the point of view of the European marauders. The hinterland appeared thoroughly inaccessible.

Colonised by the French, and with close ties to the former colonial power after independence, Ivory Coast was to become a showcase for African capitalist development – a picture of the stability and economic success of "the French experiment in West Africa" (Newbury 1960: 112). The Ivorian success story was, however, economically unsustainable and was, moreover, built upon an abuse of power from the outset.

## Brief history of Ivory Coast

History records that Ivory Coast was visited by European ships as early as the 1460s, but it wasn't until 1637 that France landed missionaries at Assinie. Early contacts were limited due largely to the notoriously inhospitable coastline but may also have been limited by settlers' "fear of the inhabitants" (US DoS 2010). According to Fage, the first account of Ivory Coast comes from Villault de Bellefond, who after his visit in 1667 remarked that "its people ate Europeans, and wore less clothing than any other West Africans" (Fage 1980: 299). Whereas most areas of West Africa involved colonial powers dealing with established local 'authorities', this was not the case of the coastal regions of Ivory Coast, "which also seems unique in that Europeans apparently neither saw nor were offered slaves there" (Fage 1980: 298), and "[a]part from some evidence as late as the 1820s it is generally accepted that Ivory Coast slave trade ceased by 1800" (Jones and Johnson 1980: 33).

Fage argues that the lack of slave trading can be explained by a shortage of local kings and the resultant sparse population "and so with a lack of economic development and of trade organized to offer goods of interest to foreigners" (Fage 1980: 299). In the early 1840s the French signed treaties with the kings of the Assinie and Grand Bassam regions, placing their territories under a French protectorate, thus securing a monopoly for French traders along the coast. Naval bases and fortified ports were built at Assinie and Grand Bassam, but "they were not intended to serve as springboards for expansion inland" (Newbury 1960: 253). The French did not get involved with local politics, and by the 1860s these trading posts were poorly situated, weakly defended and commercially unhealthy. To promote more efficient trade, Ivory Coast became a fully fledged French colony in 1893. Captain Louis Gustave Binger, as first governor, negotiated boundaries with Liberia and the Gold Coast in the early 1890s and set about "the primary task of establishing law and order along the rivers and trade routes from the coastal ports to the interior" (Newbury 1960: 112). By 1900 the budget of French Western Africa was about 24 million francs per annum, and in Ivory Coast up to 50 per cent of revenue went on administrative services, whereas "social services, health and education received 4.5 per cent" (Newbury 1960: 123).

From 1904 Ivory Coast was ruled from Paris as part of the Federation of French West Africa (until the 1956 Overseas Reform Act), and by 1915 effective French control of the territory was achieved. The process, however, was not without conflict and was secured only following a 'pacification' period (Bierwirth 1997) which included a war with the Mandinka (from Ghana) and the Baoulé (a guerrilla war that continued until 1917). The French were considered experts at this type of pacification in the region at that time. Edmund Dene Morel, British journalist and anti-slavery campaigner, pointed to the French success in applying direct taxes without bloodshed in 1901, showing, "in her handling of native questions in the land of the true Negroes ... the superiority of France's methods" (Morel 1902: 201). The French employed the mantra: "On gouverne de loin, mais on ne peut, de loin, que se borner a gouverner" (Newbury 1960: 112); 'we govern from afar, but from afar, we can only limit ourselves to govern'. This made sense at the time, when the colony was economically independent from France, with most imports coming from Britain and Germany (Newbury 1960). This attitude changed as France became more economically entrenched. Haute Volta, another French colony, was absorbed by Ivory Coast in 1933 in a bid to administer more efficiently, and by 1934 the French managed successful military recruiting in the territory – another indication of the 'superiority' of French methods (Arnett 1935).

During World War II (WWII) France's Vichy regime maintained governance until 1943, when de Gaulle took control of all French West Africa. Right up until the end of WWII, Ivorians were French 'subjects' without rights to citizenship or representation. The Ivorian Parti Democratique de la Côte d'Ivoire (PDCI) came to power after the war, as soon as political parties became legal. They lost a series of elections between 1949 and 1952 "but only because the French administration had tampered with the ballot" (Schachter 1961: 295). From 1950 Ivory Coast became dominated by immigrants and "corrupt state leaders" (McMullin 2009: 84; Wannenburg 2005). Entering politics continues to be seen as a means to criminal ends: "by capturing power, political figures gain control of a lucrative clandestine economic network" (ICG 2004: 4).

In October 1958 Guinea became the first independent French–African state. De Gaulle violently cut ties with Guinea when it refused to join a 'French Community' in the region. There was however a route to independence while still retaining close ties to France (Le Vine 1997), and this was seized upon by Ivory Coast in December 1958, when it became an autonomous republic within the French Community and then an independent (in the strict legal sense of the word) state on Sunday, 7 August 1960. By 1960 the population of Ivory Coast was about 3.3 million (and growing at about 3.5 per cent, including 1 per cent from immigration) – with about 180,000 people in Abidjan. Half of GDP derived from agricultural activities, and coffee and cocoa exports accounted for about 30 per cent of GDP. Close ties with France ensured that it was the biggest market for both exports and imports. As with most other newly independent former French colonies, Ivory Coast adopted a 'French' approach to its constitution and legal system. Le Vine argues that this was inevitable as "schooled in the French political tradition and habituated to French legal and institutional norms and forms, the African leaders were not likely to reject the political culture in which they themselves had been nurtured" (Le Vine 1986: 84). Perhaps the most pursued element of the French system was a provision which allowed for "strongly centralized leadership and control" (Le Vine 1997: 85) – very much suiting the style of the first president Félix Houphouët-Boigny and his successors. Houphouët-Boigny had cut his teeth as a member of the French parliament before taking control of the newly independent African colony.

In 1983 the capital of Ivory Coast was moved to the then small village of Yamoussoukro, which was Houphouët-Boigny's birthplace. This was a bold statement of a self-important leader who would rule the country for thirty-three years, from independence in 1960 to his death in 1993, with a repressive, kleptocratic regime. Houphouët-Boigny ruled by terror and was prone to claiming false plots against him to imprison and torture anyone that he felt was not totally loyal. He also presided over the bloody repression of two revolts. But by 1990 his regime had begun to unravel.

In 1990, struggling to cope with crippling national debt, the government attempted to cut public service salaries, but this was met with mass public defiance and "launched the biggest challenge to Houphouët-Boigny's rule since independence" (Bienen and van de Walle 1991: 404):

> In the streets themselves, popular resentment against the wealthy and the corrupt usually merged with anger over years of authoritarian rule. During an anti-government demonstration in Abidjan in March 1990, protestors chanted "Houphouet, voleur! Houphouet, demissionnez! Houphoulet, corrompu!"
>
> (Harsch 1993: 44)

Adiko Niamkey, general secretary of the general workers' union (UGTCI), demanded that the government should "repatriate the funds of those who have enriched themselves" rather than tax salaries as recommended by the IMF (Harsch 1993: 44). This was the first sign of cracks in the government's regime and was precipitated by the dire economic situation. In 1990 the teachers' union (Synares) demanded that "the immense fortunes illicitly acquired and stashed abroad should be brought back, and that personalities who obtained huge loans through state guarantees should be summoned to repay them as soon as possible" (Harsch 1993: 44). Riots were widespread, and banks and shops were attacked as far north as the city of Bouaké (Harsch 1993).

After Houphouët-Boigny's death in 1993, Henri Konan Bédié (leader of the National Assembly) took over to serve the remainder of his term (as prescribed under the constitution). In the 1995 presidential elections, boycotted by opposition parties amid allegations of voter registration irregularities, Bédié won 96 per cent of the vote. The opposition parties did, however, participate in legislative elections later in 1995, which were again hampered by similar irregularities, and the PDCI retained control of the National Assembly. In 1998 the PDCI government issued constitutional amendments that further increased and centralised the power enshrined in the president. From 1960 to 1999 the PDCI held both the presidency and a majority of seats in the National Assembly (African Elections Database 2010).

On Christmas Eve 1999 Ivory Coast experienced its first 'bloodless' military coup d'état ousting President Bédié. Justifications for the coup alluded to government corruption and incompetence. Retired Brigadier General Guéï formed a subsequent government, and a new constitution was ratified in 2000, but this constitution still contained clauses which exacerbated national divisions between North and South, Christian and Muslim.

Presidential elections in October 2000 sparked violence and attracted accusations of irregularities. The Supreme Court (as handpicked by Guéï) excluded the PDCI and one of two main opposition political parties, the Rally for Republicans (RDR), and western election monitors were subsequently withdrawn. Despite gaining fewer votes Guéï declared himself the winner. Supporters of presidential candidate Laurent Gbagbo, of the Ivorian Popular Front (FPI), took to the streets – joined by police and army – forcing Guéï to flee. The Supreme Court then declared Gbagbo president, with 53 per cent of the vote. The RDR protested as their candidate, Alassane Ouattara, had been prevented from running for office. The new government suppressed the protest; hundreds were killed in the ensuing violence until Ouattara recognised Gbagbo as president and called for peace. The violent Ouattara–Gbagbo rivalry was repeated in 2011, the outcome of which was victory for the French and UN-backed Ouattara and the arrest and transfer of Gbagbo to the International Criminal Court.

National Assembly elections in December 2000 were again dogged by violence and electoral irregularities, with most seats won by the FPI (about 40 per cent) and PDCI (35 per cent). Boycotted and violently disrupted by the RDR, turnout was about 33 per cent.

Both elections in 2000 attracted allegations of severe human rights abuses at the hands of the government, and a mass grave at Yopougon, western Abidjan, remains uninvestigated (IBP USA 2013; Seyni 2001).

In January 2001 there was another coup attempt that proved to be a relatively minor incident, and successful local elections were held peacefully a couple of months later. The RDR won a comfortable majority, ahead of the PDCI and FPI. In 2002 Ivory Coast had its first provincial elections, which again attracted accusations of electoral irregularities, and in August, President Gbagbo formed a 'unity' government which included the RDR.

In September 2002 exiled members of the military launched another coup attempt, which was said to include foreign fighters and support from the governments of Burkina Faso and Liberia (Gleditsch and Beardsley 2004: 380). This attempted coup evolved into a fully fledged rebellion, splitting the country in two. The New Forces (NF) took control of the northernmost 60 per cent of the country, whereas the government retained control of the populous southern territory. During the coup, General Guéï was killed, and the government razed shantytowns, displacing about 12,000 people. In October 2002 the government and NF agreed a ceasefire to be monitored by French military forces. However, in late November of that year, a new front developed in the conflict, in western Ivory Coast. In January 2003 the Economic Community of West African States (ECOWAS) deployed 1,500 troops to assist the 4,000-strong French force in patrolling the 'zone of confidence', a kind of buffer, or demilitarised zone that divided the country in two along an east-west axis.

In January 2003 the UN-monitored Linas-Marcoussis Accord was proposed by France and agreed to – paving the way for power sharing between the government and the NF. Seydou Diarra, as chosen by the international community, was appointed prime minister by Gbagbo (US CIA 2011). In July the National Armed Forces of Ivory Coast (FANCI) and the NF military agreed to work towards the Linas-Marcoussis Accord and disarmament.

The February 2004 United Nations Security Council (UNSC) Resolution 1528 approved the UN operation in Ivory Coast (ONUCI) which involved the deployment of 6,000 troops, joining the French 'Operation Unicorn' force of 4,000. Deadlines and goals set by the 2004 Accra III Agreement – designed to implement Linas-Marcoussis – were not met by the parties, and a deadlock had been reached. This was broken in November 2004 by the government when they launched bombing attacks on the north, including a raid on a French military installation – killing nine French soldiers. The French responded soon afterwards by destroying the Ivorian air force and taking over Abidjan. This reaction served as a reminder of the presence of the former colonial powers in the city. In November 2004 the UNSC agreed an arms embargo on Ivory Coast.[2]

The 2005 Pretoria Agreements, brokered by South African president Thabo Mbeki, formally brought peace and put the Linas-Marcoussis Accord back on track. In October 2005 UNSC Resolution 1633 extended the Linas-Marcoussis peace process for an additional twelve months and called for elections by the end of October 2006. In December 2005 the African Union (AU) designated Charles Konan Banny (then governor of the West African Central Bank) as prime minister. In 2006, realising that elections couldn't take place in time to reach the agreements deadline, the UNSC passed Resolution 1721 extending the mandates of Gbagbo and Banny until October 2007.

In March 2007 Gbagbo and former NF leader Guillaume Soro signed the Ouagadougou Political Agreement in Burkina Faso. The agreement saw Soro become prime minister, mandated elections and the dismantling of the zone of confidence. By the end of 2008, about 90 per cent of civil administration had returned to the North, and some courts were functioning and issuing birth certificates that were needed for voting in upcoming elections. Elections had been scheduled for November 2007 but were postponed to June 2008 and did not actually take place until the end of 2010.

## Developing the Ivorian economy

The Ivorian economy is based on a strong free market approach and depends heavily on smallholder cash crop production – cocoa (with 40 per cent of world supply, Ivory Coast is the largest producer in the world), coffee, pineapples, rubber and tropical woods. Agriculture employs about 70 per cent of the population (ILRF 2002). Another chief export is petroleum. This leaves the economy very sensitive to commodity price fluctuation on the world market.

The economy is also heavily influenced by the outside world, particularly by its former colonial power. Direct foreign investment accounts for about 45 per cent of total capital in Ivorian firms, and French investment accounts for 25 per cent ownership of Ivorian companies and around 60 per cent of all foreign investment capital. The stock of foreign direct investment was about US$5.7 billion (28% of GDP) in 2007. France is the main investor; other significant investors are other EU member-states, Switzerland, Lebanon, China and India. The state is part of the West African Economic and Monetary Union (WAEMU), which uses the CFA franc. The French Central Bank retains all international reserves of WAEMU states and maintains a fixed rate of 655.956 CFA to the Euro.

Ivory Coast is an important source of oil and chocolate for France and the rest of Europe. The government has surrendered monetary policy to France, and the majority of the population is at the mercy of the international commodities markets. Half of the country is under foreign ownership, a quarter by the French, and commentators have labelled the Ivorian state as susceptible to "elitist exploitation" (Clapham 1970: 8). By the 1970s Ivory Coast was widely renowned for its liberal economic policies, and a policy based on free enterprise had "been consistently pursued since independence" (O'Connor 1972: 411). At that time Shaw and Grieve argued that Ivory Coast was an "emerging economic magnet . . . for the US and other capitalist states" (Shaw and Grieve 1978: 3). Bartlett noted that Ivory Coast had long been considered "one of Africa's success stories" (Bartlett 1990: 330). The legal structure ensured that the economy was attractive to private investment, whether from domestic or foreign sources (O'Connor 1972). Tax rates remained modest, and so did the size of government (Bartlett 1990). These incentives for private capital ensured that Ivory Coast became "one of the most prosperous nations in Africa" (Bartlett 1990: 330). So how did this 'Ivorian miracle' come about, and how was it shattered?

Honohan argues that cash crops were key to success: "Côte d'Ivoire enjoyed enviable economic growth and diversification after independence, helped by the introduction of new cash crops" (Honohan 1993: 52). But this dependence may also have been part of the problem as these exports had little added value, and furthermore, profits were "more likely to be repatriated to France thanks to guaranteed convertibility, particularly when illicit and/or untaxed" (Bienen and van de Walle 1991: 394). Commentators with foresight (see, e.g., O'Connor 1972), described Abidjan as an 'island of prosperity' created for the comfort of Europeans and that the country was trading future prosperity and independence for rapid growth in the short term (O'Connor 1972).

Woods (2003) argues that the property rights regime was to blame. Land was freely (at next to no cost) available to locals and migrants alike. Whoever managed to produce something could lay claim to that land. However, declining incomes caused ethnic friction, and as Woods explains, as "the over-exploited tropical forest approaches 100% depletion, 'natives' are more likely to resort to violence and discrimination against 'outsiders' to reclaim land" (Woods 2003: 463).

At colonisation the only export was ivory (Jones and Johnson 1980). For the European powers in West Africa, business interests were paramount from the outset. Aside from any military ambitions, the ultimate goal of conquest was to bring civilised trade and commerce to the region to burgeon the home-state economy. Along the coast at Benin, the Porto Novo protectorate agreement (1863), Mellacourie treaties (1865–1866) and the treaties ceding Cotonou in 1868 and 1878 "were all initiated by mercantile pressure on French authorities on the coast" (Hargreaves 1960: 103). It is undoubtedly true that pandering to merchants, the French government built strongholds along Ivory Coast coast-line to protect trade. In the early 1870s, Verdier of la Rochelle was trading at Grand Bassam and Assinie and voiced opposition to the proposed exchange with the British of the enclave for Gambia, citing the economic potential of Ivory Coast. He was ignored by the new Third Republic's government, but they soon became more sympathetic as French politics became more republi-can and increasingly controlled by business and professionals, a small minority of whom were representatives of African merchants (Hargreaves 1960).

By 1900 the economy was doing well, and Morel noted that Ivory Coast was 'self-supporting' (Morel 1902: 198) – a situation unique for comparable colonies at that time. Bierwirth notes that the 1920s, "were euphoric times . . . a period that saw exports double in volume and quadruple in total value" (Bier-wirth 1997: 325). Plantations were established in the south in the 1920s and expanded in the 1930s, using forced labour. Commodity prices were protected in the French market, and Arnett notes that exports of cocao the "rose from 16,000 tons in 1927 to 31,000 tons in 1934 – when Ivory Coast showed a surplus" (Arnett 1935: 436).

Robinson (1951) argues that, post-WW II, the extent of 'Western penetra-tion' in the Ivorian economy explained its continuing accumulation success. One-fifth of revenue from the eight French territories came from Ivory Coast by 1949, where political activity "of a more or less western variety is most marked" (Robinson 1951: 125).

Cash crops continued to dominate the economy after WWII, and "the major effect of cash crop agriculture (cocoa, coffee) and its accompanying economic nexus was to make for fairly sharp divisions between different parts of the country, which coincided with distinct culture circles because these cash crops were spatially localised" (Zolberg 1967: 455). This led to "poorer and richer tribes" (Zolberg 1967: 455), a feature of colonial penetration, with ratios of 6:1 in income and 9:1 in proportion of children attending school between the richest and poorest areas of the country during the 1950s (Zolberg 1967).

From independence Houphouët-Boigny was keen to maintain ties with France. This was assured by pegging the Ivorian currency to the French franc "and even retaining French administrators in the government" (Bartlett 1990: 330). Segal noted that negotiations by Ivory Coast with the European Eco-nomic Community in the early 1960s were conducted with "little or no con-cern for the possible repercussions on the economies of the non-associated

African states" (Segal 1964: 77). Here, again, we encounter an attitude of 'elitist exploitation'. The economy experienced a "remarkable high rate of economic growth following independence in 1960, which was exceptional as compared with the growth rates of the other West African countries" (Haraguchi 1994: 79) and grew by an average of 8 per cent GDP in the 1960s and 1970s. Of course, GDP may not be the most accurate or reliable measure of the state's wealth as many enterprises are under foreign ownership, and there are no limits on the amount of finance expatriated by foreign or indigenous corporations. Despite a sharp fall in coffee and cocoa prices in the 1970s – to which the economy is highly susceptible – growth remained strong in the late 1970s when compared to other (non-oil-producing) nations in the region (Honohan 1993). This allowed Ivory Coast to maintain above-average growth, and by 1979 the country was the world's leading cocoa producer. The 'Miracle Ivoirien' continued through the 1970s and "[t]he main motivating factor of this miracle was rapid increases in cocoa and coffee production and export" (Haraguchi 1994: 79). However, a reversal of fortune toward the end of the decade heralded troubled times ahead (IFC 1985) despite the fact that "[f]ortuitous events, like the discovery of oil . . . and the sharp appreciation of the US dollar in the early 1980s disguised the burgeoning crisis" (Bienen and van de Walle 1991: 392).

In February 1980 World Bank President Robert McNamara launched the structural adjustment loan, or SAL (Easterly 2005). The main features of IMF and World Bank SALs during the 1980s and 1990s were fiscal adjustment, price setting and trade liberalisation (World Bank 1981a, 1981b) dictated by a general "movement towards free markets and away from state intervention" (Easterly 2005: 3). In 1981 the IMF made its first SAL to Ivory Coast in the amount US$150 million; a second and third followed in 1983 and 1986, both in the amount US$250 million (Haraguchi 1994). From 1982 the World Bank made similar loans available to states that already had IMF loans which were "designed to tide countries over until their balance of payments positions can be strengthened by changes in the structures of their economies" (Hodd 1987: 334).

Some of the conditions attached to SALs included harmonising energy and agriculture with world prices and the removal of protections on national industries. These loans would prove disastrous for Ivory Coast. Bruce Bartlett argues that any problems resulting from the SALs were as a result of "state encroachment into the private sector" (Bartlett 1990: 331) – unconvincingly citing the building of a large cathedral. However, throughout the 1980s government regulation of the economy remained modest by African standards, and considerable privatisation had taken place (Bartlett 1990). By the end of the decade, Bartlett optimistically argued that its economy "is likely to remain one of Africa's brighter lights" (Bartlett 1990: 331). However, Ivory Coast and other states in the CFA zone "continued to live beyond their means and accumulate debt" (Bienen and van de Walle 1991: 392). By the end of the 1980s, "[t]he cocoa boom in Ivory Coast was reaching its structural limits" and since independence 10 million hectares of

tropical forest had been destroyed (Woods 2003: 648). The bright light was starting to burn itself out. The deficit increased to 16 per cent of GDP and the debt
of 14 billion US dollars was estimated at 160 per cent of GNP. The outlook was
bleak "with as many as half the banks bankrupt and over a quarter of all loans
defaulted upon" (Bienen and van de Walle 1991: 392). Ivory Coast's liberal and
open economic policies that had proved so promising over the years were coming
back to haunt the country as the "signs of economic disequilibrium were more
pronounced in the Zone's richer countries which have more diversified economies and had had access to private capital" (Bienen and van de Walle 1991: 392).

In 1989 the Ivorian government succumbed to World Bank demands
and reduced the guaranteed prices offered to farmers by 50 per cent, sav-
ing the government a third of its budget but resulting in "the sacrifice of the
equivalent amount of cash income of around 500 thousand cocoa and coffee
farmers" (Haraguchi 1994: 80). Local producers of cash crops were to suffer
dramatically. Cash crops had been generally bought up by the government, and
this policy helped increase prices and output of coffee and cocoa by reducing
taxes on farmers (Honohan 1993). This guaranteed pricing system would have
worked well in a market impervious to large price fluctuation and did in fact
work well for Ivory Coast for a few years – but world demand started to fall,
precipitating a fall in cocoa prices throughout most of the 1980s (ILRF 2002),
putting a severe burden on government coffers and pressure on CFA parity
(Honohan 1993).

On top of these woes, the oil crises of the 1970s were still being felt, the
US dollar rose, industrialised countries continued increased protection of their
domestic industries and in 1983 the cocoa crop (by then still the largest in the
world) was damaged by "extraordinarily wide-ranging and destructive bush-
fires" as a result of drought, which had the knock-on effect of causing power
cuts in the Abidjan (Derrick 1984). By the late 1980s growth had slowed,
and Bienen and van de Walle argued that the overvaluation of the franc was
"demolishing the production apparatus" in affected countries and leading to
economic recession (Bienen and van de Walle 1991: 394). By the 1990s the
country started to run into severe debt problems (Bartlett 1990; Honohan
1993), leaving the state "almost bankrupt" (Haraguchi 1994: 80). The population suffered from the recession, and the International Labor Rights Forum
reported that from 1988 to 1995, the 'incidence and intensity of poverty' dou-
bled from around 18 per cent to around 36 per cent (ILRF 2002).

In 1994 the value of the CFA was halved, "thereby signalling the demise of
the Franco-African preferential monetary and trading area known as la zone
franc" (Martin 1995: 1). The rate had remained unchanged since 1948, and a
devaluation had been demanded by the World Bank and the IMF since the end
of the 1980s (Haraguchi 1994). The 1994 currency devaluation, as prescribed
by the World Bank and IMF to make Ivory Coast's exports more attractively
priced, "significantly affected the poor as their savings and purchasing power
dwindled overnight" (ILRF 2002: 8). The devaluation also increased the state's

debt burden. This devaluation and the contemporaneous structural adjustment measures, which allowed for increased aid flows, put – according to the IMF – "an end to the economic slump that had marred the Ivoirien economy for the previous eight years" (IMF 1996). The IMF had approved a SAL in the amount of US$183 million in 1995 to support economic reform, the main thrust of which was privatisation, reduction of price controls and non-tariff barriers and a scaling down of state intervention in the cocoa and coffee sectors (IMF 1995). The IMF praised the progress being made by the structural reforms:"the privatization program made great strides in 1995, and there was considerable liberalization of the regulatory framework governing economic activity" (IMF 1996). In 1996 the IMF approved a third SAL for 'enhanced' structural adjustment which included a structural reform programme that called for "a major deepening and acceleration of structural reforms" (IMF 1996).

Bolstered by especially high international commodity prices and currency devaluation, the economy grew by some 6 per cent per annum from 1994 to 1998, but it became necessary for Paris Club debt rescheduling in 1994 and 1998 (Paris Club 2011) and similarly with the London Club in 1998 (IMF 2006). By 1997 Ivory Coast was added to the IMF-World Bank list of heavily indebted countries (IMF 2006). Despite this fact the loans continued.

In March 1998 the IMF approved another loan "to address the unfinished reform agenda", which resulted in complete liberalisation of both the coffee and cocoa markets and "the sale of the state-owned bank BIAO was finalized in January 2000" (IMF 2000).

After the attempted coup of 1999, economic aid was significantly disrupted. Aid from the EU resumed in 2001, and the IMF re-engaged then too. But again, in 2002, crisis led to the cessation of foreign aid, and arrears on international loans started to build up for the government. Paris Club loans needed restructuring again in 2002 (IMF 2006). By the time the World Bank, IMF and the African Development Bank resumed lending in 2007, per capita income had declined by about 15 per cent, and in 2009, the IMF lent Ivory Coast US$565 million (IMF 2011). In 2009 both the Paris Club and London Club debt was once again rescheduled (Paris Club 2011; IMF 2009).

To "rebuild economy after years of internal crisis", the IMF loaned the Ivorian state US$612 million in 2011 (Camard 2011), which will ensure that the country continues to suffer from indebtedness.

The International Labor Rights Forum has argued that Ivory Coast is a

> perfect example of a country where the socioeconomic situation deteriorated with the arrival of the World Bank and IMF . . . a relatively stable country [which] possessed the largest economy in the West Africa Monetary Union, until it began engagement with the World Bank and IMF in 1989.
>
> (ILRF 2002: 1)

The structural adjustment programmes dictated by the World Bank and the IMF recommended accelerated privatisation, a reduction in government spending, liberalisation of the agricultural sector and severe currency devaluation.

The 'ill-advised' reforms resulted in the dismissal of around 10,000 public sector workers and produced "devastating effects on the poor" (ILRF 2002: 3; Haraguchi 1994), and the International Labor Rights Forum (ILRF) (2002) reports that the consequences of the SALs for Ivory Coast included economic instability, increased poverty and instances of child labour, a decline in the quality of education and health, and a widespread decrease in standard of living, with the poor hardest hit.

Ivory Coast's transition from colonial outpost to post-colonial 'economic magnet', based on liberal economic policies dictated by Bretton Woods institutions, has created a state in which the population is susceptible to state crime, state-corporate crime and the consequent suffering on a wide scale. In 1999 Ngoran Niamen, the Ivorian minister of finance, trying to justify the situation argued that "[g]lobalization is a fact. Globalization has been imposed on us. Globalization is marching on. The issue is how do we march with it or how will we be left behind" (IMF 1999).

Despite the apparent failure of the SAL project, the Ivorian government continues to rely on an open economy and ensures that tax, labour, environment, or health and safety laws do not impede investment. In other words the government may avoid enforcing the rule of law if in conflict with business interests. This free market approach unhindered by regulatory regimes was clearly reflected in the illegal granting of a licence to Trafigura's subsidiary (Puma Energy) and subcontractor (Tommy) in Ivory Coast as well as in the impunity afforded to the company when it was found to have contravened domestic environmental and criminal laws.

## The state's role in the dumping crime

The state of Ivory Coast's history of neo-patrimonial rule, moved from the stability and legitimacy enjoyed by the long-standing leader Houphouët-Boigny to the more unstable, 'predatory' form of state embodied by Laurent Gbagbo's administration. The Ivorian state is fragmented in the sense that constituent subunits do not always work in any coherent manner or follow shared goals. This is to be expected, and Green and Ward argue that any state "does not always or even in the majority of cases act as a unitary force" (Green and Ward 2004: 5). This was undoubtedly true of the aftermath of the dumping and can be seen, for example, from the unsynchronised and uncooperative attitudes of the various agencies operating in Abidjan port. For the purposes of understanding the criminal propensity of the Ivorian state, and in particular its role in Trafigura's dumping of toxic waste, this study has focused on health, security, port and customs services and related government departments.[3]

The director of the National Institute for Public Hygiene told the National Inquiry that his three-person team[4] boarded the *Probo Koala* on 19 August and verified the ship's documentation and checked its general condition. He stated that they found that nothing was out of the ordinary and "neither did they smell anything in particular".[5]

Similarly the port's police commissioner told the National Inquiry that the police agents who boarded the *Probo Koala* reported that nothing was out of order.

The director of Territory Surveillance stated that his agents boarded the ship and checked the ship's papers, which declared only slops and that their responsibility was thus limited to operations related to unloading slops. He stated that his officers "were never informed of the dangerous nature of the *Probo Koala*'s cargo".[6]

The head of Abidjan's Port Surveillance Department reported that his department did not intervene with transactions unless there were foodstuffs involved.[7] The commander of the Port Security Sector of the National Police stated that since 2002, following a meeting at the General Secretariat of the port, his agents were in fact no longer authorised to board ships.[8]

The director of Navigation and the Coastguard stated that the general director of Maritime and Port Affairs suspended the maritime police's activities[9] in 2004 to avoid 'agent abuse', and therefore his agents would only board a ship to locate defects in the ship and to check any equipment's suitability in accordance with International Maritime Organization standards. In this case his agents "did not detect any defects likely to cause any accidents in the sea".[10] And he stated that his department was "not alerted to any particular security or pollution problems".[11] This exchange suggested that the corruption (or perceived corruption) of the maritime police created a situation which precluded them from effectively carrying out their duties.

The oil storage facility of Abidjan[12] is supplied by a pipeline from the nearby oil refinery of Abidjan[13] and by ship via the PETROCI landing stage in the Vridi Canal. A Vridi customs officer told the National Inquiry that "he smelt a strong odour which triggered a series of sneezes. He thus asked Ugborugbo if the products were dangerous. Ugborugbo reassured him that the experts' analyses showed that the cargo presented no danger."[14] Vridi customs argued that they couldn't have known the nature of the materials being pumped from the ship to the trucks and that their "involvement was limited to control of the quantity of products discharged".[15] This contrasts to the reaction of the Amsterdam personnel, who raised the alarm on the issue of toxicity when they smelled the waste (UNHRC 2009).

Customs services are supposed to sit on a Licence Commission meeting when granting a licence such as that given to Tommy. Despite not being invited to any such formally prescribed meeting, customs services granted the probationary licence[16] to allow Tommy to act as "maritime chandler specialised in refuelling, maintenance and refuelling of ships in the Port of Abidjan".[17]

Tommy submitted its request for a maritime chandler's licence on 7 June 2006 and it was granted on 12 July 2006.[18]

The customs general director told the National Inquiry that he had, "well before the arrival of the *Probo Koala* ship, prohibited his agents from going on board oil tankers and ships which did not unload merchandise ... to avoid bothering the ships' crews".[19] This seriously hampered customs' ability to stop the importation of toxic waste and the customs services' claim to have not found out about the toxic waste until after the *Probo Koala* had departed. This demonstrated some serious problems with their intelligence collection operations, and the National Inquiry found "a malfunctioning of the Custom Administration ... contributed to the dumping of toxic waste in the Abidjan District".[20]

In the Ivorian Environmental Code, 'environment' is defined as

> all of the physical, chemical and biological elements and all the social, economical, moral and intellectual factors susceptible to having a direct or indirect, immediate or in time, effect on the development of the atmosphere, living beings and human activities.[21]

The Department for the Environment and Waters and Forests administers CIAPOL and the minister for the environment told the National Inquiry that the director general of PAA refused his agents a presence at the port. This was the same problem experienced by the maritime police and suggests a fiefdom mentality, with port authorities very protective of the territory and jurisdiction of their governmental subunit. The minister for the environment also stated, as did the director of CIAPOL and the head of the Port Authority Environmental Department, that environmental officers do not board ships.[22] The minister, on 21 August, set up a crisis committee and instructed CIAPOL to investigate the smell pervading the city. By 25 August, the minister felt that there had been a case of illegal toxic waste trafficking and informed the prime minister, who ordered and sat on an Inter-ministerial Committee. On 29 August, the minister formally notified the government council of the dumping.[23] Because the minister belatedly reacted to the dumping and violation of the environmental code (which determine his obligations), he failed to prevent such violations, and the National Inquiry argued that "the Environmental Minister did not use all the appropriate means that should have allowed him to undertake controls on the *Probo Koala* when it arrived at the Abidjan Port".[24]

On 21 August, CIAPOL, in collaboration with the Central Environmental Laboratory and the Antipollution Police Services Unit, traced the toxic waste to the *Probo Koala* but were refused boarding by its crew. They did, however, take samples of the toxic waste that had been spilled on the wharf in the course of the pumping from the ship to the trucks. Later that day CIAPOL issued a formal notice to the *Probo Koala*[25] "to immobilise the boat until the nature of its cargo had been determined".[26] The notice was sent to WAIBS as well as the Port Authority, the District of Abidjan and to the Ministry of the Environment, but none of these government agencies prevented the ship from leaving port (whether they were in a position to do so or not).

On 20 August, Bombo was officially notified of the odour of the waste from the *Probo Koala*. In the morning of the 21 August, Gossio telephoned Bombo to enquire about the odour, but Bombo "did not judge it necessary at the time" to inform Gossio of the details. Gossio was finally briefed at a meeting with CIAPOL and Bombo the next day. The National Inquiry concluded that the port authorities were 'accomplices' in the dumping and in the speedy departure of the *Probo Koala*.[27]

It is clear that the operating licence issued by the Department of Mines and Energy to Puma Energy (Trafigura's subsidiary) was granted illegally.[28] Tommy's request for an operating licence was granted without reference to the Licence Commission,[29] and the general director of Maritime and Port Affairs justified this breach of the law as a measure to avoid petitioners' direct contact with the prime minister's office as a procedural appeal,[30] and the National Inquiry concluded that "[t]his argument cannot succeed for one cannot rely on a violation to obstruct a route of appeal."[31] The licence granted legitimised Tommy as an organisation competent to receive the hazardous waste, and the circumnavigation of administrative rules in awarding the licence was a determining factor in the dumping.

The District of Abidjan had responsibility for environmental protection and the management of waste,[32] and it conceded management of the Akuédo dump to Pisa-Impex, a private company. During his hearing in front of the National Inquiry, the governor of the District of Abidjan stated: "as a District, we are not concerned with the management of industrial waste".[33] However, the 2003 law which transferred the state's responsibilities to the territorial authorities[34] does not make a distinction among types of waste, and the National Inquiry argues that the governor's statement "has no legal founding",[35] and the governor contributed to the dumping and "in no way carried out the mission to protect the environment".[36]

PETROCI,[37] the parastatal in charge of Ivory Coast's oil and gas industry which ran the berth where the *Probo Koala* docked, did not have the power to refuse the docking or unloading of the ship as all of the required paperwork was produced on demand. The general director of PETROCI considered this a 'loophole' and has since written new conditions for using the wharf.[38]

## The departure of the *Probo Koala*

WAIBS registered a 'leaving request' for the *Probo Koala* on the morning of Sunday, 20 August, with an indicated departure time of 11 p.m. that night. However, the anchor malfunctioned as it was 'blocked' or 'locked',[39] which delayed the departure of the ship. WAIBS then recommended that the Ivorian Tow and Rescue (IRES) be engaged to assist and asked Puma Energy to put pressure on the port authorities to get IRES to unlock the boat's anchor, which it did on 22 August 2006 at about 1 p.m. "upon the Port's insistence".[40] The National Inquiry argued that Bombo had insisted that IRES fix it so that the *Probo Koala* could leave quickly.[41]

Before the ship's departure the director of the CIAPOL received results of the preliminary analysis of the tests of the samples, confirmed the presence of toxic waste and began the process of immobilising the *Probo Koala*. However, an oil tanker cannot easily be contained by force, and the cooperation of the captain of the ship is required. The captain of the *Probo Koala* insisted that only Bombo could prevent the ship from leaving. The CIAPOL director went to Bombo's office to ask for help in stopping the departure, but the commander insisted that the state public prosecutor be summoned first to block the *Probo Koala*. The CIAPOL director asked for half an hour to do so, to which Bombo replied: "[a]t any rate, blocking a boat is very expensive and necessitates appropriate authorisation, in so far as the ship had actually provided all of the required documents".[42] Here, the port commander engaged in what Stanley Cohen (1993) would call implicatory denial, and at an organisational level the role of the *Probo Koala* was subjected to "cultural reconstruction" (Cohen 1993: 110). That is, the port commander employed obfuscating technical and legal terminology to justify the departure.

The CIAPOL director then requested a meeting with the general director of the Port Authority, Marcel Gossio. Upon arrival at the general director's office, Bombo was already there. The CIAPOL director made a request to immobilise the *Probo Koala*. Gossio asked for Bombo's opinion, who reported that "the ship was not at fault and thus could only be blocked at the request of the Public Prosecutor".[43] According to the CIAPOL director, Gossio then stated, "[Y]ou heard it, go and get the DA order or there is nothing I can do".[44] To which Bombo added, "at any rate the *Probo Koala* ship is already on its way".[45]

The general director of PETROCI stated that he too was "unable to block the *Probo Koala*, despite several attempts to do so".[46] The general director of PETROCI and the president of SIR Administrative Services had made repeated attempts to make contact with Gossio to ask him to prevent the *Probo Koala* leaving but were told by his personal secretary that he was unavailable. It is clear from the testimony outlined here that the *Probo Koala* – effectively a potential crime scene – was allowed to depart despite calls from various state agencies to block the ship as a result of the collusion between the commander and the director of the port.

The patchwork nature of the regulatory framework, compounded by infighting among state subunits created a space for deviant behaviour on the part of each of the state agencies involved which in turn allowed Trafigura to take advantage of an opportunity to shoddily, cheaply dispose of their toxic cargo. Although the actions of some individuals on the Ivorian side of the state-corporate relationship have been recognised as criminal by domestic courts in Abidjan, Trafigura has (to date) suffered no such prosecution and continues to deny any wrongdoing or harmful behaviour.

## Conclusion

The deviance or criminality of the Ivorian state has been readily identified and exposed by social audiences, particularly the National Inquiry. In summary the operating licence issued to Puma Energy was granted illegally.[47] Tommy's request for an operating licence was granted without reference to the Licence Commission.[48] This licence legitimised Tommy as an organisation competent to receive the hazardous waste, when it was patently incompetent to do so. The authorisation allowing the *Probo Koala* to dock was granted by Bombo, who the National Inquiry argued, had insisted (after the dumping) that the ship was not at fault and organised for the *Probo Koala* to leave port quickly.[49] The Ivorian state was also heavily criticised for operating a weak regulatory system.

The National Inquiry found that the dysfunctional customs administration contributed to the dumping.[50] The Department for the Environment and CIAPOL's agents, as well as the maritime police, were refused a presence at the port, and this prevented them exercising the requisite control. The National Inquiry argued that the minister for the environment failed to prevent violations of the Ivorian Environmental Code. The National Inquiry argued that the governor of the District of Abidjan contributed to the dumping and "in no way carried out the mission to protect the environment".[51]

This chapter has illuminated the collusion between Trafigura and the Ivorian government in particular through the illegal granting of licences and unfettered access to the port of Abidjan. The National Inquiry concluded that the port authorities were 'accomplices' in the dumping and in the speedy departure of the *Probo Koala*.[52]

Lasslett argues that any crime's 'phenomenal nature' "sets a gradient of difficulty, which will shape the practice's amenability to exposure and analysis" (Lasslett, 2012a). This is true of the dumping, which presented multiple barriers to analysis: scientific – because of the complex chemical composition of the waste; medical – because determining the health impact of the waste required specialist knowledge; legal – because the corporate veil of a close company is very difficult to penetrate; and geographical – because the location of the crime in an underdeveloped post-conflict West African country made access to information difficult. These difficulties were compounded by the reaction of Trafigura to public scrutiny. The corporation engaged in widespread cover-up and public relations management activities, making it difficult to collect and analyse data. But what has been revealed by the available data are the clear breaches of international and domestic regulatory norms by Trafigura and the Ivorian state. In the face of such deviance, the lack of significant sanction requires explanation.

## Notes

1  The official capital is Yamoussoukro.
2  United Nations Security Council resolution 1572, adopted unanimously on 15 November 2004.

3  The Office of the President, Office of the Prime Minister, Ministry of the Environ-
    ment and Forestry (including CIAPOL), Ministry of Transport, Ministry of Mines and
    Energy, Abidjan Port Authority, governor of the District of Abidjan, and the parastatals
    PETROCI and SIR.
4  A team leader, a state registered nurse and a driver.
5  The report of the National Commission of Inquiry on the Toxic Waste in the District
    of Abidjan, page 30.
6  Ibid., page 30.
7  Ibid.
8  Ibid.
9  Director of Maritime and Port Affairs note no. 10021/MEMT/DGAMP of 14 Septem-
    ber 2004.
10  The report of the National Commission of Inquiry on the Toxic Waste in the District
    of Abidjan, page 31.
11  Ibid., page 31.
12  Terminal Pétrolier d'Abidjan-Vridi or Abidjan-Vridi's Oil Terminal (TPAV).
13  Société Ivoirienne de Raffinage (SIR).
14  The report of the National Commission of Inquiry on the Toxic Waste in the District
    of Abidjan, page 32.
15  Ibid., page 31.
16  Decree 169/MT/DGAMP/DTMFL of 12 July 2006 according to the report of the
    National Commission of Inquiry on the Toxic Waste in the District of Abidjan, page 58.
17  The report of the National Commission of Inquiry on the Toxic Waste in the District
    of Abidjan, page 58.
18  Decree no. 2006–169/MT/DGAMP/DTMFL; see the report of the National Commis-
    sion of Inquiry on the Toxic Waste in the District of Abidjan, pages 18 and 20.
19  The report of the National Commission of Inquiry on the Toxic Waste in the District
    of Abidjan, page 58.
20  Ibid., page 59.
21  Article 1 of Law 96–766 of 3 October 1996, as quoted in the report of the National
    Commission of Inquiry on the Toxic Waste in the District of Abidjan.
22  The report of the National Commission of Inquiry on the Toxic Waste in the District
    of Abidjan.
23  Ibid.
24  Ibid., page 62.
25  Under Article 26 of Decree no. 98–43 of 1998 regarding graded facilities for the protec-
    tion of the environment, according to the report of the National Commission of Inquiry
    on the Toxic Waste in the District of Abidjan.
26  The report of the National Commission of Inquiry on the Toxic Waste in the District
    of Abidjan, page 36.
27  Ibid.
28  Under Article 2 of Law 92–469 of 30 July 1992, according to the report of the National
    Commission of Inquiry on the Toxic Waste in the District of Abidjan.
29  As required under Article 4 of Decree no. 97–615 of 16 October 1997.
30  Provided for under Article 8 of Decree no. 97–615 of 16 October 1997.
31  The report of the National Commission of Inquiry on the Toxic Waste in the District
    of Abidjan, page 44.
32  Under Law 2001–478 of 9 August 2001, according to the report of the National Com-
    mission of Inquiry on the Toxic Waste in the District of Abidjan.
33  The report of the National Commission of Inquiry on the Toxic Waste in the District
    of Abidjan, page 66.
34  Article 7 of Law no. 2003–208 of 7 July 2003.
35  The report of the National Commission of Inquiry on the Toxic Waste in the District
    of Abidjan, page 66.

36 Ibid., page 66.
37 PETROCI owns a 47.3 per cent share in Société Ivoirienne de Raffinage (SIR, or the Simple Oil Refinery in Abidjan [www.mbendi.com/copt.htm]).
38 In a letter dated 22 August 2006 and addressed to SIR, SMB, Customs, the Port Autonome in Abidjan and Puma Energy.
39 The report of the National Commission of Inquiry on the Toxic Waste in the District of Abidjan.
40 Ibid., page 40.
41 Ibid.
42 The report of the National Commission of Inquiry on the Toxic Waste in the District of Abidjan, page 41.
43 Ibid., page 41.
44 Ibid.
45 Ibid.
46 Ibid.
47 Under Article 2 of Law 92–469 of 30 July 1992, according to the report of the National Commission of Inquiry on the Toxic Waste in the District of Abidjan.
48 As required under Article 4 of Decree no. 97–615 of 16 October 1997.
49 Ibid.
50 Ibid., page 59.
51 The report of the National Commission of Inquiry on the Toxic Waste in the District of Abidjan, page 66.
52 Ibid.

# Chapter 5

# Explanations for impunity

Whereas sanctions and censure can be applied both informally by civil society and formally by law, impunity too can be traced to the operation of both mechanisms. This chapter will provide a criminological explanation for the apparent impunity enjoyed by Trafigura and the Ivorian state and will look at the efficacy of informal, civil society and sanctions.

Despite the fact that legal instruments aim to define and control corporate offending, "managers and corporations commit far more violence than any serial killer or [mafia-type] criminal organization" (Punch 2000: 243), and corporations have been committing crime with impunity for many years. In 1977 Conklin found that "there is little evidence that there has ever been a real effort to control business crime through criminal sanctions" (Conklin 1977: 136), and whereas criminal prosecutions of corporations in US courts were not uncommon in the 1970s, sentences were lenient. This apparent lack of legal control can be traced back to definitions of criminal law and to a lack of political will in legislating, or if enacted, for enforcing, rules designed to curtail criminal corporate behaviour.

The standard test of legal criminal liability can be summed up by the phrase *actus non facit reum nisi mens sit rea*, which means 'the act is not guilty unless the mind too is guilty'. From this well-established principle we get the two requisite legal elements of a crime: *mens rea*, the mental element of the crime, which must usually contemporaneously coincide with the *actus reus*, the offending act.[1] The *actus reus* is generally uncontroversial because it is much more easily located in the physical world. *Mens rea*, requiring a 'mind', is a more troublesome concept for the study of state-corporate crime and can only usefully be ascribed to individuals and not organisations:

> The primacy granted to notions of individual intent in criminal law, inscribed in the notion of mens rea (or 'knowing mind'), essentially excludes organisations from the normal method of attributing criminal liability and makes it difficult to attribute the blame for individual acts or omissions in the context of organisations.
>
> (Alvesalo and Whyte 2007: 59)

The construction of the *mens rea* test, devised by the common-law judiciary, ensures an enduring focus on the individual by all levels of the criminal justice system: "investigators, prosecutors, judges and juries all struggle to ascribe liability to an organisational entity distinct from the intentions, actions and omissions of one or several concrete individuals" (Hillyard and Tombs 2007: 13). The legal concept of *mens rea* is a major factor in attributing impunity for serious harm to organisations. The first US case of a corporation being tried for murder (more specifically, reckless homicide) was the Ford Pinto case. There was a failure of the US criminal justice system to appreciate the organisational nature of the crime, and Punch argues that "companies then get away with 'murder' because the law and the courts are not geared to organizational deviance and corporate violence" (Punch 2000: 243). In the UK a case against P&O for the *Herald of Free Enterprise* incident failed for similar reasons: "the judgement pointed to the difficulty in identifying a 'corporate mind' to explain the collapse of the case" (Punch 2000: 249). The technical legal difficulties of identifying, conceptualising and sanctioning corporate crime do not, however, hinder the social scientific field of criminology.

The constraints of criminal law have long led scholars of state and corporate crime to question a definitional reliance on law (Sellin 1938). As Green and Ward (2004) have argued, "A state's interpretation of its own laws should not suffice to remove its conduct from the purview of criminology".

The applicable definition of 'crime' is a heavily debated concept within criminology. The study by Alvesalo and Whyte (2007) on safety crime reveals the connections between principles of criminal law and how crime is understood: "the fundamental precepts upon which criminal law is based have an important role in providing a conceptual framework for how safety crimes are widely perceived and understood" (Alvesalo and Whyte 2007: 59). A brief analysis of the debate reveals two potential reasons for corporate criminal impunity. The corporate wrongdoing may not be against any law (and therefore not within the study of criminology when defined in the narrowest sense). Alternatively the act has been criminalized, but the organisational nature of the crime allows the deviant actor to escape prosecution (as well as escaping the scrutiny of traditional criminology and its singular interest in individual 'street crime'). Harms caused by corporations have thus tended to be left out of the criminal law altogether, and even if crimes are on the statute books or in common-law precedents, they are neither properly investigated (Alvesalo and Whyte 2007) nor enforced (Tombs and Hillyard 2004).

Although criminologists have traditionally taken the law as a starting point for their understanding of crime, increasing numbers of contemporary scholars are less wedded to legal determinations (see Walklate 2011).

As discussed in Chapter 1, this monograph concentrates on deviant behaviour, as opposed to behaviour recognised as criminal under the law. The criminological concept of 'deviance' is a complex one and requires some elaboration. Edwin Lemert (1951) first argued that deviance from informal and formal rules, and from social norms, was actually a function of society's reaction to behaviour and the subsequent attachment of a deviant label to the actor. Following Lemert, Erikson (1962) wrote: "it is the audience which eventually determines whether or not an episode of behaviour or any class of episodes is labelled deviant" (Erikson 1962: 308).

There is a weakness, or lack of formal legal rules and institutions, for their enforcement when it comes to crimes of corporations. This is especially true of crime committed on a transnational or international level. However, breaches of social norms often fall within the purview of civil society organisations and the media. In the absence of formal rules and corresponding sanctions, breaches of informal rules can be censured and labelled as deviant by civil society organisations such as human rights and environmental NGOs or by members of the press. Becker (1963) argued that rules are a manifestation of social norms held by the majority of a society, whether formal or informal, and the enforcement of 'norms' starts with a social audience bringing any breach to the attention of the general public (Becker 1963). When the formal norms of the criminal justice system are not invoked, civil society can act as a social conscience and bring wrongdoing to the public's attention (Green and Ward 2004).

## A political-economic explanation of impunity

In 1949 Sutherland famously bemoaned the fact that

> [t]he crimes of the lower class are handled by policemen, prosecutors, and judges, with penal sanctions in the form of fines, imprisonment, and death. The crimes of the upper class either result in no official action at all, or result in suits for damages in civil courts, or are handled by inspectors, and by administrative boards or commissions, with penal sanctions in the form of warnings, orders to cease and desist, occasionally the loss of a licence, and only in extreme cases by fines or prison sentences.
>
> (Sutherland 1949: 17)

Critical criminologists have focused on "the power of privileged segments of society to define crime, and to support enforcement of laws in accord with their particular interests" (Friedrichs and Schwartz 2007). These privileged interests frustrate any meaningful application state defined criminal law to state-corporate crime:

> corporate crime and state crime are obvious, heterogeneous categories of offence that remain largely marginal to dominant legal, policy, enforcement, and indeed academic, agendas, while at the same time creating widespread harm, not least amongst already relatively disadvantaged and powerless peoples.
>
> (Hillyard and Tombs 2007: 12)

Conklin (1977) echoed Sutherland's (1949) view of the role of the class system and noted that corporations were treated with leniency in the rare event of a conviction. The literature reveals that little has changed in the decades following this claim.

Academic sources reveal two particular features of capitalist society which heavily influence corporate crime and the freedom from censure it tends to enjoy. First, capital accumulation acts as a driver of crime: "capitalism provides the major incentives for organizations to use illegitimate means to achieve profit" (Kauzlarich and Kramer 1998: 146). And second, it promotes impunity for the main actors in the market sector. Fraud, for example, attracts stronger sanctions than corporate crime, not least because it is "deemed to threaten the effective functioning of capitalism" (Alvesalo and Whyte 2007: 59). It is, therefore, not simply a matter of the goals promoted by the capitalist economic system which drives state-corporate crime; it is the institutional relationship between corporations and the state, designed to protect the market, which plays a central role in ensuring that corporations are not unnecessarily constrained by law or other forms of regulatory control:

> Obviously, state-corporate crime is driven by financial interests; however, it is also sustained by key political dynamics serving to resist criminal definitions that would otherwise designate its actions as wrong and unethical. As a result, state-corporate crime persists because it is afforded impunity against prosecution.
>
> (Welch 2009: 352)

Impunity is, in this sense, embodied in the law even before the enforcement stage. Box argued that the ability of large corporations, both to affect regulations and to evade the law, may produce higher levels of small-business crime (Box 1987). This raises an interesting issue as initiatives by government to assuage calls for the control of corporate crime tend in practise to be directed at lower-level business offenders. Enforcement agencies tend to take the path of least resistance and balk at the idea of a 'complex' legal defence by tenacious barristers paid for by large firms with deep pockets (Croall 1989).

But it is not just at the legislative stage that corporations can influence the law. The state, to survive in a globalised capitalist system, cannot afford to discourage companies from investing. In Ivory Coast the state went to great lengths to create an attractive atmosphere for foreign corporate investment. Chambliss puts it this way:

> The accumulation of capital determines a nation's power, wealth, and survival today, as it did 300 years ago. The state must provide a climate and a set of international relations that facilitate this accumulation if it is to succeed. State officials will be judged in accordance with their ability to create these conditions.
>
> (Chambliss 1989: 202)

This climate inevitably encourages collusion between government and international corporations and not infrequently for the precipitation of crime in pursuit of organisational goals. In a study based in Nigeria, Lenning and Brightman argue:

> Western-based oil companies such as Mobil-Exxon, Chevron, Texaco and Shell Petroleum Development Company (SPDC) have flocked to Nigeria, creating very volatile relationships between the government that profits from their presence and impoverished citizens, millions of whom live on less than $1 US a day.
>
> (Lenning and Brightman 2009: 39)

Whyte, in similar vein, argues that capitalist regimes have had detrimental effects on African civil society:

> The rampant march of neo-liberalism has inflicted a crippling anti-protection trade regime upon many African states. It has encouraged, through strategies of privatization, the fragmentation of civil society and has created a breeding ground for civil conflict and state repression.
>
> (Whyte 2003: 598)

## Controlling state-corporate crime

The literature on state-corporate has grown apace in recent years (Tombs and Whyte 2002; Kauzlarich et al. 2003; Kramer and Michalowski 2005; Lasslett 2010b), but very few scholars have explicitly attempted to explain in detail the ways in which freedom from censure and punishment has been granted to corporations. Instead empirical studies have largely been preoccupied with explaining the prerequisite factors of the crimes.

Until recently the primary focus of the empirical literature on state-corporate crime has been on three catalysts for action. Advanced by Ron Kramer and his co-authors, this work suggests that a combination of motivations with opportunity coupled with a lack of social control can result in state-corporate crime. The motivations can be understood (albeit rather simplistically) in terms of pressure and goal attainment. Opportunity concerns the availability and attractiveness of illegitimate means. The third category, 'operationality of control', is concerned with the prevention of crime but does not engage with sanctions for criminal behaviour, and crimes are studied under this heading in terms of a failure of social control mechanisms. Three early state-corporate crime studies illustrate the point well. Kramer's (1992) study of the *Challenger* space shuttle explosion outlined various failures of internal and external corporate and government controls which, had they been sufficiently robust, may have prevented the disaster. Similarly Aulette and Michalowski (1993) point to a failure of local, regional and federal regulatory bodies in preventing a fire at the Imperial Food Products chicken processing plant in Hamlet, North Carolina. Matthews and Kauzlarich (2000) isolated the failure of the regulatory environment and a corporate culture of rule breaking in a study of the crash of ValuJet flight 592.

An important tool developed to understand state-corporate crime is the integrated theoretical model of state-corporate crime (Kauzlarich and Kramer 1998), which introduced six catalysts for action in the category of operationality of control on an institutional level of analysis: international reactions, political pressure, legal sanctions, media scrutiny, public opinion and social movements (Kauzlarich and Kramer 1998). The former three could be considered to be within the purview of the state. But the latter three are of interest to the study of civil society's capacity to act as agents of control: social movements, public opinion and media scrutiny are interrelated elements of civil society. Both social movements and the media contribute to public opinion in the struggles among civil society, the state and the market in formulating the dominant ideological hegemony. Kauzlarich and Kramer (1998) outline how these control mechanisms could operate at an institutional level and give a rather cursory account of the potentialities of social control by civil society actors:

> various forms of legal sanctions, both domestic and international, could be imposed by criminal justice or other governmental regulatory bodies. Domestic or international public opinion could pressure offending organisations, or citizen watchdog groups could exert social-control influence.
>
> (Kauzlarich and Kramer 1998: 151)

However, the model limits these 'social control mechanisms' (Kauzlarich and Kramer 1998: 151) to the prevention of crime and does not explore the utility of sanctions against criminal or deviant behaviour. Kauzlarich and Kramer argue for these mechanisms to be deployed to *block* state-corporate crime: "[a] highly motivated organisation with easy access to illegal means of goal attainment may be blocked from committing an organizational crime by one or more of these social control mechanisms" (Kauzlarich and Kramer 1998: 151). Walker and Whyte (2005) examined the accountability of private military companies (PMCs) in light of international and domestic laws and with respect to the market. The advantage to a government of employing PMCs for military operations includes the deflection of unwanted media coverage. As Walker and Whyte note, it is easier to avoid public scrutiny when PMC personnel rather than members of the military forces are killed. This alludes to an avenue of censure open to civil society that governments are keen to close, and as Walker and Whyte conclude, corporate reliance on market accountability reduces "public scrutiny and the observance of human rights and humanity to optional contract terms" (Walker and Whyte 2005: 687). Instead of providing significant sanction and censure, market accountability therefore only serves to drive deviance underground and out of civil society reach.

Corporate crimes differ from the originally conceived white collar crimes (Sutherland 1949) in that they are *organisational* in nature and are committed in furtherance of corporate rather than individual goals (Clinard 1983). Growing out of Sutherland's work, state crime and state-corporate crime form a natural extension of the organisational significance of these forms of criminality (Matthews and Kauzlarich 2007). However, two heavily contested areas of criminology as applied to corporations are, according to Matthews and Kauzlarich, "the unit of analysis and definition of crime" (2007: 46). Thus both the very conceptualisation of crime and the organisational nature of state-corporate crime contribute to problems associated with researching corporate offending. The organisational nature of the corporation is also a particularly decisive factor in the impunity afforded by criminal justice systems.

A reliance on strict legal definitions of crime has often meant that impunity for powerful crimes has been implicitly constructed as a failure of the law and its criminal justice processes as well as a lack of political will on the part of the domestic state and the international community of states. Recognising the limitations of that conception, Green and Ward (2004) introduced the notion of civil society as a powerful source of censure and sanction for deviant state and corporate behaviour (see also, McCulloch and Pickering 2005).

## Censure and sanctions

When reviewing the literature on corporate and state-corporate crime, it becomes clear that very little empirical research has been conducted into the mechanisms of impunity that operate around this class of criminality. This book critically engages with the impunity afforded Trafigura from the vantage point of both law and civil society and investigates the hypothesis that civil society could act as an effective censuring and sanctioning mechanism for the crime. This study involved empirical inquiry into the crime, the corporation, the Ivory Coast state and, more particularly in light of Green and Ward's (2004) work, international NGOs (INGOs) and that section of Ivorian civil society which might have played a significant role in applying censure and sanction. The study provides the opportunity to empirically test the significance of civil society in imparting informal regulation in the form of sanctions that were absent from the legal justice systems of the jurisdiction where the crime was directed (London) and the jurisdiction where it occurred, its harmful effects were felt and the victims are located (Abidjan, Ivory Coast).

The original aim of this research was to survey relevant civil society organisations to determine their capacity to apply sanctions. Data gathered in Ivory Coast revealed that the ability of civil society organisations to resist the crime was severely limited by both internal and external factors and by the disproportionate power of the corporate entity. However, once fieldwork was underway, it became apparent that elements of civil society, or groups masquerading as CSOs, were taking advantage of the general impunity afforded the corporation to exploit the victims of the dumping for financial gain, a crime that persists to this day. The implications of this discovery suggested a new emphasis in the direction of the research, and the behaviour of these deviant civil society organisations in Abidjan was investigated.

To better understand civil society's capacity to challenge impunity in cases of state-corporate crime, a Gramscian theoretical lens was applied to civil society actors in Abidjan and INGOs in Europe. Gramsci's theory of civil society as an 'arena of struggle' (1971) provides a framework for interpreting the data collected in London and on a field trip to Abidjan and in understanding the impunity afforded to Trafigura for the deviant act of dumping. A powerful counterbalance to struggles against impunity is denial, and Cohen's (2003) theory of state crime denial is employed throughout to explain some of the tactics deployed to counter sanctions and censure efforts by civil society actors.

## Civil society's promise

Many aspects of the toxic waste transport and dumping analysed in this book could be considered to be violations of law – whether administrative (document forgery), environmental (including violation of Regulation 5 of the Marpol Convention and Articles 6 and 13 of the Basel Convention) or criminal (e.g., the UK's Corporate Manslaughter and Corporate Homicide Act 2007). The question is why weren't these crimes addressed by the relevant legal authorities? A further possible explanation for the impunity afforded to Trafigura lies in the international nature of the corporation and the transnational nature of the state-corporate crime, directed from London and committed in Ivory Coast. As already mentioned Michalowski and Kramer (1987) argue that transnational corporations engage in crime that falls in 'the space between laws'. The criminal legal system deploys various tactics to avoid the prosecution of transnational corporate harms and state crime. These can be explained by the legal fiction of jurisdiction, an aspect of the international law principle of sovereignty (Lauterpacht 2011). Dutch prosecutors refused to investigate the crime as it lacked jurisdiction to pursue Trafigura for a crime committed in Africa (Greenpeace 2011). International criminal law, similar to the treatment of crime by most domestic legal systems, only recognises the criminal liability of individuals, and corporations cannot be tried or sanctioned by the International Criminal Court (ICC) (Bantekas and Nash 2007). Former Ivorian president, Laurent Gbagbo, does not enjoy the same 'technical' immunity and has since been transferred to the ICC in The Hague for crimes against humanity committed between 28 November 2010 and May 2011 in many of the same neighbourhoods of Abidjan that experienced the toxic dumping as well as in the west of Ivory Coast.[2]

The exploration of civil society as a mechanism for sanctions against powerful offenders is suggested by the apparent failure of legal definitions of crime to provide sanctions to corporations. Green and Ward's (2004) work concerns the organisational nature of crime, and is underpinned by a recognition of the limiting nature of strictly legal approaches. Furthermore, the role of civil society is taken from the periphery and centrally located as a key analytical concept in the sanctioning and censure of state-corporate crime actors. This presents an attractive theory to assist when trying to understand the mechanics of state-corporate crime and the possibilities of controlling it. The dumping of toxic waste in Ivory Coast provides an illuminating case study of the potential and limitations of civil society's role in the censure and sanction of state and state-corporate crime.

Kramer in his early work expressed greater confidence in processes of criminal justice and only cautious optimism in relation to external controls:

> Corporations . . . are subject to the criminal justice system, a wide variety of regulatory agencies, the media, labour unions, consumer and environmental groups, and public opinion. While these external controls are generally quite weak and ineffective, their sheer numbers guarantee at least a modest measure of oversight.
>
> (Kramer 1992: 234)

However, ten years later, Kramer and his colleagues retreat a little from their reliance on formal mechanisms of social control for powerful crime and consider the fact that civil society actors, with their less formal methods, could indeed be considered as agents of effective control:

> The theory of state-corporate crime suggests that formal social control is but one, and perhaps the least effective, way to control organizational crime and deviance. Real control must grow from social movements, grass-root activities, a truly aggressive and inquisitive media, and most important, open and democratic participation in the political process.
>
> (Kramer et al. 2002: 279)

Despite the apparent relegation of civil society actors to preventative measures only, there have been glimpses of the role of civil society in sanctioning corporate behaviour. Tombs and Whyte (2007) focus on the regulation of safety crimes and highlight the importance of domestic and international protest and social movements in enforcing safety crime regulations against corporations and criticise 'consensus' and 'capture' theories of regulation for marginalising these group.

So how did Ivorian civil society fare in the censure and/or sanction of the dumping in Ivory Coast?

## Notes

1  Crimes can also be couched in terms of omissions or failures to act.
2  Warrant of Arrest for Laurent Koudou Gbagbo, No. ICC-02/11, 23 November 2011.

# Chapter 6

# Civil society's role

Inadequacies in the application of criminal law and state inaction to bring justice to victims of state and state-corporate crime have presented civil society with the role of labelling and sanctioning the crimes. This chapter aims to provide a theoretical framework which will facilitate a greater understanding of the modest successes and catastrophic failures of civil society in exposing the fatal crime of toxic waste dumping in Abidjan in August 2006. The deviance of an act is determined not merely by illegality under the criminal law of a state or the international community but also, and predominantly, from this author's perspective, by reference to social harm (Hillyard et al. 2004) and violations of human rights as recognised by a social audience (Green and Ward 2004). The failure of criminal justice systems to deter and sanction state and (importantly, for the purposes of this book) corporate wrongdoing opens the way for civil society to do so. Another, less likely, avenue of sanction might emanate from the private sector itself, but as Parker argues; "[i]f the law itself fails to recognise and protect substantive and procedural rights, then business will doubly fail to do so" (Parker 2007: 4).

Parker (2007) proposes that meta-regulatory law could recognise and empower corporate governance standards promoted by INGOs and other non-state actors and foresees a future where we could see "international 'networks' of regulation in which state law, transnational voluntary codes, global civil society organisations and so on reinforce one another to regulate corporate conscience" (Parker 2007: 25). However, Parker acknowledges that this type of regime "generally only comes about through considerable struggle and conflict" (Parker 2007: 49). The ideal of an effective meta-regulatory regime has not yet come to pass. In the interim the role of civil society organisations is becoming increasingly recognised, and the ability to censure and sanction state-corporate criminal behaviour is worthy of exploration.

The elements of civil society examined here include NGOs in Ivory Coast and 'global', or 'foreign' or 'international', NGOs — sometimes referred to as INGOs. To employ the contested notion of civil society in understanding the processes of sanctioning state-corporate crime, a working theoretical framework is first proposed.

## Defining civil society

Even as it is used as a social scientific term, 'civil society' lacks clear definition. The definitional uncertainties are further confused by an academic divergence between civil society as a normative ambition and civil society as an empirical reality (Pearce 2000). Despite these ongoing issues useful definitions and conceptualisations of civil society as a cultural phenomenon have emerged and have been developed through the literature.

Although its origins are murky (Pelczynski 1984), the idea of 'civil society' as distinct from 'political society' is thought to have originated in eighteenth-century Enlightenment Europe in the work of Adam Ferguson (Edwards and Foley 2001). It was later developed by Hegel who also emphasised the state-civil society distinction (Hegel 1821). Hegel used the term 'burgerliche Gesellschaft', which can also be translated as 'bourgeois society' – a meaning famously adopted by Marx to describe a social class based on the ownership of private capital. The modern theory of civil society is attributed, in the main, to the work of Hegel as developed by Alexis de Tocqueville and Gramsci (Whaites 1998b). The idea was 'forgotten' for some time but rediscovered by counter-hegemonic intellectuals in communist Eastern Europe (Lewis 2001) and in the 1970s and 1980s by social movements resisting dictatorships in South America and Central Europe (Trentmann 2003). These counter-dictatorship origins are retained in popular understandings of civil society, with Madison arguing that civil society is "everything that totalitarianism is not" (Madison 1998: 12).

The definition adopted here derives from a concept of civil society introduced by Ferguson, developed by Hegel and then Marx, and crystallised by Gramsci. A parallel modern formulation of Hegel's work was developed by de Tocqueville, but he employed normative assumptions of civil society as an altruistic force for good. For Ferguson, civil society encompassed civilisation (meaning a departure from our natural state or 'rudeness') and the emerging modern standards of living as a result of specialisation; his main concern was that increased specialisation promoted an untenable diversification of interests that would lead to the fragmentation of society (Ferguson 1782). Both Ferguson and Hegel saw civil society as separate from and contrasted to the state, and Hegel argued that the solution to Ferguson's problem of fragmentation was a modern, enlightened state (Edwards and Foley 2001).

Hegel's philosophically original and 'problematic' (Pelczynski 1984) recognition of a 'civil sphere', as distinct from a political sphere (which regulated it), was criticised by Marx, who sought to eliminate the theoretical distinction between civil society and the state. Marx reconceptualised the Hegelian idea of the primacy of the political sphere, preferring to theorise civil society as the site of political discourse and change (Pelczynski 1984). Gramsci continued Marx's work but reached different conclusions based on a Hegelian notion of civil society: "Gramsci does not derive his concept of civil society from Marx but is openly indebted to Hegel for it" (Bobbio 1988: 149). In Gramsci's view

"civil society was the site of rebellion against the orthodox as well as the construction of cultural and ideological hegemony" (Edwards 2006: 8); in other
words the struggle that is central to civil society allows lower or under classes
to challenge the hegemony maintained by the ruling class as embodied in the
state (Edwards and Foley 2001). Hegemony, as refined by Gramsci (1971) in his
*Prison Notebooks*, is the organisation of public consent, through the institutions
of civil society, to the dominant ideology of the political and economic spheres.

Whaites (2000a) illustrates two visions of civil society: the Tocquevillean
approach, which centres on groups that organise around issues, and not 'kin',
and the view of Jean-François Bayart, which is more wide-ranging in that it
includes associations based on language and ethnicity. De Tocqueville's work is
based on the premise that a strong state acts as a stimulus or catalyst to civil society. However, others contend that a 'strong' and 'vocal' civil society can emerge
in those states that fail to provide basic services. The weakness or strength of a
state is not a function of its size but of its independence from elite social groups
who can hold the state to ransom, as was the case in Nigeria, Brazil, the Philippines and Thailand (Whaites 1998b).

Mercer (2002) acknowledges an increasing trend in the voluminous literature on the subject towards conceptualising civil society (and by extension
NGOs) through the theoretical lenses of Hegel, Marx and Gramsci. However,
some scholars doubt the usefulness of the very concept of 'civil society'; they
(see, e.g., Edwards and Foley 2001; Heinrich 2005) argue that the term should
be abandoned because of the multiplicity of views applied to civil society: "it
would be difficult to claim that the concept represents a distinctive 'paradigm'
for social scientific inquiry" (Edwards and Foley 2001: 5). Although acknowl-
edging the complexity, generalities and ambiguities presented by the notion of
civil society, a Gramscian model of civil society holds considerable explanatory
value for the study of state-corporate crime.

Van Rooy (1998) adopts a definition of civil society as, "the population
of groups formed for collective purposes primarily outside of the state and
marketplace", whereas other commentators argue that it is the political space
which is found between the state and the household or the family (Urry 1981;
McIlwaine 1998). This latter conceptualisation implies that the market, or private enterprise, may exist in this political space, and in this light Colás argues
that Gramscian civil society is "associated with the capitalist market and the
contest between hegemonic and counter-hegemonic forces that arise from this
'private' sphere of social relations" (Colás 2002: 10). Certainly the market, and
specifically the illicit market, did enter Ivorian civil society, but its penetration
suggests not the eclectic or plural nature of that civil society but rather its weakness. A more convincing interpretation of the Gramscian view of civil society
entails "counter-hegemonic struggles against the market as well as the state"
(Pearce 2000: 34).

For Gramsci civil society is intertwined with his theory of hegemony (Buttigieg 1995) and is "the sphere where the dominated social groups may organ-
ize their opposition and where an alternative hegemony may be constructed"

(Forgacs 2000: 420). Counter-hegemonic forces therefore contribute to the construction of an alternate hegemony. Parker's (2007) meta-regulation provides a framework for the exercise of a shifting concept of hegemony, which as 'cultural, moral and ideological' leadership (Forgacs 2000) is dynamic, and for Levy and Egan, hegemony "depends on an alignment of forces" (Levy and Egan 2003: 810). The first force is the power encompassed by the economic system (including production, taxation and sales). The second is organisational capacity (of corporations, the state and members of civil society). The third is the "discursive structure of culture, ideology, and symbolism that guides behaviour and lends legitimacy to particular organizations, practices, and distributions of resources" (Levy and Egan 2003: 810). From the point of view of civil society, the relationship between the second and third 'forces' is instructive; the organisational capacity of civil society organisations determines its ability to contribute to culture and ideology to ultimately guide behaviour, and "Gramsci's theoretical approach to understanding the process of social contestation can be extended to encompass multiple social actors competing for influence over the rules, institutions, norms, and policies that structure markets and economic relations" (Levy and Egan 2003: 824). And for Gramsci the 'actors' of civil society include "trade unions and other voluntary associations, as well as church organizations and political parties, when the latter are no part of the government, are all parts of civil society" (Forgacs 2000: 420). NGOs as 'voluntary associations' of civil society are "part of the public domain of governance" (Tandon 1991: 12). And for Parker (2007), INGOs and other non-state actors may someday complement state law in the regulation of corporate behaviour.

Whereas Gramscian civil society is "the ideological arena in which hegemony is secured . . . the relative autonomy of civil society turns the ideological realm into a key site of political contestation among rival social groups and ideas" (Levy and Egan 2003: 806). This concept of 'contestation' or of a 'war of position' is described by Gramsci using a military metaphor as he describes a battleground to challenge hegemony. The competing nature of the victims' organisations observed on my field trip to Ivory Coast, and the discourse between Trafigura and global civil society, resonates with Gramsci's theoretical understanding of civil society as a 'battleground' (Gramsci 1971; Hearn 2001). Whereas civil society can be methodologically conceptualised as independent of political power, it has a symbiotic relationship with the government (Buttigieg 2005) and can access the political sphere. The constituents of civil society are 'amphibious' (Taylor 1990) – with the ability to operate politically when required. Civil society actors that do not take advantage of this political potential may limit their possibilities for resistance (Lasslett 2012a). The struggle can also move the other way, "with the state attempting to penetrate and control civil society" (Harvey 2002: 205). Gramsci argued for a strategic approach in counter-hegemonic activities:

> avoid a futile frontal assault against entrenched adversaries; rather, the war of position constitutes a longer term strategy, coordinated across multiple

bases of power, to gain influence in the cultural institutions of civil society, develop organizational capacity, and to win new allies.

(Levy and Egan 2003: 807)

Although civil society organisations may employ either or both strategies – the 'frontal assault' or 'coordinated positional approach' – the very basis of what civil society actually lacks is clarity. There is no generally accepted, 'correct' view of civil society, but there is confusion about the term as a normative concept (i.e., what civil society ought to/aspires to be) and an empirical one (i.e., what it is). This book is, at once, concerned with the variance between the normative and empirical descriptions of civil society in general, and in Ivory Coast in particular, and with the way in which that variance played out in the reaction to a major state-corporate crime.

Edwards and Foley argue that "as an analytical concept, the contemporary notion of civil society and the sectoral models to which it is attached (i.e. the state and the market) ... suffer from acute definitional fuzziness" (Edwards and Foley 2001: 4), which can be attributed to (inter alia) the treatment of civil society and the sectors as ideal, normative types. Civil society can be described neutrally as "a sociological counterpart to the market in the economic sphere and to democracy in the political sphere" (White 1996: 178). However, some definitions assume an idealistic model of what civil society *ought* to be, in that it is expected to provide a bulwark – protecting people against the abuses and domination of the market and the state. Harvey argues that the various conceptualisations of civil society treat it "as much as a normative concept as an analytical tool" (Harvey 2002: 205). The problem with the confusion between the normative and empirical views lies in the assumption that civil society is always or necessarily 'a force for good' under the normative, idealised view – a confusion compounded by a misplaced fusion of visions of Tocquevillean and Gramscian civil society. Mercer (2002) is dismayed to find that there is no obvious distinction in the literature between commentators who adopt a Tocquevillean perspective (civil society is 'good', and therefore all NGOs are 'good things') and those who adhere to a Gramscian one (civil society as a contested space). Harvey (2002) adopts White's definition of civil society as an "intermediate associational realm between state and family, populated by organisations enjoying some autonomy in relation to the state and formed voluntarily by members of society to protect their interests or values" (1996: 182). The distinctiveness of this formulation, as Harvey points out, is that it is so wide as to include organised crime or death squads and does not make assumptions that civil society is always a "positive force for development" (Harvey 2002: 205). Furthermore, 'some autonomy' is not equivalent to "complete separation or independence" (Harvey 2002: 205), and Buttigieg argues that it is an "error of thinking that civil society is or can ever be sealed off from political society and the economic sphere" (Buttigieg 2005: 45). Gramscian hegemony too rejects the idea of a definable schism between government and civil society and holds any distinction to be purely methodological (Buttigieg 2005).

A general lack of literature outside the North American and Western European contexts means that comparisons between the North and South[1] are difficult, and this difficultly extends to the fashionable (but poorly problematised) concept of 'global civil society' (Edwards 2006). The term 'global civil society' has attracted the labels 'fuzzy' and 'contested' (Giddens 2001) or "an elusive metaphor which doesn't make much sense empirically" (Kaldor et al. 2004). However, Cox (1993) argues for a 'globally conceived civil society' to link social classes within the constituent nations. And Tandon argues that "[t]he challenge to the power of multinational corporations . . . necessitates strengthening international linkages across Civil Societies" (Tandon 1991: 13). Kant too proposed the idea of a global (or 'universal') civil society regulated by a cosmopolitan rule of law enshrined in international treaty (Kaldor 2003).

There are two liberal-cosmopolitan approaches to global civil society (Berry and Gabay 2009). First, it is that space between the family, the state and the market where action is undertaken for good on a transnational level (Berry and Gabay 2009; Naidoo 2003). This corresponds to a non-global Tocquevillean notion of civil society and suffers from the corresponding assumptions of civil society as a force for good. The second, Gramscian, approach outlines a global level beyond the concept of nation-states (Berry and Gabay 2009) and is involved in defining and redefining social orders (Colás 2002), but there is no inherent assumption of 'good' under this view. However, despite this, elements of such an assumption persist in the global society literature.

## Hijacking civil society

Civil society is primarily composed of organisations – such as religious institutions, charities, NGOs and INGOs, and a myriad of community groups – all of which are set up with overtly altruistic or moralistic ambitions. Anheier and Carlson describe the organisations that constitute the infrastructure of modern civil society as

> [v]oluntary associations, and non-governmental or non-profit organisations, social movements, networks and informal groups . . . they are the vehicles and forums for social participation, 'voice' processes, the expression of values and preferences, and service provision.
>
> (Anheier and Carlson, undated)

The assumption embodied in this quote, and often made by state crime scholars – that civil society organisations are inherently a 'force for good' – is too simplistic and does not allow for explanations of the full complexity of civil society and NGO activity in Ivory Coast.

The normative view of an inherently reformist civil society characterises the NGO literature (Clark 1995), and Fontana argues that "since the middle of the 1980s, the term civil society has been used as a kind of mantra and a panacea" (Fontana 2006: 1). The literature has tended overwhelmingly to portray

NGOs and civil society in positive light, but as this book suggests, such a view obscures the ambiguous and countervailing impact that civil society organisations can have. As Mercer argues, "[A] more contextualized and less value-laden approach to the understanding of the political role of NGOs" is required (Mercer 2002: 5). The assumption is widespread, and some scholars even go as far as to crudely count up the number of NGOs in a given region and "predict a positive correlation between their density and the vitality of democracy" (Trentmann 2003: 5). Todaro and Smith, for example, argue that NGOs are often perceived to be more trustworthy and more credible than companies or governments (Todaro and Smith 2006).

The World Bank is a leading exponent of this perspective and has defined NGOs as "private organizations that pursue activities to relieve suffering, promote the interests of the poor, protect the environment, provide basic social services, or undertake community development" (World Bank 1989). This definition makes unjustifiably optimistic and value-laden assumptions of NGOs which cannot always be sustained. World Bank sentiment is often applied uncritically to the expanding cohort of domestic NGOs in Africa today (Lewis 2001).

Applying altruistic and optimistic characteristics to civil society actors and ignoring the possibility of self-serving, deviant and criminal actors provides a distorted concept. And as the findings of this research suggest, an assumption that civil society is inherently a force for good can lead to a hijacking of that assumed goodwill. Beliefs in the inherent moral value of civil society are prevalent in the African context, and Sesan argues that civil society in Africa has assumed the role of "custodian of the people's hopes" for a better life (Sesan 2006: 5). Reading an inherent benevolence into civil society organisations and adopting an uncritical approach "can do more harm than good" (Whaites 1998: 130) as the potential for deviance is ignored. A lack of due diligence (at the least) by the Ivorian state and assumptions made by Ivorian victims about the nature of the organisations, purportedly acting in their interests, have led to the exploitation of these victims by deviant, mafia-style organisations. Although promising to work for the benefit of victims these organisations, in the guise of civil society, they have in fact been *commodifying victimhood* for profit. From a Gramscian perspective, NGOs can be seen not only to challenge state incursions into civil life but also to reflect and illuminate the more fundamental struggles within capitalist society (Mercer 2000). When the toxic waste was dumped, the first reaction of many in the community was to organise into victims' organisations, of which there were soon to be hundreds. The deviant organisations among them used force, bribery and intimidation to profit from the victims' suffering. This 'capture' of sections of civil society can be understood only in terms of the political and economic particularities of Ivory Coast, which is usefully described by Luckham (1996) as a *democradura*, or illiberal democracy. Whereas Ivorian governments are ostensibly democratically elected, election results are normally fiercely contested by defeated parties and not infrequently result in civil war. The instability of Ivory Coast political society allows for a larger political space between the state and the family. Organised crime "typically takes root and flourishes where the state is weak" (Sands 2007: 219) and will also seek to capitalise on the "vacuum created by an ineffective state" (Green and Ward 2004: 87). It is in this context that data was collected in Ivory Coast to assess the nature of emergent post-disaster civil society and its ability to fill that space and to resist state and state-corporate crime.

The propagation of victims' organisations in Ivory Coast is reminiscent of 'civil society gridlock' (Blair 1997), which is not just confusion or disjointedness caused by the volume of civil society organisations but the process by which claims on the state for services and resources are multiplied, thereby actually contributing to further weakening state institutions (Lewis 2001).

Green and Ward (2004) argue that one of the functions of civil society is its capacity to "label state actions as deviant" (Green and Ward 2004: 4) in the absence of the state defining its own acts as criminal. Furthermore, a well-developed civil society can be "a major constraint on state crime" (Green and Ward 2004). Green and Ward's (2004) definition of state crime is broad and ranges "from trade unions to television channels to single-issue pressure groups to revolutionary movements". Although it might be expected that the loudest voice of civil society in Ivory Coast would come from the local community of human rights NGOs (along with local branch offices of INGOs) and trade unions, significant questions were raised by the data collected in Ivory Coast in relation to the suitability and capacity of these types of to constrain or sanction of state crime.

In developing and post-conflict countries, civil society is often associated with the proliferation of NGOs (Howell et al. 2006), and the idea of NGOs as the manifestation of civil society is not a novel one. The World Bank usually sees civil society solely as "the new professionalized service and advocacy groups" (Edwards and Foley 2001: 4) – that is, NGOs – and does not subscribe to a wider definition that would include unions, community groups or non-profit organisations. Mohan (2002) also argues simply that civil society is composed of NGOs. NGOs have been growing in number throughout the world and have experienced a 2,000 per cent growth in numbers from 1964 to 1998 (Malhotra 2000). The 1980s and 1990s saw a particularly rapid rise in the number of NGOs, which can be attributed to the ascendancy of neo-liberalism and the corresponding reduction of the state (Malhotra 2000). Structural adjustment programmes (SAPs) in this period required drastic cuts in education and health spending, which provided encouragement for NGOs to substitute for government activities (Whaites 1998a). In June 2011, 3,337 NGOs were registered with consultative status at the United Nations – up nearly 50 per cent from 2003 (Todaro and Smith 2006). Forty-eight of these were based in Ivory Coast.

There are two primary ways to categorise NGOs: first, by the type of activity or project they pursue, more specifically by orientation – "welfare, development, advocacy, development education, networking and research" – and second, by the level on which they operate, including local, national, and international. But, as Vakil (1997) argues, an NGO may have several orientations, and to categorise NGOs by level of operation may also be an overly simplistic formulation. Many African NGOs have links beyond Africa (Lewis 2001), and horizontal, transnational links imply that NGOs do not challenge the state 'from below' but are instead 'contemporaries' of a wide range of civil society and political institutions (Ferguson 1998). But the fact that many domestic NGOs remain grassroots organisations, despite international funding, is suggestive that despite transitional network links, they may still be forms of resistance to the state from below. However, without supporting data, it cannot be assumed that all NGOs will challenge the hegemony of the prevailing state. Further assumptions made about NGOs by commentators include: independence, trustworthiness, and credibility and the ability to assist weak or corrupt states to function (Todaro and Smith 2006). A good example of the respect the literature affords NGOs, based on these assumptions, can be seen in the work of Lawrence and Nezhad, who argue that NGOs can, among other things,

> better address the needs of the community it is serving . . . can often bring innovative techniques and solutions to regions in need . . . provide public goods to sections of the population that might be socially excluded . . . the preservation of common property such as forests and rivers . . . teach sustainability techniques to people who would otherwise have limited incentive to conserve. They can act as an advocate of those who would otherwise not be heard within their own nation.
>
> (2009: 76)

This final point is important from the point of view of a counter-hegemonic struggle against the world view of the perpetrators of state-corporate crime. In Ivory Coast, human rights NGOs were expected to react to the abuses associated with the dumping and to provide the voices of victims of the dumping so that their views and experiences of the event would become part of the social discourse.

NGOs in Africa have particular strengths which Shastri (2008) outlines as strong links with grassroots, empirical expertise, innovative ability, democratic work culture, cost-effectiveness and long-term commitment. But weaknesses may include lack of experienced manpower, limited financial assistance, focus on short-range objectives, political influence, legal obligations, the high rate of growth in number of NGOs and a high corruption rate (Shastri 2008; Lawrence and Nezhad 2009). The rate of corruption is particularly important for this study. The data collected shows that the Ivorian victims' organisations set up in response to the dumping are involved in a range of corrupt practises in pursuance of organisational and individual goals. The developing critique of NGOs in the literature identifies four main themes: a neo-liberal orientation; relationships between INGOs and domestic NGOs; relationships with the state;

and limited theory and research focused on NGOs (Pearce 2000). It is worth exploring each thematic in some detail to better understand the NGOs surveyed in this book.

My research reveals that the civil society sphere in Ivory Coast was 'hijacked' and that organisations operating in this space can be used as vehicles for the pursuit of goals differing from, and often to the detriment of, the organisation's stated intended beneficiaries. One of the key findings from this research is that a range of organisations, masquerading as civil society organisations, were in fact engaged in the exploitation of the victims of the dumping of toxic waste created and owned by Trafigura in August 2006. The corruption of civil society in Ivory Coast was further compounded and exacerbated both by Trafigura's and the Ivorian government's lack of transparency and accountability. At a global level civil society fared better than its domestic Ivorian counterparts, but the struggle to label Trafigura's actions as deviant by INGOs was met by an effective cover-up operation by the corporation.

## NGOs and neo-liberalism

NGOs commonly advance a neo-liberal idea that the responsibility and solutions to social problems lie within the private and civil society spheres, leaving the poor with self-exploitation (or self-help) as the only option to meets their needs (Petras 1997). This approach is based on a theoretical misconception that a separation of the spheres of society exists:

> it is asserted that economic activity belongs to civil society, and that the state, must not intervene to regulate it. But since in actual reality civil society and state are one and the same, it must be clear that laissez-faire too is a form of state 'regulation', introduced and maintained by legislative and coercive means.
>
> (Forgacs 2000: 210)

This takes us back to a Gramscian formulation: civil society + political society = the state. However, it remains questionable whether civil society "has a global affinity with peace, democracy, and human rights, or is it yet another Western disguise for promoting individualism and market capitalism by other means?" (Trentmann 2003: 6). Even without an overt neo-liberal agenda, there is a risk that civil society is perceived as "a tool for the promotion of democracy, the market economy or capitalism" (Harvey 1998: 205). Civil society organisations will therefore be "assumed to be independent from the state and a fundamentally positive force" (Harvey 1998: 204). Harvey's critique is aptly illustrated in Ivory Coast, where all human rights NGOs interviewed in Abidjan were at one time or another funded by the National Endowment for Democracy (NED), a staunch proponent and promoter of the neo-liberal agenda.

## North-South transfer

Global civil society institutions operate within a North–South resource transfer paradigm (Malhotra 2000), with funding forming the basis of the relationships between INGOs and their domestic NGO partners. However, since the 1990s, the UN, some states and even NGOs in the developing world have questioned the legitimacy of 'northern' NGOs to represent the interests of poor people in the developed world (Howell et al. 2006). Commins, writing about northern NGOs, argues that there has been a backlash against them in which they are characterised as "useful fig-leaves to cover government inaction or indifference to human suffering" (1999: 71). Holloway (1999) relays that "[t]he word on the street in the South is that NGOs are charlatans racking up large salaries . . . and many air-conditioned offices" (in Pearce 2000: 21) and that some NGOs in Africa appear to be motivated by profit. Whereas there is debate about the relationship between northern and southern NGOs, the interdependent nature of these networked NGOs may not be conducive to viewing the entities as truly separate (Mohan 2002; Bebbington 2004). There are significant links among domestic groups and regional and global organisations (e.g., the local chapters of Amnesty International and Club African Union in Ivory Coast receive financial and technical support from their parent organisations[2]), but most Ivorian human rights NGOs are independent from other organisations and are, in fact, completely isolated from a globalised civil society. This isolation also limits their capacity to resist state-corporate crimes through organised regional and international networks.

During the 1990s the idea of an African civil society was often subject to enthusiastic debate in African politics and those debating tended to define it rather too narrowly and idealistically (Orvis 2001). As a result the debate did not portray African civil society accurately: "African civil society is more rooted in and representative of African society as a whole than the pessimists have admitted, but also less internally democratic and less likely to support liberal democracy than the optimists assert" (Orvis 2001: 17). The African NGO sector is characterised by external financial dependence and an external orientation (Hearn 2007), and the 'pessimistic' view is borne out by data collected from human rights NGOs in Ivory Coast.

## NGOs and states

NGOs may not be non-governmental at all (Petras 1997) as a considerable number receive funds from overseas governments to which they are ultimately accountable. This can create conflicting interests between the NGOs and the communities that they are supposed to serve. Contingencies attached to funding can limit services to a narrow range of the community, or section thereof, without being accountable to that community. NGO work is generally project based without any commitment to social movements (Petras 1997). The result of the scramble for donor money can make NGOs more accountable to the donors than to those they were constituted to assist and could even imply support for economic liberalisation (Hulme and Edwards 1992). Of the NGOs surveyed in Ivory Coast, all were funded to some extent by foreign states (including Canada, Denmark, Germany, Switzerland and the United States). In the struggle between civil society and the state, there is competition for donor funds, and as a consequence African NGOs are often taken under government control (Sesan 2006). In Ivory Coast it was reported during interviews that the government had set up its own NGOs precisely to secure international donor funds. Hearn (2001) argues that African civil society as an 'autonomous social force' is a spurious assumption and as discussed may be an assumption that any working definition should avoid.

There is a 'rather selective geography' (Mercer 2002) of the empirical literature on NGOs and civil society. And those most frequently referred to include Brazil, Chile and the Philippines, followed less frequently by Bangladesh, India and Kenya, with less literature again on South Africa and Thailand (Mercer 2002). This restricted knowledge base restricts the literature to the experiences of only a few countries and with a limited number of NGOs. Furthermore this literature has the danger of promoting de-contextualised normative ideals against which the performance of NGOs in other countries might be measured.

## Notes

1  North and South are used here to refer to the developed and developing world.
2  Interview, Abidjan, September 2010 (Club UA 2010).

# Chapter 7

# Researching civil society in Ivory Coast

Under a Gramscian formulation, civil society is a sphere of society "where an alternative hegemony may be constructed" (Forgacs 2000: 420). Human rights NGOs are obvious candidates for the constituents of civil society in the state-corporate crime context given their potential to label corporate and state actions as deviant and their potential to apply sanctions to those deviant actors. Human rights NGOs and victims organisations in Ivory Coast might have been expected to propose an alternative to the discourse of the state and Trafigura following the toxic waste dumping. However, as the data analysed here revealed, "to regard [the oppressed, the marginalized, and the voiceless] as tantamount to civil society can only result in a false understanding of the complex dynamics of power relations within, among, and across States" (Buttigieg 2005: 35).

The Gramscian distinction between the two major superstructural levels of society – the state and civil society – is not organic but methodological. Therefore, whereas the distinction may be analytically beneficial, it does not reflect the reality of the overlap between the state and civil society institutions (Forgacs 2000). Bearing this limitation in mind, this chapter aims to synthesise the relevant criminological and development studies literature to come to a broad working definition of civil society. This definition has both empirical and theoretical aspects and can be summarised as follows: (1) the space between the state and the family, distinct from the market (White 1996), and (2) a Gramscian battleground in which a struggle against the dominance of the state and the market takes place as well as the space in which members of civil society vie for position (Gramsci 1971). The empirical element of the definition assisted in locating participants for a case study, whereas the Gramscian framework allowed for a theoretically grounded analysis of data collected in the field.

In addition to the economic and political difficulties faced by Ivorian NGOs (common themes for African NGOs), my data revealed that they are particularly reticent to work with each other and suffer from an isolationist attitude: there is no genuine collaboration. "In other countries, when governments take a decision and civil society does not agree with the decision, they resist collectively. But in Ivory Coast, this is not the case."[1] Furthermore, NGOs did not assist victims of the dumping in any significant way. This was a calculated stance and was taken to avoid any association with corrupt, government-backed victims 'organisations (discussed further as follows).

The value of Gramsci's articulation of civil society for this study lies in its ability to assist in understanding and assessing the potential of human rights-orientated grassroots organisations in defending people against criminal actions of the state and international corporations. It also assists in understanding the very real limitations and ambiguities of civil society in sanctioning large-scale state-corporate crimes. My research focuses on voluntary organisations, in the form of INGOs, NGOs and victims' organisations. These are the Gramscian institutions of the superstructure.

NGOs were the primary subject of the field trip because they were seen to be at the vanguard of labelling and sanctioning deviant behaviour. Whereas in Europe, governments and NGOs, or similar civil society organisations, have a vast corporate-style Internet presence, this was not the case in Ivory Coast. Although many NGOs stated that they "have a site that needs updating",[2] most are not readily available to the most popular search engines and, if they are, contain little information.

## Participant NGOs and victims' organisations

For the analytical purposes required by this research, civil society in Abidjan has been divided into pre-existing human rights NGOs and the newly formed 'Trafigura victims' organisations'.

The study population for the focused interviews was initially selected based on convenience of location and purposive sampling to include all relevant local human rights NGOs – that is, NGOs that should or would have investigated and reacted to the case being researched. Two field trips were originally considered, an exploratory one in September 2010 with an option to follow-up in January 2011, but civil war broke out soon after the first trip, and the follow-up field trip became impossible for security reasons.

The NGOs surveyed can be split into the following four categories: domestic human rights organisations – APDH, LIDHO, MIDH and FIDHOP;[3] local chapters of international, regional and/or transnational organisations – Amnesty International, Ivory Coast (AI CI) and Club UA;[4] international or regional networks of associations – RAIDH and WANEP;[5] and other, less influential associations with human rights aspects attached to their stated mission – OFACI[6] and Transparency Justice.[7] These organisations as a group are representative of the relevant social audience for the violations of social norms by the state and by Trafigura. However, not all interviews with representatives of these organisations were suitable for data analysis. AI CI did not engage with the incident as they deferred to their parent organisation. RAIDH is an umbrella NGO, a federation of small human rights organisations, and did not consider the dumping to be the kind of incident within its remit: "we leave it to our members to act" was the response when an interview was requested.[8] RAIDH membership includes APDH, MIDH and Club UA. WANEP is only concerned with peace building.[9] OFACI did not consider the dumping specifically a women's issue and therefore not within its remit.[10] Transparency Justice is concerned with government transparency and, again, claimed not take on cases of this. The research therefore focused primarily on the data collected from four organisations: APDH, MIDH, LIDHO and Club UA, identified as major 'players' in the human rights field in Ivory Coast at the salient time.[11] A fifth notable human rights NGO, FIDHOP, is a newer organisation established in 2009,[12] after the crime examined here. FIDHOP has not been involved with the dumping at any level,[13] despite the presence of ongoing harmful effects. The validity of the selection was ultimately confirmed by the data supplied by participant organisations. According to APDH, "there are three major NGOs for the defence of human rights – LIDHO, MIDH and APDH".[14] MIDH stated that "there are three major organisations that work in the defence of human rights, three major NGOs in Ivory Coast – MIDH, LIDHO and APDH".[15] Unsurprisingly, when asked, FIDHOP included themselves in the list; "there are five NGOs: LIDHO, MIDH, APDH, Club UA and FIDHOP its representative claimed. These are the serious ones."[16] Club UA sees the main players in the field as LIDHO, MIDH, CEFCI[17] and RAIDH.

Apart from these 'major' NGOs, APDH reported that there are between twenty and twenty-five specialised human rights NGOs fighting for the rights of women, children and the disabled. Club UA claimed they were "in permanent contact with about fifteen human rights NGOs".[18] However, from my own observations, corroborated by a range of journalists, the participant NGOs form the core of the domestic human rights organisations in Ivory Coast and may therefore be seen to be representative of the relevant social audience. The ancillary NGOs, in terms of size and focus, were not chosen as participants, and none have surfaced in the literature or media reports as having been involved with the dumping.

Individuals at the participant NGOs were all well placed to answer the questions posed and included the president of the national executive of APDH,[19] the president of the MIDH,[20] the president of LIDHO[21] and the vice-secretary general of Club UA.[22]

However, whereas the NGOs under study were identified as the main human rights organisations, only two reported that they were either 'seized' by the issue at that time or were involved in the foundation and organisation of victims' organisations. One hundred and twenty of these victims organisations were established, either organically or with the assistance of local NGOs, and they in turn organised into (at least) four larger, 'umbrella' federations. Upon learning of these organisations, it was decided that they may be the civil society NGOs that this study should be concerned with, and arrangements were made to interview them.

This study was primarily concerned with six victims' organisations or federations: Union des Victimes des Déchets Toxiques d'Abidjan et Banlieue

(UVDTAB), Fédération Nationale des Victimes des Déchets Toxiques de Côte d'Ivoire (FENAVIDET), Réseau National pour la Défense des Droits des Victimes des Déchets Toxiques (RENADVIDET), Coordination Nationale des Victimes des Déchets Toxiques de Côte d'Ivoire (CNVDT), Fédération des Associations de Victimes de Déchets Toxiques de Côte d'Ivoire (FAVIDET) and Victimes Unies contre les Catastrophes Humaines (VUCAH).

Interviews were conducted with senior members of participant organisations including the founder president of UVDTAB, the president of CNVDT, the president of FAVIDET and the vice president of FENAVIDET. Information regarding RENADVIDET and VUCAH (who were scheduled for interviews during the aborted follow-up field trip) was found instead in the reports of journalists. Participant victims' organisations were chosen with the help of local and international journalists and NGOs and by asking the organisations themselves. For example, CNVDT suggested that apart from UVDTAB, FAVIDET would be useful participants.[23]

Access to these organisations was more difficult. The problems associated with accessing this type of organisation raised subjective suspicions in the researcher's mind. The representatives of victims' organisations were harder to meet than NGO representatives (taking weeks in some cases to respond and in others only allowing interviews with junior staff in the first instance); no recording was allowed at one and was limited at another. These issues of restricted access raised questions about the nature of the organisations themselves. One of the four victims' organisations approached for interview, CNVDT, was run by a former "high ranking"[24] member of Fédération Estudiantine et Scolaire de Côte d'Ivoire (FESCI), a 'mafia-type' student organisation (HRW 2008: 99). These organisations generally had security personnel on their premises or in the room during interview. This was observed at one NGO too (FIDHOP) but was much more pronounced at the victims' organisations.

What became apparent quite quickly was that a number of victims' organisations appeared to be extorting money from victims: offering promises of compensation from overseas or domestic civil damages cases, or from the government of Ivory Coast, even though no case or claim had been running. My research revealed that these victims' organisations were offering an elaborate registration process for a fee, and one group issued membership cards in an attempt to out-manoeuvre rival organisations in the 'battleground' for revenue or recognition. One organisation was keen to display an official government press certificate of authenticity to bolster claims of legitimacy; another simply 'muscled in' on victim-bound compensation, managing to convince an Ivorian court that his was the most 'official' victims' organisation.

## The topography of domestic NGO resistance

Together APDH, LIDHO, MIDH and Club UA represent the vanguard of Ivorian civil society concerned with human rights. These organisations would be expected to be an important measure of the capacity of civil society in Ivory Coast to resist state and state-corporate crime. Lasslett argues that a determination of the capacity of civil society organisations to resist state crime "must take into account the movement's class composition, the institutional pockets of opposition from which it can draw support, and the movement's capacity to employ the right balance of tactics" (Lasslett 2012a: 4). Ndegwa's (1996) study of African NGOs reaches a similar conclusion in relation to resistance: "for NGOs and other organizations in civil society to advance democratization (for instance, through successful opposition to state control of civic activities), four conditions must obtain: organization, resources, alliances, and political opportunity" (Ndegwa 1996: 1). The following analysis begins by examining the composition, institutional resources and internal processes of the Ivorian NGOs, before turning to external networked links to a wider civil society and the state.

LIDHO employs three people: the permanent secretary, the guardian/watcher and someone who runs errands for the organisation. LIDHO claims to have about 3,000 voluntary workers in fifty-six sections around the country.[25] This appears to be a significant membership, whereas other organisations claim serious personnel problems. However, the LIDHO website lists the email addresses of only six of its sections,[26] raising doubts that an organisation of this size and capabilities could effectively sustain 3,000 volunteers. MIDH staff are all said to be voluntary workers. However, there are five people to whom they "pay concessions to be permanent at work".[27] MIDH boasts four hundred members; a hundred of whom are "really committed" to the organisation.[28] APDH has four salaried staff: the secretary, the accountant, the cleaner and someone to run errands. They have twenty permanent volunteers.[29] Club UA has more than two hundred members and ten permanent staff, five of whom are salaried – the accountant, the secretary, the vice-secretary general, the staff member responsible for elections and the staff member in charge of conflict related to land – and the rest are paid expenses for transport.[30] The main four human rights NGOs therefore employ a total of only seventeen salaried staff – of whom only half are involved in human rights activities, with the remainder working as accountants, cleaners or errand runners. The number of salaried staff across the sector is low in a country of 20 million people but is relative to an official employment rate of 4 per cent (IRIN 2005).

During interviews, this problem of personnel was a recurring theme. APDH stated that it was their main problem, and it is not just a case of finding the funding as they felt that "it's quite difficult to find volunteer workers".[31] Even when funding is forthcoming, LIDHO reported that funds put at the organisation's disposal are strictly targeted to specific projects and cannot be used to pay salaries, rent or transport[32] (this problem of 'project-based funding' is discussed further as follows). Club UA sees two major inter-linked problems facing NGOs in Ivory Coast today: training and funding. Without trained personnel organisations are unable develop sophisticated project management strategies to attract funding. And even if they do manage to attract funding, they don't have the personnel with the competence to deal with it.[33] This problem of unskilled staff is related to the inadequacies of state institutions in the Ivorian state. Education is underdeveloped, with illiteracy standing at about 50 per cent,[34] and the average length of schooling is reportedly six years (US CIA 2011).

The human resources of these NGOs are severely limited, particularly when compared with those of Trafigura. Trafigura can offer attractive wages to highly educated individuals. The local NGOs have difficulty in finding and hiring skilled staff due to both a lack of funds and suitable candidates. This imbalance suggests that the local NGOs would struggle to meet the demands of sanctioning and censuring large-scale state-corporate crime in the face of significant corporate power.

## Data collection and dissemination

The Ivorian NGOs' lack of capacity is further exacerbated by the fact that their offices are all centralised and based on the south coast of the country. They demonstrate a significant urban-rural divide, compounded by infrastructural deficiencies. There is also a north-south divide, the country having been effectively partitioned for years. Making contact with the NGOs is very difficult from outside of Abidjan as there is a limit to the advocacy and support that can be provided via the underdeveloped mobile telephone network. The small size of the organisations, along with their apparent financial and human resource constraints, limits their capacity to send personnel into the interior of the country to serve individual victims of human rights abuses outside of Abidjan.

Similarly it is not easy for these NGOs to communicate their messages electronically to rural populations as most Ivorian civil society organisations and individuals are not online, and Internet connectivity is very low.[35] The websites of the NGOs' studied provide an indication of the communication structures of the organisations. APDH had a website (www.apdh-ci.org), but it was not working as of August 2011. MIDH claims to have a website, but the president did not know the address.[36] LIDHO has a website (www.lidho.org), but "that needs to be updated";[37] and Club UA has a website (www.clubua-ci.org) with eight pages, but half of these are devoid of content.[38]

A lack of modern communication tools severely hampers an organisation's ability to censure the criminal actions of the state and large corporations by disseminating information on abuses to domestic and international audiences. The domestic audiences to be reached by online campaigning would be predominantly city elites and the educated middle class given that Internet connections are relatively expensive at US$20 per month.[39] Improved modern communications structures would certainly assist the NGOs in getting their messages across to the general public as well as provide a platform for reports and statements that censure the deviant actions of states and corporations. Better communications would also facilitate collaboration among NGOs.

## Decision-making and accountability

The following section analyses how decisions are made within the organisations and by whom. It also explores the accountability of the organisations involved – important in understanding any restraints on individuals within the organisations. The issue is not just whether the organisations are transparent and can be held to account but also a question of who can hold an organisation to account – often determined by the funding streams that the organisations rely on for survival. Decision-making and accountability procedures impact upon the organisations' capacity to resist state-corporate crime. The speed at which an organisation can gauge and respond to a major human rights event is an important measure of resistance, as is their capacity to critically reflect on this response and modify future strategy.

The domestic NGOs deal with complaints from individuals, as well as proactively designing projects to promote human rights and democracy. APDH reports that they receive complaints of human rights abuse from "two or three persons per day and throughout the month it may be near 50 persons".[40] They also run seminars every three months in the interior of the country, which attract about fifty attendees each time.[41] Over the course of a year MIDH provides services for fifty to sixty individuals.[42] These individuals are dealt with on a case-by-case basis, and any decision to assist is based on the 'merits' of each case. No criteria were outlined for assessing the merits influencing decisions to take on cases. This creates the possibility of clients being arbitrarily refused assistance and could expose the client recruitment process to claims of discrimination on ethnic or gender grounds, clientelism and the misplacement of resources on cases that the organisation does not have the capacity to effectively deal with.

With respect to project work, NGOs in Ivory Coast must focus on a discrete range of abuses so that limited resources can be used effectively. The decision-making process for taking on projects and individual clients is important as it determines where the energies of the organisation are focused and which human rights abuses may be neglected. Based on an apparent lack of action in the Trafigura case, this decision-making process was explored as well as any assessment and auditing mechanisms in place.

The question asked – "Who decides what projects to work on?"[43] – was one of the most challenging in terms of eliciting an answer and required rephrasing and repeating during the majority of interviews in Abidjan. The problems stemmed, in some cases, from a misunderstanding of the question. All NGOs interviewed eventually answered that their management board makes all decisions as to which projects will be undertaken, and this decision was usually made democratically by that board. However, none of the management boards proposed projects and could only decide whether to pursue a project which had been recommended by a special department of the NGO or its president. The decision as to which projects should be rolled out will necessarily be influenced by the likelihood of receiving funding (the problem of project-specific funding is discussed next).

APDH's board consists of ten members: the president, two vice presidents, the secretary general, the secretary general for finance, an organiser, the secretary in charge of communication, the secretary in charge of women and children, the secretary in charge of training and projects, and the secretary in charge of social affairs. Decisions are reached by consent and voting if necessary: "generally speaking it is by consent and it is rare that they go to voting".[44] MIDH have a similar five-person board presided over by the vice president (in charge of projects) and includes the president, the staff member in charge of investigations, and the two staff members in charge of projects. The staff member who proposed and drafted the project is also in attendance to take part in the discussion. They discuss the project and decide whether to proceed. When asked whether all board members must agree to proceed with a project, the president answered, "[G]enerally, this is the case".[45] LIDHO works in teams to assess potential projects, determining their viability before submitting to partners for financing.[46] LIDHO was working on two projects when visited as part of the research: a project of 'cohesion' in the border regions between Liberia, Guinea and Ivory Coast and a training and capacity project around the issue of decentralisation in which local populations are trained to get involved in the development of their own area.[47] At Club UA the president, once elected for a term of five years, appoints a twelve-person board (which includes all the permanent members of staff), and this board makes all strategic decisions. The president also reports to the general assembly of all members every two years.[48] Whereas on paper these processes appear to be transparent and democratic, it would be difficult to assess the impact of influential members of the boards. Furthermore, the composition of the board itself can be heavily influenced by the head of some organisations – with the entire board of Club UA being appointed by its president.

The reality of these decision-making processes was hard to discern and, as noted, the question raised difficulties. It is possible that projects are chosen on the basis of their human rights impact and correlation with the NGOs' stated missions. However, in the scramble for funding, it is likely that applications are made when funding opportunities become available for projects and that the organisations will choose projects based on those opportunities.

Another marker of an organisation's transparency and organisational capacity relates to the mechanisms of oversight that are applied to individual projects. MIDH, APDH and Club UA evaluate their human rights projects using questionnaires that are submitted to participants.[49/50/51] MIDH also claimed that they measure a project's effectiveness by the number of congratulatory phone calls they receive.[52] The only organisation which moves beyond congratulatory phone calls or questionnaires was LIDHO, which has a staff member responsible for writing project evaluation reports. The lack of proper assessment mechanisms necessarily reduces an organisations' capacity to act as an agent of censure given that a lack of accountability erodes the legitimacy of its operations and will impact its ability to generate or influence public opinion. From a practical point of view, it also hampers their ability to learn from previous campaigns. These NGOs lack reliable data sets that could be used to empirically evidence their organisational deficiencies and strengths. Without a resistance strategy that is informed by critical reflection and rigorous data sets, it could be argued that these organisations risk repeating practises that are inappropriate, ineffective or counterproductive.

The internal organisational limitations of the NGOs are amplified if they are compared with the internal practises of the corporations they are required to challenge. In 2008 Trafigura agreed to a £9 million management training programme following an organisational audit.[53] The weaknesses identified in the organisational audit at Trafigura were not dissimilar to those of the Ivorian NGOs and included poor data quality, lack of expertise at senior levels of the organisation and lack of adequate oversight at the management level. But although the problems may be shared at one level, the NGOs lack the financial resources and expertise needed to deal with them. This, of course, is a product of the broader political-economic environment in which they operate. Indeed Makumbe explains that civil society in Africa is generally "fairly weak and beset with constraints of a financial, organizational, operational and even environmental nature. Some of these constraints have been generated by Africa's history, while others are the result of the continent's present social, cultural and political condition" (Makumbe 2008: 316–317). Here Makumbe is specifically referring to the effects of colonial regimes, which "made strenuous efforts to ensure that no civic groups would emerge in their colonies to challenge them for violating people's rights, for imposing authoritarian governance and for pillaging the Africans' human and natural resources" (2008: 310). It is clear then that each NGO's internal characteristics are determined to some extent by the environment in which it operates. The next section will look at the external factors that influence the NGOs' capacity to identify and resist state crime.

## Funding and access to government

According to Lasslett (2012a), if resistance movements are to be effective, they must possess "the right measure of financial assistance, complemented by a range of avenues for legal and direct action" (Lasslett 2012a, 4). He adds that these determinations are always relative to the crime itself and the campaign of denial mounted by the powerful. This section discusses how the human rights NGOs are funded, the influence donors have over the organisations' operations and the effect this has on their capacity to act as agents of resistance. Avenues for legal action and censure are explored in the following section.

Makumbe (2008) argues that funding secured by most African NGOs is ring-fenced and inadequate. Project agendas are set by external donors, and NGOs must ensure that funding applications and project delivery fit with the aims of these donors. This was also the case in Ivory Coast, but even when funding is forthcoming for the Ivorian human rights organisations, it tends to be relatively paltry and project based.[54]

The majority of APDH's project funding in 2010 was from three external partners: the Swiss Embassy, the US Embassy and the local UN office. The average project budget is about 10 million CFA (about €15,000) over one or two years. Project accounts are self-audited internally and audited externally when required by external partners.[55]

Initially, when first formed, MIDH collected money from members, but it proved an unstable funding stream, so they now only seek funding from external partners.[56] This highlights a problem faced by most NGOs working in Ivory Coast: the conflict of interest between donor requirements and members' needs. MIDH's main external partners are Oxfam, the National Endowment for Democracy (NED), the Canadian Embassy, the German Embassy and the US Embassy. The average project budget is €35,000 to €100,000 for projects that run from one to three years.[57] MIDH has both internal and external audits. Internal audits are conducted by independent auditors, and external partners use external auditors to oversee their respective projects.[58] The main venture that MIDH is currently working on is a three-year project on prisons, funded by NED.[59]

LIDHO has two main external funding partners – the Danish Refugee Council and the European Union (EU). They also secured limited funding from the International Rescue Committee (IRC). In the past they have been financed by Oxfam and NED. The 2010 project budgets range between 2 and 50 million CFA (about €3,000 to €75,000). In the past, when it was financed by Oxfam Novib, LIDHO had a project worth 200 billion CFA (about €300,000) over three years.[60]

CLUB UA's main projects concern children's rights (principally exhorting parents to obtain birth certificates for their children), land rights and training the population on how to vote. The most recent project had a budget of about 10 million CFA (about €15,000), and their accounts are audited internally and externally by a firm of auditors.[61] Club UA does collect funds from its members and also has external funding partners: the Canadian Embassy, US Embassy, the European Union, NED, Organisation International de la Francophonie, Ecole le Paix de Grenoble (School of Peace, Grenoble) and "an organisation in Switzerland".[62]

Clearly the local NGOs are heavily funded from outside the state, and most of the aid is specifically project based and from foreign government sources (with the notable exception of France, the post-colonial power). This creates a number of problems which reduce the capacity of Ivorian NGOs to challenge both state and international corporate crime.

First, the NGOs are beholden to foreign funders who have their own specific political agendas which may not necessarily be allied to the interests represented. For example, a number of the NGOs received funding from NED, which has a history of funding projects and movements that further the US neo-liberal agenda in the developing world. NED uses the cloak of civil society to operate politically (Blum 2002) in countries important to US interests[63] and claims that its "nongovernmental character gives it a flexibility that makes it possible to work in some of the world's most difficult circumstances, and to respond quickly when there is an opportunity for political change".[64] Blum (2002) argues that "NED likes to refer to itself as an NGO because this helps to maintain a certain credibility abroad that an official US government agency might not have. But NGO is a misnomer. NED is, in essence, a GO" (Blum 2002: 179–180). NED is funded by the US Congress with oversight provided by the US Congress and the US Department of State and has an annual grant budget of about US$100 million[65] (NED 2011). NED's engagement in the country has steadily increased over the years; in 2005 and 2006 NED committed about US$400,000 each year to Ivory Coast. In 2010 this figure rose to US$1.1 million. More than 67 per cent of the funds were channelled to three NED sister institutions ('the NED institutions'): the National Democratic Institute for International Affairs (NDI), chaired by Madeleine Albright, the International Republican Institute (IRI), chaired by John McCain, and the Center for International Private Enterprise (CIPE), which has a stated mission of strengthening democracy through corporate interests and market-oriented reform. The remaining funds are distributed among the local NGOs. This includes US$450,000 to MIDH (which is 9.2 per cent of the total funds distributed by NED in Ivory Coast between 2005 and 2010 inclusive), US$145,000 to Club UA (3 per cent of total), US$160,000 to APDH (3.3 per cent), US$68,000 to LIDHO (1.4 per cent) and US$95,000 to RAIDH (2 per cent). All the funding was project based, with no allowances for institutional funding. The projects ranged from those concerned with prison conditions (MIDH) to much more general undertakings, for example, to "improve civil society oversight of public institutions" or "strengthen women's knowledge of civil rights and democracy". Whereas NED is a major contributor to the human rights NGOs, it is funded by other governments too. When funding is obtained from foreign governments, Ivorian NGOs must be sensitive to the investment goals of the relevant foreign mission.

Second, as Ivorian NGOs lack direct budgetary funding, any human rights project must go through a cumbersome process of application of review. These projects take some time to propose and initiate and that limits the NGOs' response times and could go some way to explain a lacklustre reaction to the dumping. Without contingency funds an NGO must await funding approval before moving forward with any project. An alternative stream of funding could in theory come from the Ivorian state, but the reality of the relationship between NGOs and the state does not support the transfer of funds from the state.

Project money from embassies tends to be imperialistically applied to further foreign policy objectives of the donor state and as such can be interpreted as a form of neo-colonial control. The funds cannot be employed to run projects without the explicit approval of donors, the vast majority of which are states (through embassies and NED). As a result, according to Grugel, "a number of African NGOs have responded chiefly to governments rather than their supposed clientele. Others have lost local legitimacy through their dependence on funding sources from outside the country" (Grugel 2000). The scramble for funding has thus had the effect of encouraging NGOs to see accountability lying with donors as opposed to those they were constituted to assist. To attract follow-on funding, donors' expectations must be satisfied, and most aid has conditions attached. The vast majority of funding for human rights NGOs comes from overseas aid, and as a result NGOs tend to be answerable to large organisations that are far removed from the realities of local life.

The type and nature of projects cannot be dictated by the boards of NGOs as they are dependent on the funding that is available. Ensuring that funding is inadequate assures the NGOs' dependence on the donors for survival. Grugel (2000) argues that the presence of external donors challenges NGOs to maintain two policy agendas: "their own, based on a notion of civil society as people-centered development and democratization; and that of their funders, who use the term to mean capitalist modernization and liberalization" (Grugel 2000: 103). One of the major donors, NED, has funded projects for all of the NGOs under study here at one time or another. This has led to the development of programmes which suit donors' call for funding, as opposed to those which the local NGOs may feel are necessary, which is underlined by the relationship between states and civil society.

Tombs and Whyte (2003) argue that studies of state-corporate crime examine the complex relationships between harm and economic, political and social power. The next section sets out the landscape of the interrelationship between the political (state) and social (civil society) powers in Ivory Coast. We look first at the support, or lack of, provided to NGOs by the government and then at attempts to untangle the political influences on the NGOs and the social influences of civil society on the government.

## NGOs and the state

It appears that the NGOs, despite their history, distance themselves from the suggestion that they are aligned to any political actors in Ivory Coast. However, fieldwork raised significant questions about the support and encouragement provided by the government to the NGO community.

The Ivory Coast government has never, it appears, directly encouraged APDH to take on any projects, nor are they financed by the government. And whereas their advocacy and project-based activities are not facilitated by the government, they claim to take a complementary approach and "are associated to some activities that the government undertake".[66] Although APDH aims to complement governmental tasks, this has not always been the case, and its activity has tended to assume the actual role of government. According to one official within APDH "the government does not play its role so [APDH] are obliged to".[67] Even though APDH finds itself substituting for government, it also claims that the government has never impeded their work.

Although this may be true of the 'official' government based in Abidjan, there have been territories outside the Ivorian state's control at one time or another, and in June 2010, during a campaign in the northern part of the country, APDH were attacked by "well armed rebel forces", the Forces Nouvelles army which controlled that territory.[68] It is not clear why the group was attacked, but NGOs have been accused of siding with one side or another during periods of civil war that Ivory Coast has experienced. In 2002, for example, the minister of justice accused MIDH of working for the rebels, an accusation which led to assaults on NGO members by the public.[69]

Despite these accusations MIDH has received encouragement from the government to take a more active role in pursuing projects but "not openly".[70] The reasons for this lack of 'openness' is unclear, but it may be to do with the political considerations involved in engaging with an NGO in a way that acknowledges government failure. Or it may be to avoid association with organisations that have been accused of political ties to the opposition in the past.

MIDH substituted for government with its prison projects in Bouake and Daloa, which concerned providing assistance to prisoners, "normally a government task".[71] Whereas MIDH claims that the government has never directly impeded their work, its first president and his replacement were both exiled to the United States for highlighting human rights abuses by the government.[72] LIDHO claimed that the government has neither encouraged nor impeded their work but acknowledged that human rights NGOs are sometimes threatened by the government, organisations or individuals.[73] Club AU reported that apart from the signing of its incorporation documents, it has never received encouragement from the government to take a more active role in any area of its work. Rather it claims that it has experienced obstructive practises by state officials, especially in the interior of the country, and attribute this to ignorance on the part of those officials as to their role and a "rivalry between their actions and those of the government".[74]

It may be that the government is considered an indirect impediment to work or, alternatively, that participants were careful not to criticise the government explicitly in interviews – but no participant attempted to convey dissatisfaction with the government either off tape or off the record. This is not surprising given evidence of clear attempts by the government to suppress criticism, such as the threats to civil society organisations reported by MIDH, LIDHO and Club AU. These threats will undoubtedly promote caution on the part of NGOs when criticising government human rights abuses, and the resulting atmosphere of oppression appeared to depress and to limit NGOs' abilities to censure government activity.

It would appear that elements of the Ivorian state have at times employed force, or the threat of force, to shape how institutions of resistance within civil society strategically pursue their cause. When NGOs have acted in ways that complement the government, they have received encouragement from the Ivorian state. However, when they have reacted in ways that threaten the goals of existing governing projects, they have been harassed with some NGO staff forced into exile. As a result of this state oppression, the range of desirable strategies available to Ivorian NGOs when challenging state-corporate crime has been limited, thus weakening their capacity to censure. It is apparent from this that the Gramscian 'struggle' for civil society is played out within the NGO sphere – and that this battle is more obvious between the specifically constructed victims organisations, as we shall see later. The evident 'rivalry' among these groups also revealed a potential struggle between civil society, represented by NGOs, and the state. Investigative interviews (with journalists, among others) raised the issue that the following allegiances existed: LIDHO with Front Populaire Ivoirien (FPI); APDH with Front Populaire Ivoirien (FPI); MIDH with Rassemblement des Républicains (RDR); and Club UA – a Gadaffi-inspired group.[75]

APDH reported no connection to any political parties but acknowledged that other NGOs in Ivory Coast do because of "their willingness to control some NGOs and civil society". Those NGOs allied with explicit political affiliations were not generally perceived as powerful actors on the ground; according to APDH, "they are legless, they are not significant". APDH refused, however, to name any of these NGOs.[76] When asked whether his NGO had any connection to a political party, the president of MIDH answered, "No", but with the caveat: " as soon as you get out of this office and you ask anybody in Ivory Coast, they will say RDR [*Rassemblement des Républicains*]". The reasons for this were explained as follows: the first president of MIDH, Zorro Ballo, was the judge who signed the nationality certificate of Allassne Ouatarra, then president of RDR. Ouatarra was formerly the deputy director of the IMF and became the president of Ivory Coast in 2011, after the UN and French forces overthrew Gbagbo on his behalf. The fact that a former president of MIDH was from the North and the majority of the organisation's members are also from the North was also significant – RDR is therefore seen as a party of people from the north. MIDH however, continued to deny the claim of party affiliation: "I can assure that they have no particular link with this political party."[77]

The president of MIDH reported that there was a general perception that APDH was close to Laurent Gbagbo's *Front populaire ivoirien* (FPI) but expressed the belief that this was merely a perception: "after long discussions with the president of this NGO, I know how the man is and I cannot say that he is from a political party."[78/79] He went on to explain that at the beginning of the Ivorian crisis, in 2002, APDH supported the position of the president, so some of those in power participated in creating LIDHO as politically neutral. However, the previous president of LIDHO had been the financial director of the Labour Party.[80] When asked whether the interview at LIDHO could be recorded, the president answered, "LIDHO is a non-political, non-governmental organisation concerned with the defence of human rights, so they have nothing to hide."[81] When asked whether any of the large NGOs in Abidjan are politically motivated, the vice-secretary general of Club UA claimed he didn't know,[82] but his organisation was inspired by Muammar Gadaffi (former prime minister of Libya).

Clearly Ivorian NGOs were reluctant to acknowledge any links with specific parties. Nevertheless, whereas this may be politically expedient on their part, from a sociological perspective, the capacity of NGOs to resist the crimes of the powerful depends on their ability to establish relationships with institutional organs within the state and civil society. A capacity to work with opposition political parties avails NGOs with governmental resources and forums which can potentially increase their strategic ability to expose and censure crime.

As Lasslett (2012a) argues resistance should be mounted by movements and networks of actors. In Ivory Coast, the NGO community has been at pains to remain independent from politics. Despite the heritage of political involvement, NGOs have few viable connections with the state and reported no conduits in government to work through. Furthermore, as we shall see, lawyers are well represented among NGO staff but rarely make use of the judicial system. The Ivorian Ombudsman does not provide an avenue into the state apparatus as it is widely recognised as a weak institution with no legal powers.[83] Struggle and resistance, along with the mechanism of sanction and censure may benefit from cooperative relations with other civil society actors and the exploitation of certain state institutions. As Lasslett has argued a lack of these connections will weaken resistance movements, and in Ivory Coast this resultant weakness was manifest (Lasslett 2012a).

## Applying significant sanctions

With state-corporate crime, there are two principle actors – the state and the corporation. The significance of sanctions applied will differ from each actor's point of view. A corporation strives primarily for profit (and, to a lesser extent, growth with a view to increasing future profit generation capacity). To achieve the profit goal, a large international corporation must pursue power and influence to be a preferred commercial partner. Typical sanctions applied against corporations include legal actions (with a view to fines) and public campaigns (boycotts, sanctions and divestment) that damage a corporate reputation and, by extension, future profitability (at least in the short term). Campaigns targeting public opinion are likely to be more effective against consumer-facing companies, which Trafigura is not, and fines would have to be very large to make an impression on Trafigura's annual turnover. Therefore, arguably the most effective sanctions that could be applied to a large close business would be to affect their power to influence governments for favourable treatment and industry-friendly laws. One powerful tactic in this respect is legal action. Major legal actions can mobilise public support for human rights issues while exposing offenders to prolonged periods of negative publicity. In Ivory Coast, where NGOs lack the capacity to mobilise the public through political campaigns, the law remains one of the few conduits open to them. Nevertheless, as we shall now see, legal strategies were employed unevenly and conservatively by Ivorian human rights NGOs.

Human rights law in Ivory Coast is enshrined in both international and domestic law instruments by international treaty and domestic constitutional arrangements. Serious crimes tend to involve human rights abuses, and criminal charges under domestic law can be made against individuals as well as organisations. The human rights NGOs appear to have some capacity, in terms of staff and legal standing, to challenge state and corporate criminality by filing legal complaints against the government. Most, however, do not take advantage of this channel. Although this may be a result of a lack of confidence in the independence of the judiciary, the inability or unwillingness of civil society organisations in Ivory Coast to access justice through the legal system allows state, state-organised and state-corporate crime to flourish.

APDH receives legal support from a board known in English as the Commission of Legal Affairs and Judiciary Assistance. The APDH executive board and administrative staff includes three lawyers, two magistrates, three people working in justice, a secretary of justice and eight law graduates.[84] APDH have, in the past, lodged complaints on behalf of civilians against abuses by government military forces at a military tribunal. They also began proceedings against a student union (namely, FESCI, discussed as follows) by lodging complaints with the attorney general which were not acted upon. Since 2008 they have acted on behalf of twenty people in criminal legal proceedings, suggesting some experience at interacting with the criminal justice system.[85]

MIDH has a legal department with five lawyers and four law graduates. It has never filed an action against the government within the domestic legal system, but MIDH has initiated two separate proceedings against the Ivorian state at the African Commission on Human and Peoples' Rights (cases 246/02 and 262/02). Both cases alleged, with some success, that the Ivory Coast constitution contained provisions which are discriminatory to some citizens.[86] From 2008 to 2010 MIDH launched about ten criminal actions against individuals, including against policemen for extortion. Although it is difficult to gauge the success of such actions, the status quo has been maintained, and even state crime researchers are prone to extortion by Ivorian police.[87] MIDH has also assisted a student union to file a criminal legal complaint against another student union following the rape of one of their members.[88]

When faced with legal issues, LIDHO consults with their former chair, a professor of law and a lawyer, and the third president, who is also a lawyer.[89] LIDHO has never considered legal action against a corporation, but they do provide assistance to victims in finding legal representation. LIDHO has considered legal action against a student union but has never considered legal action against the government or an individual.[90]

Club UA does not have a legal department but do have 'legal officers'. They have never considered legal action against the government, a corporation or an individual.[91]

Thus we see a sparing use of law by Ivorian NGOs as a tool to resist the crimes of the powerful and the capacity to deal with only a limited number of individual complaints. Furthermore, none mentioned that they were involved in any project that dealt with the human rights abuses that resulted from Trafigura's toxic waste.

## Censuring Trafigura

To censure a large company such as Trafigura, which is engaged in complex forms of crimes, resistance groups need to be exceptionally well resourced and employ extensive links to nodal points within the state and civil society through which they can act.

It is extraordinarily difficult to match the resources of a large, powerful organisation like Trafigura to censure that organisation, and the analysis to this point has revealed that Ivorian NGOs are isolated with few or no connections with state institutions of accountability. This isolation drastically limits the possibility of effective censure. NGOs were aware of the dumping from the outset, and APDH provided a succinct version of events:

> A ship that came from Europe, declared that it had onboard waste water but in reality it was toxic substances. They gave the waste to a company for treating and dumping. This company was not competent in treating the substances, and immediately dumped the toxic substances in Abidjan. Immediately, on the morning of the dumping, all of Abidjan was invaded by bad odours and people were intoxicated. Officially, 500,000 victims were intoxicated and 21 dead. These are official figures, provided by the state of Cote d'Ivoire, Ministry of Health.[92]

APDH were approached by victims of the toxic waste dumping but acted slowly. Four years after the event, they claimed to be considering the matter and possible future legal action against the government.[93] However, the legal system is arguably insufficiently independent to be relied upon to provide relief against the government. Moreover, the lack of experience in legal challenges by human rights NGOs suggests only the possibility of a haphazard and poorly resourced response.

MIDH claims to have had "un peu"[94] involvement with the toxic waste case of 2006. They investigated the matter in collaboration with la Fédération International des Ligues des Droits de l'Homme (FIDH), a Paris-based association of NGOs, of which LIDHO and MIDH are member organisations.[95] FIDH, LIDHO and MIDH published a report in French in April 2011 outlining how this crime was dealt with by the domestic and international justice systems. It is indicative that neither LIDHO nor MIDH published independent reports on the issue, and it is only their relationship with this INGO (and not with each other) that has produced results. MIDH also claim to have assisted the UN special rapporteur when visiting Ivory Coast to investigate the matter.

Club AU did investigate the toxic waste dumping and visited numerous dumping sites before making a declaration "to condemn vehemently what was considered as a real violation of human rights in Ivory Coast".[96] However, they did not produce any documentation or reports on the crime, arguing the issue was outside its expertise.[97] Club UA highlight here another aspect of the mismatch with Trafigura – a small, underfunded NGO cannot command the same scientific 'knowledge' as the international corporation, and this lack of knowledge limits the capacity to act.

It appears that domestic NGOs did not have the capacity or willingness to challenge, in any significant way, the state-corporate crime of dumping and as a result did not pursue civil or criminal legal justice. MIDH chose to largely ignore the crime because it had been tainted by profiteering: "when people see you more active, they immediately think that you want to have money".[98] For this reason they only provide advice to victims and not representation.

Thus it would appear that whereas domestic human rights NGOs were aware of the dumping, and its significance as a human rights violation, they fundamentally failed to respond in a decisive fashion. At first glance this might be seen as a simple result of organisational preference. However, it would appear the factors underlying this lacklustre response lie in the weaknesses of human rights organisations in Ivory Coast. These organisations lack financial resources, skilled personnel, and reflective strategy. Moreover, Ivorian human rights NGOs are isolated, seeing this isolation as a virtue rather than a limitation. However, without links to organs of opposition and accountability within the state, or to counter-hegemonic institutions within civil society, these organisations lack the capacity to react to the crimes of the powerful or formulate a carefully theorised, well-resourced censure strategy. The relative strength of the offender compounded the weakness of human rights NGOs.

None of these processes occurred within a vacuum. The state has attempted to suppress civil society. And while this has not totally overcome dissent, it has ensured that it is expressed in ways that are more tolerable to the state. Moreover, as NGOs are dependent on project funding, they are also beholden to foreign states. In the case of Trafigura, this meant that they simply lacked the resources to respond through more conservative means (legal actions and research studies), whereas more radical courses of action were closed off by a lack of inter-linkages with political groups, unions and churches.

## Conclusion

As noted earlier Gramsci's conceptualisation of civil society provides a valuable means for understanding and assessing the potential and limits of human rights-orientated grassroots organisations in defending people against criminal actions of the state and international corporations. Gramsci (1971) describes civil society as a site of rebellion, where a counter-hegemonic struggle against the excesses of the state and the market takes place. This theoretical approach leads to an understanding of the very real limitations and ambiguities of civil society when contributing to the effective definition, censure and sanctioning of large-scale state-corporate crimes.

The present study reveals that – relative to those they were challenging – Ivorian domestic NGOs had little capacity to expose, control, constrain or sanction the large-scale state-corporate crime the toxic dumping represented. The failure to mount a comprehensive resistance was found to be the result of a combination of internal and external factors. Internally NGOs suffered from a lack of institutional funding, resources and quality personnel. Externally there was an apparent unwillingness by Ivorian NGOs to pool resources and expertise with other civil society organs (e.g., trade unions, the church, community groups and probably, most importantly, other NGOs) as well as an inability to maintain a working relationship with elements within the state which could aid resistance (e.g., an ombudsman office, the judiciary or sympathetic political parties). It will be suggested that the underdevelopment of NGOs in Ivory Coast – which fundamentally weakened their capacity to censure Trafigura – is a manifestation of successive colonial and post-colonial government policies, the imperial agendas of foreign states and Ivory Coast's peripheral role in the world economy.

Employing Lasslett's (2012a) relational paradigm of resistance, this chapter gauged the capacity of domestic NGOs in Ivory Coast to resist state-corporate crime – specifically the dumping as explored in Chapter 2 – and demonstrated the general weaknesses of NGOs in Ivory Coast to define, expose and resist a state-corporate crime of the order the dumping. Lack of funding, staff and expertise was a common feature and a function of the economic and political environment in which the NGOs found themselves. Most of the funding (when it is forthcoming) derives from foreign governments and is project based so that the organisations are essentially prevented from using the resource to develop institutional capacity. Perhaps the most surprising failure was the isolationism manifest by all NGOs studied, with Club UA capturing the essence of the problem: "[t]here is no genuine collaboration. In other countries, when governments take a decision and civil society does not agree with the decision, they resist collectively. But in Ivory Coast, this is not the case."[99] This lack of collaboration among NGOs to 'resist collectively' is a serious limitation and precludes the establishment of an effective resistance movement to single-issue events like the dumping. When asked about the advice offered to victims who approached them about the dumping, the president of MIDH stated that they would redirect them to the local victims' organisations. But he was clear to state that he would not advocate victims' organisations or federations. MIDH distances itself from these federations because of the "issue of money" and the struggle for profit among these federations.[100]

While researching human rights NGOs on my field trip to Ivory Coast, it emerged that the interests of the victims of the dumping were not being served by the existing human rights NGOs based in Ivory Coast. Rather newly formed, bespoke organisations and federations – victims' organisations – emerged as apparent 'champions' of toxic waste victims. The next chapter reveals how these victims' organisations, facilitated and encouraged by the state, took up roles normally expected to be within the purview of the state or of the well-established human rights NGOs. Further investigation revealed that these victims' organisations were in fact self-serving, corrupt and often criminal. Victims were thus left without genuine representation and worse were exploited because of their status as victims. It is to these victims' organisations that this study will now turn.

## Notes

1  Interview, Abidjan, September 2010 (Club UA 2010).
2  Interview, Abidjan, September 2010 (LIDHO 2010).
3  Action pour la Protection des Droits de l'Homme (APDH), Ligue Ivoirienne des Droits de l'Homme (LIDHO), Mouvement Ivoirien des Droits Humains (MIDH) and La Fondation Ivoirienne pour les Droits de l'Homme et la Vie Politique (FIDHOP).
4  Amnesty International Côte d'Ivoire (AI CI) and Club UA.
5  Regroupement des Acteurs Ivoiriens des Driots Humains (RAIDH), an umbrella organisation that includes as its members APDH, Club UA, MIDH, Organisation des Femmes Actives de Côte d'Ivoire (OFACI) and West African Network for Peacebuilding Côte d'Ivoire (WANEP) – established in 2003 by five NGOs, including Club UA.
6  Organisation des Femmes Actives de Côte d'Ivoire – focuses on the human rights of women.
7  Concerned primarily with justice system reform.
8  Interview, Abidjan, September 2010 (RAIDH 2010).
9  Interview, Abidjan, September 2010 (WANEP 2010).
10  Interview, Abidjan, September 2010 (OFACI 2010).
11  Interview, Abidjan, September 2010 (Comité International de la Croix-Rouge 2010).
12  Interview, Abidjan, September 2010 (FIDHOP 2010).
13  Ibid.
14  Interview, Abidjan, September 2010 (APDH 2010).
15  Interview, Abidjan, September 2010 (MIDH 2010).
16  Interview, Abidjan, September 2010 (FIDHOP 2010).
17  Centre Feminin pour la Democratie et les Droits Humains en Côte d'Ivoire, an organisation focusing on women's rights and established in 2003; see www.cefci.org/.
18  Interview, Abidjan, September 2010 (Club UA 2010).
19  Interview, Abidjan, September 2010 (APDH 2010).
20  Interview, Abidjan, September 2010 (MIDH 2010).
21  Interview, Abidjan, September 2010 (LIDHO 2010).
22  Interview, Abidjan, September 2010 (Club UA 2010).
23  Interview, Abidjan, September 2010 (CNVDT-CI 2010).
24  Email correspondence with international press correspondent, November 2011.

25  Interview, Abidjan, September 2010 (LIDHO 2010).
26  See http://lidho.org/section_interieur.html, accessed November 2011.
27  Interview, Abidjan, September 2010 (MIDH 2010).
28  Interview, Abidjan, September 2010 (MIDH 2010).
29  Interview, Abidjan, September 2010 (APDH 2010).
30  Interview, Abidjan, September 2010 (Club UA 2010).
31  Interview, Abidjan, September 2010 (APDH 2010).
32  Interview, Abidjan, September 2010 (LIDHO 2010).
33  Interview, Abidjan, September 2010 (Club UA 2010).
34  According to data from UNICEF's Multiple Indicator Cluster Survey, reported in the United Nation's Development Programme – Human development indices, available at http://hdr.undp.org/en/media/HDI_2008_EN_Tables.pdf, accessed November 2011.
35  Reportedly at 4.5 per cent of the population (2011). Source: www.internetworldstats.com/stats1.htm#africa
36  Interview, Abidjan, September 2010 (MIDH 2010).
37  Interview, Abidjan, September 2010 (LIDHO 2010).
38  Interview, Abidjan, September 2010 (Club UA 2010).
39  According to the International Telecommunication Union, the price basket for the Internet is calculated based on the cheapest available tariff for accessing the Internet twenty hours a month (ten hours peak and ten hours off-peak), www.nationsencyclopedia.com/WorldStats/ADI-price-basket-internet.html
40  Interview, Abidjan, September 2010 (APDH 2010).
41  Ibid.
42  Interview, Abidjan, September 2010 (MIDH 2010).
43  Interviews, Abidjan, September 2010.
44  Interview, Abidjan, September 2010 (APDH 2010).
45  Interview, Abidjan, September 2010 (MIDH 2010).
46  Interview, Abidjan, September 2010 (LIDHO 2010).
47  Ibid.
48  Interview, Abidjan, September 2010 (Club UA 2010).
49  Interview, Abidjan, September 2010 (MIDH 2010).
50  Interview, Abidjan, September 2010 (APDH 2010).
51  Interview, Abidjan, September 2010 (Club UA 2010).
52  Interview, Abidjan, September 2010 (MIDH 2010).
53  Particulars of Claim of Olswang LLP in Kieran Looney v Trafigura Beheer BV [2011] EWHC 125 (Chancery Division).
54  Interview, Abidjan, September 2010 (LIDHO 2010).
55  Interview, Abidjan, September 2010 (APDH 2010).
56  This is a stark contrast to the victims' organisations (see Chapter 4) who survive solely on membership fees.
57  Interview, Abidjan, September 2010 (MIDH 2010).
58  Ibid.
59  Ibid.
60  Interview, Abidjan, September 2010 (LIDHO 2010).
61  Interview, Abidjan, September 2010 (Club UA 2010).
62  Ibid.
63  IRI, 2011, Message from the President, Lorne W. Craner, available at www.iri.org/learn-more-about-iri-0 (accessed November 2011).
64  See www.ned.org/about.
65  See www.ned.org/sites/default/files/IndependentAuditorsReport2010.pdf.
66  Interview, Abidjan, September 2010 (APDH 2010).
67  Ibid.

68  Ibid.
69  Interview, Abidjan, September 2010 (MIDH 2010).
70  Ibid.
71  Ibid.
72  Ibid.
73  Interview, Abidjan, September 2010 (LIDHO 2010).
74  Interview, Abidjan, September 2010 (Club UA 2010).
75  Interviews, September 2010, Abidjan.
76  Interview, Abidjan, September 2010 (APDH 2010).
77  Interview, Abidjan, September 2010 (MIDH 2010).
78  Ibid.
79  It was noted that this was a personal perspective that would require corroboration.
80  Interview, Abidjan, September 2010 (MIDH 2010).
81  Interview, Abidjan, September 2010 (LIDHO 2010).
82  Interview, Abidjan, September 2010 (Club UA 2010).
83  See www.lemediateur.ci/inst.htm#.
84  Interview, Abidjan, September 2010 (APDH 2010).
85  Ibid.
86  Interview, Abidjan, September 2010 (MIDH 2010).
87  Observation, Abidjan, September 2010; at a checkpoint, on a Saturday evening, the researcher's taxi was stopped on the bridge that connects the neighbourhoods of Deux Plateaux and Plateau and was forced at gunpoint to pay €30 or risk spending a night in a police station.
88  Interview, Abidjan, September 2010 (MIDH 2010).
89  Interview, Abidjan, September 2010 (LIDHO 2010).
90  Ibid.
91  Interview, Abidjan, September 2010 (Club UA 2010).
92  Interview, Abidjan, September 2010 (APDH 2010).
93  Ibid.
94  Interview, Abidjan, September 2010 (MIDH 2010).
95  See www.fidh.org/Cote-d-Ivoire-In-view-of-the-intensification-of, accessed November 2011.
96  Interview, Abidjan, September 2010 (Club UA 2010).
97  Ibid.
98  Interview, Abidjan, September 2010 (MIDH 2010).
99  Interview, Abidjan, September 2010 (Club UA 2010).
100  Interview, Abidjan, September 2010 (MIDH 2010).

Chapter 8

# Organisational crime and the 'commodification of victimhood'

One of the most surprising findings of this study related to the emergence of 'victims' organisations' as organised crime networks. The victims' organisations which flourished in the wake of the toxic dumping turned out to be in the business of producing victimhood for a fee: that is, as an 'organised crime' or, as Woodiwiss defines it, "systematic criminal activity for money or power" (Woodiwiss 2001: 3). Whereas this definition is wide enough to include inter alia corporate crime (Green and Ward 2004), it is applied here to organisations that purport to be civil society organisations – that is, would-be 'champions of the people' – but which have, in fact, the ulterior and hidden motives of capital accumulation at their clients' expense. As will be shown the more 'successful' victims' organisations in Ivory Coast were set up by opportunists and crime entrepreneurs.

Using such a broad interpretation of organised crime also avoids the pitfalls of legal definitions, the unresolved discourse in academic attempts at a definition or an association with enduring stereotypical mafia-type organisations or 'syndicated crime'. Legal definitions are too restrictive for present purposes.

As for academia, Levy argues:

> Very few academics would defend the analytical utility of the term organized crime, with its crude binary organized/unorganized distinction which means that there is more variation within the category of organized that there is between organized and unorganized . . . many have shifted towards using the term 'enterprise crime'.
>
> (2002: 887)

As will be seen in this chapter, the organisations acted in a disorganised, ad hoc manner, and the crude binary that Levy (2002) refers to fails to account for the behaviour observed.

The attractiveness of victimhood to local members of the community could be based on two premises. The first is that they have indeed been the victim of the state-corporate crime and seek recognition of this fact, and the second is the promise of a future claim for compensation.

The previous chapter analysed a range of factors which weakened the response of domestic NGOs to the toxic dumping. Underpinning this analysis was a criminological assumption that those censuring state-corporate crime are necessarily a force for 'good' and social justice. This chapter challenges that assumption. While data-collecting on my field trip, it became apparent that the civil society actors spearheading domestic efforts to censure Trafigura were in fact embedded in organised crime. Victimhood became a commodity which they attempted to manufacture by encouraging victims to come forward and *pay* to join non-existing class actions which were to take place in foreign courts. This chapter will examine the infiltration of civil society by organised crime groups and describes how the dumping incident created the opening for organisations to exploit victims, essentially criminalising resistance.

The chapter begins by exploring the relationship between the nation-state and various forms of organised crime, "which ultimately defines organised crime's power, character and persistence" (Green and Ward 2004: 104). The next section of the chapter discusses the precedent of the transformation of a student union (FESCI) from a resistance organisation to a criminal gang. By exploring this historical example, some indictors of the mechanism of such a transformation become clearer. The chapter finally examines how criminal groups took advantage of an absentee government to exploit victims of the dumping and reveals the conditions "for organised crime to fill the vacuum created by an ineffective state" (Green and Ward 2004: 87; Sands 2007).

## Background of organised crime

There is a base level of organisational crime in Ivory Coast, against the background of which the newly formed victims' organisations should be analysed. In 2004 about 64 per cent of the total population was under twenty-four years old. A lack of formal employment for a large, young population fuelled the expansion of an informal sector – a sector dominated by criminal networks in West Africa (Wannenburg 2005). The informal sector in Ivory Coast is significant, and even the National Council of Ivorian Employers (CNPI), according to Integrated Regional Information Networks (IRIN 2005), encourages companies to "exploit opportunities in the informal sector". The drivers of organised crime in Ivory Coast have changed during the state's short history and have been both of an internal and an external character.

The enduring conflicts in Ivory Coast have had a marked impact on the prevalence of organised criminality. There are a number of dimensions to this factor. First, as McMullin (2009) argues, organised criminal groups are "involved in a wide array of activities within conflict states" (McMullin 2009: 76), and civil wars in conflict states have brought about "cross-border demand for arms, soldiers and natural resources" (McMullin 2009: 88). Second, Wannenburg argues that human trafficking in West Africa "is exacerbated by civil wars, refugees, internal displacement, the recruitment of child soldiers and economic conditions"

(Wannenburg 2005: 11). Third, the UN claims that West African conflict states[1] have "played a significant part in international drug trafficking, diamond smuggling, human trafficking, cigarette smuggling, forgery, money laundering, armed robbery and arms trafficking" since 1995 to generate revenues for combating internal threats (UNODC 2005: 13). Fourth, armed groups that are spawned by conflict interact with the established criminal groups: "armed groups co-opted, displaced or co-operated with existent criminal groups" (McMullin 2009: 84; and see Wannenburg 2005: 8 and UNODC 2005: 38). Thus the endemic civil conflict that has punctuated Ivory Coast's modern history has generated a variety of opportunities for organised crime groups (in the traditional sense and under the definition employed here) to flourish under the protection of a state that welcomes the revenues generated by these illicit industries (ICG 2004: 4). Regional conflict fuels demand for weapons, and the "highly porous, largely unpatrolled borders" (Small Arms Survey 2006: 256) are a failure of Ivorian government to secure the state's territory, allowing for the illicit trade. Fighters and tens of thousands of weapons (UNODC 2009) circulate among war-torn states in West Africa whose borders are "revolving doors of trafficked arms and de-mobilised soldiers of one state re-recruited to fight in another" (McMullin 2009: 88). According to Amnesty International (2008), the main players in arms trafficking weapons in Ivory Coast are private Ivorian and European brokers. However, the government is also proactively involved in the arming of pro-government militias and has "provided support for some ten thousand ill-disciplined militia fighters" (HRW 2005: 1). These militias are highly criminogenic "but enjoy impunity due to their relationship with the government" (Small Arms Survey 2006: 255). Human Rights Watch also claims that these militias have perpetrated "serious crimes with impunity" (HRW 2005: 1). On the other side of the conflict, the Forces Nouvelles de Côte d'Ivoire "engage in serious human rights abuses such as extrajudicial executions, torture, arbitrary detentions and confiscation of property" (HRW 2005: 1).

However, although significant, war is not the only factor fostering organised crime. In a country where government is dominated by a form of patrimonial politics, the state has been treated as the private property of the ruling factions. Using state power these factions have been able to extract personal wealth as well as funding for war chests (Global Witness 2007) from the economy through the use of cocoa and coffee marketing boards. The International Crisis Group (ICG), for example, claims that Houphouët-Boigny's 'slush fund' was fed by the complex arrangement of the cocoa marketing board and its associated organisations referred to as the cocoa *filière*:

> The labyrinthine cocoa filière, a kind of Enron-type structure of front companies, secret bank accounts, and transfer of funds with multiple layers of insulation between the criminal acts and their eventual beneficiaries, is the ultimate testament to their sophistication.
>
> (ICG 2004: 4)

The *filière* system, which was originally designed to guarantee a minimum price for cocoa and coffee payable to farmers, "operates through a nexus of interconnected institutions that make up the cocoa and coffee marketing system" (ICG 2004: 5) and up to the 1980s received about 60 per cent of the cocoa and coffee revenues, leaving farmers with about one quarter of world market prices (ICG 2004).

The cocoa *filière's* role is to regulate the market, but cocoa institutions have, claim Global Witness, "directly contributed to the war effort by providing the government with money, vehicles and weapons, using money from cocoa levies" (Global Witness 2007: 24). The ICG reports the allegation that US$100 million was extorted from one of the institutions of the *filière* system "and later used to buy weapons in a deal managed by an off-shore company" (ICG 2004: 5). A World Bank official told Global Witness that "[w]e know that the revenues collected from cocoa are used to fund the military" (Global Witness 2007: 24).

In March 2002, at the request of President Gbagbo, a government inspector François Kouamé Kouadio (of L'Inspection Générale d'Etat [IGE]) started investigating the reformed *filière* system. He reported on accounting anomalies in the form of gifts and 'loans' of about US$200 million, and in August 2002, shortly after his report was leaked, he was beaten up in Abidjan. This report had also warned that the state bank holding cocoa proceeds might not be "able to resist (possible) demands for funds from the Ministry of Economy and Finance" (Global Witness 2007: 56). He has since been fired from the IGE and reportedly remains in hiding (ICG 2004; Global Witness 2007).

Others reporting on corruption within the *filière* system have suffered a similar fate to Kouadio. In April 2004, for example, Guy-André Kieffer[2] was kidnapped in Abidjan. He had been working on reforming the cocoa sector and had been investigating Ivorian corruption as an independent journalist. His whereabouts remain unknown, but he was reportedly tortured to death (Global Witness 2007). Several months later, in November 2004, Xavier Ghelber[3] was kidnapped in Abidjan during his EU audit of the cocoa sector. At gendarmerie headquarters in Abidjan, Ghelber was reportedly threatened at gunpoint before he managed to escape with the help of French troops (Global Witness 2007). A French judge is looking into both the Kieffer and Ghelber cases: "[t]he judge's preliminary findings indicate that three of Xavier Ghelber's kidnappers belonged to . . . the president's private security force" (Global Witness 2007: 57). The disappearance of Guy-André Kieffer and the attacks on Kouadio and Ghelber expose "the very real dangers of denouncing corruption and other abuses in the cocoa sector" (Global Witness 2007: 59) and does nothing but discourage civil society's role in resisting these crimes.

Not surprisingly, in a country that has been burdened by civil wars and state corruption, formal economic opportunities are few and largely unattractive (for reasons that have already been outlined). This has created the incentive for a variety of illicit trades based around smuggling (drugs, humans, natural resources and weapons) and money laundering. The following section briefly outlines these activities.

At the time of the dumping, drug production in Ivory Coast was on the increase but is limited to low-grade cannabis[4] (Gonto 2010), grown by farmers trying to avoid the volatile cocoa and coffee markets and the exploitative *filière*. The financial advantages of growing marijuana are obvious: "whereas coffee and cocoa get the seller an average of FCFA 500 (US$ 1) per kilogram, and of this sum, a host of taxes is still deducted centrally, one kilogram of marijuana can get the seller a tax free FCFA 4000 (US$ 8)" (Gonto 2010: 25). The country is one the four main producers of cannabis in West Africa[5] and supplies – by way of criminal organisations – local or regional markets (Wannenburg 2005). However, despite a lack of 'hard drug' production in the state, Gonto (2010) argues that the expanding regional trade is headquartered in Abidjan. Drug traffickers use the territory as a hub for transporting heroin (from Asia) and cocaine (from South America) to Europe and the United States (Adamoli et al. 1998; Gonto 2010). Increased policing of drug trafficking in the ports of Nigeria has driven criminal networks to the less policed coastline and waterways of Ivory Coast,[6] and the "vast and porous land, riverine and seaports and extensive corruption among government and customs officials provide an ideal environment for illicit trade" (Wannenburg 2005: 11). This 'ideal environment' is one of the reasons for the toxic waste being repelled from the Nigerian ports and being accepted in Ivory Coast and is another indication of how the Ivorian state facilitates crime. But it is not just the corruption of customs regime on the coast that has allowed smuggling to thrive; the northern borders are also porous and have facilitated a range of illicit industries.

During the partitioning of Ivory Coast from 2002, the north became a kind of "free trade zone" (Wannenburg 2005: 10). Cheap cigarettes are imported from Guinea and sugar is imported from Burkina Faso and Mali. Cotton, cultivated exclusively in the North (IRIN 2005), is exported to Burkina Faso and Mali. All these transactions are illegal, and no duty is payable to the Ivorian state treasury. However, charges are levied by rebel forces (Wannenburg 2005) who argued that "government taxes would be used by the presidency to buy arms and prolong the war" (IRIN 2005), a view confirmed by Global Witness (2007).

The volume of the illicit market is significant. In the 2004 and 2005 seasons, about 220,000 tonnes (about 55 per cent of total production) of cotton were illegally exported to Mali and Burkina Faso (IRIN 2005). The UN argues that the volume of Asian sugar being illegally imported damages local industry and is "undermining local production" (UNODC 2009: 23). Northern Ivory Coast, outside the full control of the state centralised in Abidjan, is the second-largest market for illicit cigarettes in the region with 17 per cent of West Africa's illicit cigarette market (worth US$104 million per annum and 23 percent of the regional total): "the trade is rife in the unstable north but almost non-existent in the south" (UNODC 2009: 31). The UN also argues that 'a large share' of oil stolen from Nigeria is refined in Ivory Coast (as well as in Ghana and Cameroon) (UNODC 2009: 23). This suggests state involvement in criminal activity as the only oil refining facilities in Ivory Coast are government owned (Wild 2010).

Ivory Coast is also a well-documented human trafficking route (Wannenburg 2005), especially for children (Chanthavong 2002; International Institute of Tropical Agriculture 2002). The number of trafficked children working on plantations in Ivory Coast ranges from 12,000 to 15,000, which is between 9 per cent and 12 per cent of the total child workforce in the industry (Ellenbogen 2004). In an international press offensive, to avoid a boycott of Ivorian chocolate, the government insisted that "it should be seen as the victim, not the perpetrator of child trafficking. It says that it had no idea what was going on its plantations" (Blunt 2001).

Funds from these organised criminal activities usually find their way to Abidjan, the financial hub of West Africa, and are laundered along with the proceeds of regional organised crime. The cross-border trade in cocoa (and to a lesser extent diamonds) "generates contraband funds that are laundered into the banking system via informal moneychangers" (US DoS 2008). A lack of government oversight and regulation facilitates these financial crimes.

The discussion thus far would suggest that organised crime is a central feature of Ivory Coast's political economy. Moreover, organised crime has infiltrated the state and vice versa. Thus organised crime in Ivory Coast is both instigated and facilitated by the state. In such an environment it is perhaps not surprising that no sector of civil society has remained untainted by the influence of organised crime. This is certainly the case with the victim groups that were set up in the wake of the dumping. However, the hijacking of civil society by criminal gangs is not new. The case of the main Ivorian students' union, FESCI, demonstrates how a resistance organisation can be transformed into a vehicle for organisational deviance. An analysis of this students' union has two roles: to look at the context in which resistance can be criminalised and also to discuss the links between FESCI and the victims' organisations.

## FESCI and the criminalisation of civil society

This section looks at the transformation of the FESCI from a genuine pro-democracy student group engaged in the resistance against state crime to a violent, repressive criminal organisation. The union was originally founded in 1990 as "a platform for students to air their grievances" (IRIN 2007: 40). However, because of its opposition to the government, FESCI was driven underground and appears to have emerged in the late 1990s as a criminal gang. Despite the apparent criminality of FESCI, the group is considered to be a training ground for future leaders of the Ivorian state: "FESCI is the best school for leaders there is. You come out battle hardened and ready to do politics"[7] (HRW 2008: 1). This section charts the union's transition and links the changes to the criminalisation of resistance.

FESCI started out in 1990 to seek reform of the Ivorian one-party system and from the outset was funded by opposition parties, including the Front Populaire Ivoirien (FPI). Consequently Houphouët-Boigny and his PDCI viewed FESCI as subversive, and after the state's first presidential election (Houphouët-Boigny versus Gbagbo) in 1991 saw Houphouët-Boigny win amidst accusations of electoral irregularities, "the organization was formally banned and forced underground soon after its creation, with many of its leaders hunted and jailed" (HRW 2008: 7). This period also saw allegations of collaboration between FESCI and the army. Human Rights Watch claims that a government inquiry into a raid into a university dormitory led by General Guéï in 1991 and including both soldiers and FESCI 'foot-soldier' members resulted in the rape of at least three women and a number of beatings. Guéï was not sanctioned by the government for his involvement (HRW 2008), which may suggest that he was carrying out acts in pursuit of the state's organisational goals.

The majority of FESCI's leaders were gaoled during the 1990s. Martial Ahipeaud (FESCI founder), Eugene Djué (FESCI founder), Guillaume Soro (rebel leader and prime minister) and Charles Blé Goudé (Young Patriots founder) were all considered by Amnesty International (1992) to be 'prisoners of conscience'. Outside of the leadership of FESCI, Gbagbo (and his wife) and the president of LIDHO were arrested and sentenced to prison terms for activities related to the union (Amnesty International 1992; HRW 2008).

FESCI re-emerged in 1997 but with an apparent shift in character. Following the 1999 coup General Guéï allowed the union to resume full operations (US DoS 2001). Since the early 2000s FESCI has "[b]een responsible for politically and criminally motivated violence, including assault, extortion, and rape" (HRW 2008: 6) and has been accused of attacks on the state (including ministers and judges), civil society (including human rights NGOs and journalists) and individuals. The group was especially violent towards those opposed to the Gbagbo administration, and in 2004 FESCI lynched the communist party leader (US DoS 2006). Furthermore, "FESCI is routinely associated with 'mafia' type criminal behavior including extortion and protection rackets" on and around university and high school campuses (HRW 2008: 99). FESCI's victims have been primarily the students it purports to represent, but it has also targeted other civil society actors.

The bulk of FESCI's criminal activity takes place on campuses, university residences and the surrounding areas of Abidjan; the group allegedly aims to "control political thought, student activities and even commerce on campus" (LIDHO, quoted by IRIN 2007: 40). Academic freedom is threatened, and students report "harassment and extortion by FESCI members" (IRIN 2007: 40) as well as cases of rape and torture (IRIN 2007). University professors and lectures are also targeted: "[o]ne teacher's face was disfigured in an attack, prompting his colleagues to halt work for two weeks" (IRIN 2007: 41).

HRW claims that since 2002, FESCI has "exhibited an increasing tendency to criminally appropriate and allocate key university facilities and services"

(HRW 2008: 52). Students are forced to pay monthly stipends to remain in student residences, and small-traders selling food and drinks on campus must pay monthly 'taxes' to FESCI (IRIN 2007). This protection racket for the merchants includes a system of 'justice' that would normally be provided by the state. A FESCI member interviewed by HRW in 2007 explains:

> If a merchant we protect has a problem with a thief, he will bring them to us. He'll come to whoever is on duty that day who listens to both the thief and the merchant and then decides what to do. Usually he decides how much the thief owes to the merchant and takes a commission from the thief as well. Often the thief is beaten too. Merchants prefer to come to FESCI because we're more efficient than the police where you risk things not going anywhere. Police have no right to come to our territory. If they come, we chase them away. They are usually afraid of us anyway. So even if a citizen goes to the 8th precinct to say they have a problem with FESCI, the police will tell you they can't do anything about it.
>
> (HRW 2008: 55)

This interview reveals the substitution of the state's justice system by FESCI and also highlights the relationship between the student group and the police. The impunity afforded to FESCI was also reported by participant human rights NGOs, both by the inaction of the police and the criminal justice system.[8]

In May 2007 LIDHO and APDH headquarters were attacked and ransacked by members of FESCI, causing damage estimated at €60,000.[9] The apparent motive was the NGOs' support of strike action by university professors, but it has been claimed by members of LIDHO and APDH that "FESCI's real goal was both the elimination of files and records that contained details regarding FESCI's misdeeds, as well as punishment for having publicly denounced FESCI's actions in the past" (HRW 2008: 71). Police were present at one of the attacks and stood by (HRW 2008). This incident illustrates how agencies of the state have facilitated the repression of the censure capabilities of local NGOs and also highlights the volatile relationship between FESCI and the human rights NGOs.

APDH started proceedings against FESCI following the attack by lodging complaints with the attorney general. These complaints were not acted upon.[10] LIDHO was forced to abandon its former headquarters after the attack.[11] LIDHO also considered legal action against FESCI but did not follow through.[12] Following the rape of one of its members, MIDH assisted a student union in filing a criminal legal complaint against FESCI.[13] Nothing came from these legal complaints, and the next section explores the relationship between the student group and the state with a view to explaining the impunity that FESCI enjoys.

The head of FESCI from 1995 to 1998, Guillaume Soro, became the secretary general of the Forces Nouvelles (FN) and then the prime minister of Ivory

Coast, in a 'unity' government, from March 2007 to October 2010 (Global Witness 2007). His rise from student leader to government leader is not unusual as "FESCI appears to have become a training ground for emerging Ivorian leadership" (HRW 2008: 93). Many FESCI leaders have moved on to lead the youth wings of many of the major political parties, and other former leaders have set up their own parties. Another example is Charles Blé Goudé,[14] leader of FESCI from 1999 to 2001. The atmosphere created by the FESCI 'political nursery' promotes the creation of "a generation of leaders who have cut their political teeth in a climate of intimidation, violence, and impunity" (HRW 2008: 8).

The secretary general of FESCI has denied that the organisation is politically motivated or violent but did admit that that whereas there have been violent incidents, "we remind the instigators to be orderly" (IRIN 2007: 41). Calls to orderliness are in effect insignificant and suggest that the individuals involved in violence are pursuing organisational goals. HRW claims that the head of the Ivory Coast army supported FESCI when it attacked the national television station and supported the student group generally during the anti-UN riots in January 2006 (HRW 2008). This close-knit relationship between the government and the student group has both contributed to state-organised crime and the criminal impunity "associated with nearly all offenses perpetrated by members of FESCI" (HRW 2008: 82).

Indeed interviewees for Human Rights Watch's report claimed that FESCI's political power and its criminal behaviour are a result of governmental support – the group is "protected by power" and "supported by the FPI" (HRW 2008: 81). University residences are known as a "no man's land" because of the "absolute control exercised by FESCI and the inability or unwillingness of state security forces to intervene in the face of criminal conduct by FESCI members" (HRW 2008: 82). Judges and police interviewed by Human Rights Watch in 2007 explained the impunity in terms of fear for their career and personal or family safety as well as "the unpredictability of taking action against those they believe to have enormous political cover" (HRW 2008: 84). So whereas the criminal activities of FESCI are well documented, it is well protected, and "government authorities have only rarely investigated, arrested, and prosecuted those FESCI members responsible" (HRW 2008: 81).

FESCI is thus, in effect, a large criminal organisation operating in Abidjan with impunity. This is a form of state-organised crime facilitated by the organisation's inter-linkages with the state. But the particular interest in the FESCI group for this study is that fact that as a student union, it might be expected to be a 'force-for-good' member of civil society. However, any positive role it played as the representative voice of students has been changed into a quasi-state body role dictated by close links with political parties and senior politicians. This has created the framework in which its role to "control political thought" on campus, on behalf of the political elite, has allowed the group to generate rents through supplementary rackets and extortion activities. This commodification of civil society appears to be a phenomenon with deep roots in Ivory Coast. When the toxic dumping looked like generating a significant monetary windfall, it is not surprising that 'victimhood' itself became commodified under the direction of organised criminal groups. FESCI was, as will be seen, involved in this process.

## Victims' organisations

Examining the reaction of the government to the dumping, it is clear that Ivory Coast was an ineffective state. The UN special rapporteur[15] who visited Ivory Coast in August 2008 was clear that the Ivorian government was not in a position to deal with the dumping:

> it is fair to say that the Government did not have the capacity and was not prepared to handle a crisis of this magnitude . . . [and] . . . while various relevant Ministries were mobilized to deal with the crisis, many did not have the capacity or the budget to respond adequately.
>
> (Ibeanu 2008)

Green and Ward (2004) warn that

> there is a tendency in weaker states . . . for organised crime to fill the vacuum created by an ineffective state. In these circumstances organised crime is able to flourish and even to compete with the state in terms of specific administrative and political functions.
>
> (Green and Ward 2004: 187)

The inaction of the government left a vacuum that was filled with a myriad of new bespoke voluntary organisations which attracted numerous allegations of corruption and extortion. Although criminal in intent and operation, the victims' organisations can't accurately be described as traditional organised crime or enterprise crime organisations as there is no penetration of a formal or informal market as such. In a sense, however, they have generated their own market by commandeering victimhood. They attracted funding and generated a return based solely on the perceived victimhood of their members, who were enticed through false promises and propaganda.

Six victims' organisations or federations were the subject of fieldwork interviews by the author: UVDTAB, FENAVIDET, RENADVIDET, CNVDT, FAVIDET and VUCAH (see glossary for long-form names). As shown there are a number of commonalities among these organisations. All were purportedly set up in late 2006 and early 2007, claim to have many thousands of 'members' and have similar stated missions. Significantly they also share mechanisms by which to extort fees from victims for some hypothetical and unlikely future compensation claims. Furthermore, as the data reveal, many of these groups claim to be the one-and-only official group set up by the president and to have been involved with the class action launched in London by Leigh Day & Co solicitors.[16]

UVDTAB was founded on 26 September 2006 and is staffed by volunteers. The president of UVDTAB claimed the organisation had attracted 560 volunteers. It is difficult to imagine how an organisation the size of UVTAB would have the logistical capacity to sustain so many volunteers,[17] and no evidence was presented to support the claim. UVDTAB also claims to represent about 100,000 victims and offers them registration: "we list them, so these people can also receive the status of victims and receive medical care".[18] The first stated objective of UVDTAB is the identification of all victims, with a view to organising to resist the perpetrators of the crime; "we have to get united to fight together".[19] Another objective is the identification of toxic waste sites, located throughout the city and its suburbs, which have been neglected by the authorities "to identify as well places that have been forgotten by the state of Ivory Coast, places where there are toxic wastes".[20] Its third objective is the "absolute decontamination of all polluted sites".[21] Fourth, UVDTAB is asking for the construction of a medical centre to assist all the victims. Its fifth objective was pursuing compensation for victims that is "proportional to the crime committed".[22] Finally, it would like to see a study of the medium- and long-term consequences of the toxic waste on human health and on the environment, arguing that such a study has never been carried out.[23]

CNVDT claims to have been originally formed in 2006, three weeks after the dumping – when it "saw the scope of the disaster" – under the name 'Association pour les Victimes d'Abidjan'. About two years later, from the end of 2008 to February 2009, about forty victims' organisations that had been independently formed merged to form the CNVDT federation.[24] The federation claims to have been instructed by Leigh Day & Co solicitors who are running the class action claim in the UK. Leigh Day, however, denies any such instruction (Brown 2009). CNVDT is staffed by forty-two people, each president of the forty original associations, in addition to two paid members of staff, the secretary and the head of the IT service. CNVDT claims to represent 289,000 people, 134,000 of whom are children, across all the districts of Abidjan. It has four main objectives: first, to better organise those affected by the dumping; second, to fight for compensation for the organisation's members; third, to arrange health care for victims; and finally, to lobby political leaders to legislate to prevent this kind of disaster happening again.[25]

FAVIDET formed in March 2007. It is a federation of twenty-three associations and organises meetings of up to one hundred victims' associations. FAVIDET has a central committee of four people. They also have two doctors and two lawyers as well as members responsible for security and communications – all staff members are volunteers. FAVIDET acknowledged that it did not have an accurate record of victim members and was "surveying the issue" in the hope of having a clear sense of the numbers within six months.[26] The stated objectives of the federation are the identification of all victims of the toxic waste, the compensation of all victims, and the provision of health care to victims. When asked whether there were any other similar organisations, the president said that some federations had been created, but he refused to name them.[27] FAVIDET was originally a local, district-specific victim support group and claims to have been legally founded with the help of LIDHO. At the president of Ivory Coast's request, it then organised as a federation, again with the help of LIDHO, who sent PhD students to assist them. FAVIDET says that it has absolutely no resources, and 100 million CFA was promised to them by the state, after the government had reached a settlement with Trafigura, but it never materialised. FAVIDET claims that it was also involved (as was CNVDT) with the class action of Leigh Day, and assisted – along with other organisations – in compiling details of victims.[28] My interview with the president took place at a conference venue during an event organised by the federation to roll out its new registration identification cards (see the Appendix for a sample that was provided for the purposes of this monograph). These 'victim cards' were part of the paraphernalia of the federation and its membership and appeared to be produced as a token of legitimacy to entice victims to join it.

FENAVIDET was formed on 24 February 2007[29] "at the invitation of the head of state" after officers attended the presidential palace on 7 December 2006. FENAVIDET claims that the president stated he would take "important measures to find a solution to the problem"[30] and that "private organisations such as theirs should take important measures to defend the victim's rights for the benefit of justice for all".[31] It appears that the state was deferring to the victims' organisations, and "for that reason, the president offered 40,000,000 CFA and suggested that they create well organised federations to best fight for their objectives".[32] FENAVIDET claims that the organisation "has been created, by all the organisations that the president welcomed at that time".[33] This claim again echoes the claims of other groups to be the only official victims' organisation.

FENAVIDET is reported as employing fifteen permanent, paid members of staff: "[the] majority are volunteer workers except that they receive compensation just to encourage them to work";[34] "it is not a salary as such . . . they are all volunteers but receive compensation regularly".[35] From May to September 2010, FENAVIDET claims it was also paying some forty-five computer 'scientists'[36] to design and administer the organisation's database of victims. In Ivory Coast such a grand mobilisation of computer scientists is highly unusual, and the validity of this claim is doubtful. It is made all the more dubious by the fact that the office only contained about ten computers, whereas the database itself would in all likelihood require no more than two or three IT specialists.[37]/[38] The dubious claims made by FENAVIDET were part of a broader theatrical production that appeared to be designed simply to entice victims. When I entered its office, volunteers showed me computers and an array of one-metre-high stacks of documents purported to be registrations of victims. Another theatrical prop employed by FENAVIDET is membership cards, which were also handed out by other groups. When asked how many victims it represents, FENAVIDET claimed that "it is impossible to give a precise number of victims"[39] and that it "cannot answer because it needs to be careful".[40] FENAVIDET's stated mission is "[f]irst and foremost the decontamination of the Abidjan environment"; second to provide medical assistance to all victims, and third to secure reparations from Trafigura – "Trafigura need to compensate all the victims."[41] FENAVIDET claims that it is financed by any external organisation and that this "is one of the biggest problems that we are facing".[42] FENAVIDET claims that it is for this reason that membership fees are charged.[43] Representatives would not reveal how many members the organisation had nor how much the membership fee was. When asked who was responsible for the dumping, FENAVIDET stated, "There is only one responsible – one that is believed to be the most powerful, the richest able to corrupt everybody and even violate international conventions and to commit crimes of such dimensions – it is Trafigura."[44] This statement in indicative of the general approach the victims' organisations took to Trafigura – elevating the company to the status of an all-powerful demon which only they can defend against.

It was apparent to the author, following the interviews with the victims' organisations, that many of their claims were incredible. Indeed, unlike domestic human rights NGOs, these organisations claimed to be mobilising significant technical and human resources in an extremely challenging and competitive environment. Moreover, they also appeared to have extensive links with the class action in the UK and the Ivorian president. All of these claims were supported by paraphernalia designed and positioned to lend credibility to those claims. However, the spectacular claims did not end here.

## Funding, legitimacy and capacity to represent victims

UVDTAB reported that they are funded in a variety of ways, including donations from local individuals, from NGOs and individuals in Switzerland and France, and from partnerships with TV and radio channels such as BBC, Al Jazeera, CNN and other press organisations and journalists.[45] Although possible, it seems unlikely that this organisation received significant financial support from international press organisations, and the whole operation appeared underfunded and little more than a one-man operation[46] (despite the claims of having 560 volunteers). During the interview it became clear that whereas the leader of the organisation had a strong and apparently energetic, charismatic personality, the facilities of the organisation were lacking. The interview took place in a room with wooden benches along the walls, separated by a curtain from seamstresses busily working away[47] in a sewing workshop. Another office across the road had no furniture but was covered floor to ceiling in what the organisation claims to be thousands of victim registration documents.[48]

The president referred frequently to the organisation's legal initiatives, but I saw little evidence of the capacity of UVDTAB to carry out its objectives using the law. The president mentioned working with barristers and solicitors on an ongoing civil case at the High Court of Justice in London. There is, however, no record of this case. It may be they were referring to the settled case with Trafigura run by Leigh Day & Co, but the only ongoing issue in that case is a disagreement regarding the £105 million legal costs bill filed by Leigh Day & Co in 2010 (Dowell 2010). The president also discussed his organisation's intervention in a case in Ivory Coast in September 2008, but there is currently no civil or criminal case relating to the dumping pending in Ivory Coast. UVDTAB is preoccupied with its legal legitimacy as outlined by one[49] of five booklets handed over during the interview. These booklets – with titles and subjects ranging from legal capacity, 'Mission to Europe 2010', press book, *Universal Periodic Review* and stories of victims – give a valuable insight into the priorities of the organisation.

The 'legal capacity' booklet contains a copy of meeting minutes establishing the organisation on 26 September 2006, complete with official judicial stamps. It also contains a copy of the official receipt for filing the legally required incorporation documents for the organisation, exactly a year later in September 2007, and another similar receipt in August 2008, both issued by the Ministry of Interior. The booklet also contains a copy of an official journal extract, which the president claimed showed his organisation to be the only officially recognised victims' organisation in Ivory Coast[50] – a claim surprisingly redolent of other victims' organisations. The UVDTAB entry in *Journal Officiel de la Republique de Côte d'Ivoire*[51] is brief and states that the organisation's aims are to assist in a complete identification of victims and to ensure support for patients but makes no reference to the *Probo Koala*.

The 'Mission to Europe 2010' booklet is a catalogue of fourteen photographs of the president with individuals or outside offices of organisations around Europe. (The booklet contains only images with the only text being captions to the photographs.) The president also pointed out several photographs of people on his 'office' wall, which he claimed to be supporters. He insisted that a photograph be taken of our meeting, which will undoubtedly end up on the wall with the rest of his 'supporters', thereby exploiting this limited connection with me and King's College London as a medium for the organisation's legitimacy. The press book included clippings from French and Dutch newspapers that incorporated a photograph of the president as well as more photographs of the president with journalists from around the world and a BBC lawyer.

UVDTAB also claims it is the only group recognised by the UN and refers to a report it submitted[52] to the UN's *Universal Periodic Review* in 2009. This submission, however, demonstrates only that the UN recognises its existence and does not imply in any sense that it is the only legitimate victims' organisation. The organisation is also listed on the UN civil society database,[53] but again this does not amount to recognition and simply requires the organisation to fill out a short online form. The president also produced a letter from the UN in Geneva claiming that it was an invitation to attend the UN buildings, but the letter (which was in English) merely outlined the general security arrangements at the UN buildings in Geneva.

These revealing booklets were concerned only with the legitimacy of UVD-TAB to represent victims, and it appeared that all the energies of the organisation were focused towards promoting this impression. The final booklet on stories of victims was the only one dedicated to the mission of the organisation and profiled alleged victims of the toxic waste along with pictures and text describing their experiences. Some of the injuries sustained by the victims profiled, such as amputated limbs, do not, however, match with the medical evidence presented by studies in Abidjan.

FENAVIDET's office had a long queue of victims waiting to register when I visited for the interview, and the door entrance was blocked by two large men who appeared to be acting as security guards.[54] The interviewees angrily expressed that they were upset that they weren't the first victims' organisation that was visited to participate in the research because they felt that theirs was the most legitimate organisation,[55] and it was only after profuse apologies and an explanation that any research project requires meticulous planning to ensure that it achieves its objectives that the interview was allowed to proceed. The organisation had been created in 2007 at the invitation of the head of state: "[a] ll those associations that were spontaneously formed to defend victim rights have been invited by the Republic on December 7th 2006 to attend the presidential palace."[56]

According to FENAVIDET, the Ivorian president (at that meeting) declared he would take measures to find a solution to the problem. For that reason, the president offered 40 million CFA (about €60,000) "to create well organised federations".[57] FENAVIDET claim that the federation was created by all the organisations that the president welcomed. This is very similar to the stated circumstances around the founding of CNVDT and FAVIDET. At the end of the interview, FENAVIDET admitted that they didn't have any ideas on how to proceed with compensation claims, despite the fact that they were busily registering victims in the next room, and asked me if any ideas or assistance could be provided to them.[58] This would suggest that the organisation is more interested in obtaining fees from victims, whereas little or no consideration has been given to the pursuit of justice using those fees.

CNVDT claim that in December 2006, they met state officials and all the victims' organisations with the president of CNVDT as the spokesman and received the one-off payment of about 40 million CFA to establish itself – this is the same sum reported by FENAVIDET. Apart from this funding, CNVDT claimed that it received funding and material support primarily from private individuals.[59] It does not have a legal department but claims to have lawyers working for it. CNVDT have not taken legal actions at the domestic level but stated that they have taken legal action against Trafigura: "[s]o it's now in the London tribunal, through the firm called Leigh Day & Co."[60] CNVDT had claimed in 2009 that they held a mandate from all claimants to receive and distribute the compensation from this case. However, Leigh Day & Co has vigorously denied that this is the case (Leigh Day 2009).

FENAVIDET claim that they have an "international judiciary action"[61] in process but could not give details.[62] There is no evidence of any such action, and the claim has not been verified. FENAVIDET say it is 'preoccupied' with civil action against Trafigura and admitted that although the action was criminal, only civil actions were 'profitable' "and will provide tangible results, to decontaminate all the sites that are still contaminated in Abidjan".[63] FAVIDET launched its identification process in September 2010. It included the issuing of an identification card, with photo, name, date of birth and residential area for each of the victims. FAVIDET reportedly claim that the cards will "help every victim of toxic waste to be recognized as such" [64]. And to achieve this legitimacy, it sent letters to the Ivorian institutions and the United Nations Operation in Côte d'Ivoire (UNOCI) to ask that the card be formally recognised. It states that every victim will be considered if new compensation is forthcoming. It also claimed that victims' descendants would also benefit from health care "if by chance there is evidence that their illness is related to toxic waste" [65]. Each victim must pay 5,000 CFA (about €8) for the cards (Assi 2010).

FAVIDET claimed both an intention to launch a civil action against Trafigura, once it had compiled its list of victims, and to have engaged an Ivorian lawyer for this purpose.[66]

It is apparent from the interviews with victims' organisations that their stated source of funding is dubious at best. The modest offices of these organisations (with the notable exception of CNVDT) contribute to suspicions about the funding claims. Nevertheless, what is apparent is that the victims' organisations all claim to be undertaking or preparing to undertake legal actions, sometimes falsely reporting their role with the class action in the UK. This is despite the fact that the organisations in general suffer from a distinct lack of legal expertise and were unable to provide any details of pending or planned cases.

The claims, it would appear, are part of a broader theatre that these organisations use to lure victims or people wishing to obtain the status of victimhood. In almost cult-like fashion these organisations offer people the promise of extensive payouts in return for a subscription fee. The proof they offer is the successful Leigh Day action that continues to pay out via CNVDT. These promises are bulwarked by a 'stage set' designed to impress in the mass scramble for victims. This is a competitive process; each victims' group must essentially outdo the other in an effort to secure a larger share of the victim market. By victim market I mean people who are prepared to subscribe to these organisations, through some form of payment, in the hope of gaining a share of promised compensation payments. As a result of this process, local Ivorian television proclaimed that "the associations of victims of toxic waste grow each day like mushrooms since the disaster".[67]

UVDTAB are convinced that Trafigura is responsible for what happened to the victims: "[i]t's Trafigura and Trafigura and Trafigura."[68] After four years of involvement with the issue, CNVDT concluded that the crime was the result of a vast international conspiracy involving "Trafigura and all the harbour authorities of the Occident to Africa". The president initially refused to elaborate on the details, referring me to his yet-to-be-published work on the issue – "I say it in my book. I won't say it now" – but did go on to accuse the board of Trafigura and the authorities of the UK and Switzerland for not controlling the corporation after previous crimes – "it's not Trafigura's first 'blunder' with this kind of disaster in the world" – and bemoaned the fact that the UK and Switzerland still allow the company's headquarters to be based on their territory. CNVDT also believes that Trafigura's blaming of the company Tommy is "a way of escaping. It's shocking and scandalous for us."[69] When asked who was responsible for what happened, FAVIDET replied, "Oh, but it's Trafigura. For us it's not the Society Tommy."[70] FAVIDET reported that the best outcome for them would be free medical care for the victims.[71] Although the victims' organisations have missions that require some sort of legal or advocacy action against Trafigura and/or the Ivorian state, none have such an action in place. The only activity observed was that of registering and charging fees to the self-identified victims of the dumping. In this way these organisations profited from victimhood without providing concrete proposals for obtaining justice (by way of compensation or otherwise) for those who suffered at the hands of the state-corporate crime.

## The scramble for victims

Since its founding FENAVIDET claims that the organisation has been working to identify all the victims of the dumping for an international legal action against the 'polluter' but also states that one of the organisation's major objectives is to differentiate itself from the "arnaqueurs ... adventurias ... et ... opportunistes" or "scammers ... adventurers ... and ... opportunists".[72] FENAVIDET claims that others have forged victim registration documents to "rip off the poor people seeking compensation".[73] In 2010 the FENAVIDET website announced that a senior member of the group "has defected"[74] and was no longer associated with FENAVIDET. This former member of FENAVIDET has since set up Victimes Unies Contre les Catastrophes Humaines (VUCAH), another victims' organisation, which claims to have 24,000 members (Tape 2010). This defection and foundation of a 'competing' organisation is a further indication of the struggle among victims' organisations.

In July 2011 RENADVIDET organised a sit-in outside the offices of the Ministry of Justice protesting the recent suspension by CNVDT of the compensation process. It alleged that the money had been embezzled and that CNVDT had diverted the funds (Cheikna 2011c). RENADVIDET argued that the stalling of compensation payments was facilitated by and a direct result of a secret agreement between Leigh Day and CNVDT.

The conflict among some victims' organisations was not limited to words, and the RENADVIDET president claimed he was physically assaulted by CNVDT strongmen in February 2011 and that court security staff intervened on his behalf and locked him inside the office of the prefect for his own safety. Later in February 2011 two hundred people claiming to be victims of toxic waste and represented by RENADVIDET went to the offices of the prefect of Abidjan to demand their compensation from CNVDT before the second round of presidential elections. RENADVIDET declared that "we are tired and we need this money to be returned before the second round of the presidential election". According to RENADVIDET this action was the culmination of a month-long protest movement. There have also been legal battles among the groups, and RENADVIDET argued that an 'executive order' warrant against their president for the defamation of CNVDT was arbitrarily taken out (Yelly 2011).

Gendarmerie police officers, armed with automatic weapons and displaying UN security guard badges on their uniforms, were stationed outside the CNVDT building when I visited for interviews. When asked about their presence, CNVDT's president answered, "Because the organisation is in charge of the compensation, the accounting database needs to be protected so it's just for the security of the building." However, accounting databases can be encrypted, and the guards had not been present on an earlier visit to the building, when the president was not there, and it is likely that these guards were protecting him.[75]

Tigana (2010) reports on "a battle between the presidents of associations" and the vice president of a new federation, Collectif des Présidents des Associations des Victimes des Déchets Toxiques (CPAVNDT), claiming that FENAVIDET made the unilateral decision to take 15 per cent of the government compensation due to be paid to victims and that the president of FENAVIDET refused to hold elections after his two-year term expired. CPAVNDT is composed of 15 presidents of victims' organisations formerly associated with FENAVIDET (Tigana 2010). CPAVNDT claimed that it was negotiating with Trafigura on behalf of its 42,000 (APA 2010) victim members (Coulibaly 2008). VUCAH also claimed to be in negotiations with Trafigura who are "willing to pay" (Tape 2010). When asked about how confident he was of further compensation, the president of VUCAH stated, "I'm sure as a victim first and a child of God, I do not pose without the advice of the Lord. The victims will be compensated" (Tape 2010). As with other groups, there is here a distinct lack of detail on just how compensation is due to be obtained for members. This study has not identified any viable route to compensation by any victims' organisation.

## The extortion of compensation

By the middle of 2008, the Ivorian government had paid out about 16 billion CFA (€25 million) in relation to the dumping: 10 billion CFA was reportedly distributed to about 50 per cent of the 100,000 victims recognised by the government, 1.5 billion CFA to families of fifteen people killed, 1.75 billion CFA to 'economic victims' (mainly small business) and 2 billion on ten clean-up projects. The Treasury of Abidjan claimed that they had a further 9 billion CFA to hand out to victims but have not yet accounted for the remainder of funds paid by Trafigura for immunity from prosecution, which was about 75 billion CFA (about €110 million).

Gonto reports on "extensive fraud committed in the compensation of victims": "the FCFA 100 billion, disbursed by Trafigura under an agreement with the State of Côte d'Ivoire, has been squandered already. The dumping sites have not been rehabilitated. No monitoring is done on the use of this fund" (Gonto 2010). In September 2009 Trafigura paid about €34 million into a Leigh Day account in Abidjan as compensation for the dumping. In early 2010, before the money could be paid to victims, the Court of Appeal in Abidjan – in what Leigh Day called "a terrible judgment" (Leigh Day 2010) – ordered the money to be transferred to the bank account of CNVDT. CNVDT attempted to draw down the funds but was prevented from doing so as a result of "police and political intervention" (Leigh Day 2010). The case was due to be heard in the Supreme Court, but Leigh Day was not prepared to let it go that far in fear of a similar result:

> the forces in Abidjan that had persuaded the Court of Appeal to make their decision in [CNVDT's] favour seemed likely to also prevail in the Supreme Court. As a result Leigh Day has felt it has had no alternative but to enter into talks with the CNVDT lawyers to see if there is a way of trying to ensure as much of the compensation as possible ends up in the pockets of the claimants rather than in the CNVDT bank account.
>
> (Leigh Day 2010)

It is clear from this statement that the British law firm had lost confidence in the Ivorian judiciary and alluded to a lack of judicial independence. It also seems that the firm had given up on the possibility of 'all' the compensation reaching the indented recipients. According to RENADVIDET, of the 30,000 victims involved in the UK class action, more than 15,000 victims have yet to be compensated by CNVDT (Cheickna 2011c).

By the end of 2011 the situation in Abidjan with regard to these victims' organisations remained unchanged. The Amsterdam public prosecutor was seeking a fine of about €2 million to be applied to Trafigura for forgery, illegal carrying of waste and the concealment of the hazardous nature of the waste.[76] This case did not include provision for compensations for victims of the dumping. However, the victims' organisations are taking the opportunity to 'sell' this case to the public: "[s]ome of these NGOs are making the most of the current appeals court process in Holland to say – look, we are bringing Trafigura to court – give us money quick so we can give you your membership card!"[77]

## Conclusion

The actors at the centre of the deviant behaviour detailed in this chapter are the Ivorian state and the newly formed victims' organisations. As the perpetrators of an organisational crime, they are two actors in one interrelationship. The rules that have been violated include domestic law and the dictates of social morality as judged from the point of view of the relevant social audience. Potentially significant sanctions range from legal punishments (e.g., fines, revocation of licence to operate or conviction of members of staff), censure by the public and the press (both national and international) and resistance in the form of protest by the state's own population. The social audience is civil society – represented by INGOs, local human rights NGOs and victims' organisations – which, in the Gramscian sense, is the space "occupied in particular by organisations such as pressure groups, voluntary associations, religious bodies, the mass media and academic institutions, to the extent that they enjoy real independence from the state" (Green and Ward 2004: 4).

As has been seen the victims' organisations activities can be understood as organised crime. The assumption that those censuring state-corporate crime are necessarily a force for 'good' has been fundamentally questioned by the chapter, and civil society actors are exposed as commodifying victims by forcing payment for membership cards and fees in return for the chance to be compensated by non-existing class actions in foreign courts.

Civil society has been hijacked by state-organised crime, and the opportunity to do this is as a direct result of the dumping, historic practises of state corruption, and Trafigura's continuing impunity. The dumping of toxic waste created the victims in question. And the impunity afforded to Trafigura has meant that the company has not been compelled to admit liability and compensate the victims, nor has the corporation been formally required to clean up the waste sites.

The implications of the issues raised by the data analysed in this chapter are far-reaching. In examining the role of civil society in labelling and sanctioning state and state-corporate crime, it should be borne in mind that common assumptions made of NGOs and victims' organisations are here misplaced. Civil society is more usefully conceptualised as a Gramscian space in which members of civil society vie for position (Gramsci 1971). In Ivory Coast, victims' organisations have been set up to pursue criminal goals, assisted by the state, and have successfully taken advantage of normative assumptions of civil society to exploit the victims of the toxic waste dumping.

## Notes

1 Including Ivory Coast, Sierra Leone, Liberia and Guinea.
2 A French-Canadian journalist.
3 A French lawyer.
4 Known locally as 'dagga'.
5 The other three being Nigeria, Ghana and Senegal.
6 As well as to Togo, Ghana and Senegal.
7 Former leader of FESCI, interviewed by Human Rights Watch, October 2007 (HRW 2008: 1).

8  Interviews, Abidjan, September 2010 (LIDHO and APDH 2010).
9  Interview, Abidjan, September 2010 (APDH 2010).
10  Ibid.
11  Ibid.
12  Interview, Abidjan, September 2010 (LIDHO 2010).
13  Interview, Abidjan, September 2010 (MIDH 2010).
14  In 2006 Goudé was the head of the Young Patriots (an ultranationalist pro-government group).
15  Okechukwu Ibeanu.
16  [2009] EWHC 1246 (QB) Case No: HQ06X03370.
17  Observation, Abidjan, September 2010 (UVDTAB).
18  Interview, Abidjan, September 2010 (UVDTAB).
19  Ibid.
20  Ibid.
21  Ibid.
22  Ibid.
23  Ibid.
24  Interview, Abidjan, September 2010 (CNVDT).
25  Ibid.
26  Interview, Abidjan, September 2010 (FAVIDET).
27  Ibid.
28  Ibid.
29  Interview, Abidjan, September 2010 (FENAVIDET) and www.fenavidet-ci.com/index. php?option=com_content&view=article&id=68:declaration&catid=1:latest-news&Item id=76.
30  Interview, Abidjan, September 2010 (FENAVIDET).
31  Ibid.
32  Ibid.
33  Ibid.
34  Ibid.
35  Ibid.
36  Ibid.
37  Ibid.
38  Observation, Abidjan, September 2010 (FENAVIDET).
39  Ibid.
40  Ibid.
41  Interview, Abidjan, September 2010 (FENAVIDET).
42  Ibid.
43  Ibid.
44  Ibid.
45  Interview, Abidjan, September 2010 (UVDTAB).
46  Observation, Abidjan, September 2010 (UVDTAB).
47  Ibid.
48  Ibid.
49  UVDTAB: Capacité Juridique, undated (copy with author).
50  Interview, Abidjan, September 2010 (UVDTAB).
51  State journal of record for publishing legal announcements (similar to the *London Gazette* in the UK).
52  Available at http://lib.ohchr.org/HRBodies/UPR/Documents/Session6/CI/UVD TAB_CIV_UPR_S6_2009_F.pdf (accessed November 2011).
53  See http://esango.un.org/civilsociety/showProfileDetail.do?method=showProfileDetails& profileCode=617302.

54 Interview, Abidjan, September 2010 (FENAVIDET).
55 Observation, Abidjan, September 2010 (FENAVIDET).
56 Interview, Abidjan, September 2010 (FENAVIDET).
57 Ibid.
58 Ibid.
59 Interview, Abidjan, September 2010 (CNVDT).
60 Ibid.
61 Interview, Abidjan, September 2010 (FENAVIDET).
62 Ibid.
63 Ibid.
64 Ibid.
65 Ibid.
66 Interview, Abidjan, September 2010 (FAVIDET).
67 From an RTI TV2 report, video (in French) available at www.fenavidet-ci.com/index.
   php?option=com_content&view=article&id=72&Itemid=80, accessed November 2011.
68 Interview, Abidjan, September 2010 (UVDTAB).
69 Interview, Abidjan, September 2010 (CNVDT).
70 Interview, Abidjan, September 2010 (FAVIDET).
71 Ibid.
72 See www.fenavidet-ci.com.
73 See  www.fenavidet-ci.com/index.php?option=com_content&view=article&id=68:
   declaration&catid=1:latest-news&Itemid=76.
74 See  www.fenavidet-ci.com/index.php?option=com_content&view=article&id=61%3
   Acommunique-pour-les-victimes-enrolees-au-baron-de-yopougon-au-banco2-au-terminus-
   42-yopougon-andokoi-yopougon-koweit-abobo-doumeyopougon-niangonmaroc-
   carrefour-anadoryopungon-wassakara&catid=3%3Anewsflash&Itemid=55.
75 Observation, Abidjan, September 2010.
76 Amsterdam public prosecutor press release, Hoge geldboetes geëist in hoger beroep
   Probo Koala, 17 November 2011, available at www.om.nl/algemene_onderdelen/uit
   gebreid_zoeken/@157755/hoge-geldboetes/, accessed November 2011.
77 Email correspondence between the author and an international press correspondent,
   November 2011.

# Chapter 9

# Cover-up and denial

## The battle in Britain

This chapter uses Cohen's three forms of state crime denial to assist in under-standing the criminal nature of the events and relationships associated with Trafigura's dumping. The three forms of denial are: (1) 'denial of the past', (2) 'literal denial', and (3) 'implicatory denial' (Cohen 1993: 108–110). It is argued that each of these categorisations can assist in unravelling the tactics employed by Trafigura in what can be understood as an elaborate cover-up of the dumping. 'Denial of the past' at an organisational level involves "the organised attempts to cover up the record of past atrocities" (Cohen 1993: 108). 'Literal denial' can also be revealed by organised cover-ups and involves "the simple lie or fraud where facts are accessible but lead to a conclusion which is knowingly evaded" (Cohen 1993: 109). 'Implicatory denials' "seek to negoti-ate or impose a different construction of the event from what might appear the case", one of the most common forms of which is 'denial of responsibility' (Cohen 1993: 110). Cohen's work supports the use of his ideas in a corporate setting, and Sykes and Matza's original formulation of criminal denial does not preclude any form of organisational crime (Sykes and Matza 1957). Cohen uses a comparison between states and corporations when outlining the counter-arguments to objections to the inclusion of state crime as a genuine crimi-nological endeavour and argues that a state can commit crime and engage in denial despite its organisational nature – just as the corporation can.

Because "we can approach the process of denial through its opposite: the attempt to recover or uncover the past" (Cohen 1993: 109), the two responses of international civil society analysed by this chapter are a civil legal case against the corporation and a struggle for and against a cover-up. The relative power of the key actors within the arena of struggle (Gramsci 1971) was a determining factor in the success of goal attainment.

INGOs and specialist law firms have made attempts to hold the corpora-tion to account for the dumping. A network of civil society actors launched a coordinated attempt at labelling the corporation's actions as deviant. This group included Greenpeace Nederland, BBC's *Newsnight*, de Volkskrant, the Norwe-gian Broadcasting Corporation (NRK), the *Guardian*, Al Jazeera and Amnesty International.[1] These organisations formed a strategic issue-based alliance centred on the dumping. The law firms associated with this network include Sherpa and Leigh Day & Co solicitors. Sherpa is a Paris-based civil rights law association specialising in corruption in former French colonies. Lasslett argues that for any resistance movement, the institutions it can work through "in a specific conjuncture is a vital determinate of its strength" (Lasslett 2012a: 4). The INGOs along with their media partners shared information and strategised against the ongoing impunity enjoyed by the company to such an extent that a director of Trafigura implied that his organisation had been 'attacked' by this group: "it's an organised campaign by Greenpeace. We don't know why they are attacking us on this subject" (McElroy 2009). Here we witness what Cohen (1993), referring 'the official state discourse', calls 'pure denial'. Just as a state may exclaim that the international community of states is "picking on us" (Cohen 1993: 104), the Trafigura director bemoans attention being drawn to the dumping by a community of international civil society organisations.

Throughout this chapter it will be seen that agents of Trafigura, the law firm Carter-Ruck and reputation managers Bell Pottinger were deployed to great effect by the corporation. David Hooper, a former partner at the law firm Carter-Ruck, claimed that the firm's founder, Peter Carter-Ruck, "created the modern libel industry, was a dedicated liar and a reactionary with a lust for cash ... [and] ... he did for freedom of speech what the Boston Strangler did for door-to-door salesmen" (Hooper 2003). Bell Pottinger executives claimed to have privileged access to government (including to the British prime minister, his chief of staff and closest advisor, and the British foreign secretary) and that it was "possible to use MPs known to be critical of investigative programmes to attack their reporting for minor errors" (Newman and Wright 2011). Both firms, therefore, provide Trafigura with potential access to institutions of government and law through Carter-Ruck's experience, expertise in the judicial realm and Bell Pottinger's claimed access to sources of legislative and executive power (Newman and Wright 2011).

Approaching the concept of denial, as Cohen (1993) suggests, through its opposites of censure and public shaming, this chapter will examine, first, efforts to label the corporation as deviant and, second, at attempts that were made to sanction Trafigura.

## Labelling deviance

Local human rights NGOs labelled the dumping as a deviant action by Trafigura. And the National Inquiry could be seen to have carried out a civil society function when it investigated and reported that "the Trafigura group, through the behaviour of its employees ... infringed the Marpol and the Basel Convention".[2]

Trafigura's actions have also been labelled as deviant by international civil society organisations, especially by international press organisations. Gramsci included the press and media, albeit in ambiguous terms, when he outlined the institutions of civil society (Gramsci 1971) and "some institutions like the media, while essentially based on market organisations, nonetheless have significant civil society elements" (Anheier and Carlson, undated). The *Guardian*, BBC's *Newsnight*, the NRK and de Volkskrant shared the Daniel Pearl Award for Outstanding International Investigative Reporting[3] for exposing Trafigura's dumping of toxic waste in Ivory Coast.[4] By way of contrast the Ivorian press does not enjoy the same freedom as its European counterparts, and there is a lack of independence of the media, with "many newspapers in Abidjan . . . affiliated with a political party" (ICG 2004), as well as state repression of journalists critical of government (Gonto 2008).

International civil society that responded critically to the dumping with statements or reports included the European Union (Dimas 2006) and the United Nations (UNHRC 2009). European Commissioner Stavos Dimas described the dumping as "not only unethical in the most profound sense of the word, but . . . criminal" (Dimas 2006), and he planned "to put forward a proposal to criminalise certain environmentally damaging practices such as the one perpetrated" (Dimas 2006). The European Parliament resolution made since the dumping states:

> The toxic waste was dumped by a Greek-owned, Panamanian-flagged tanker leased by Trafigura Beheer BV, a Netherlands-based company; whereas such sharing of responsibilities creates a systematic and unacceptable problem with regard to the enforcement of Community legislation.[5]

The UN special rapporteur concluded that "there seems to be strong prima facie evidence that the reported deaths and adverse health consequences are related to the dumping of the waste from the Probo Koala" (UNHRC 2009: 10). Bell Pottinger, acting for Trafigura, responded in September 2009 that the UN report was "inaccurate" and "potentially damaging" (Leigh 2009d). This is a form of implicatory denial, and by challenging the accuracy of the UN report, Trafigura attempted to construct a different version of events to that observed by the UN investigators. In early September 2006 the WHO sent a team "to support the Ministry of Health in dealing with an environmental health emergency caused by toxic waste" and "to determine the extent and severity of poisoning" (WHO 2006). This team included a clinical toxicologist, an environmental health specialist and a 'further' technical specialist (WHO 2006). The WHO is the largest international organisation involved with the incident, but they have yet to produce any report on the health consequences of the dumping, and a search of the WHO website for 'Trafigura' reveals no results.[6] The WHO would have been in an excellent position to dispel the myths propagated by Trafigura in relation to the nature of the waste and its effects on the local population, and its failure to report on the matter requires further explanation.[7]

The BBC's defence to the May 2009 libel action by Trafigura against *Newsnight*'s feature on the dumping stated:

> It is admitted that the programme [*Newsnight*] alleged that Trafigura was culpably responsible for causing or permitting the unlawful dumping of highly toxic waste with an obvious potential to cause serious harm to the public as in fact it did. It is further admitted that the actual consequences alleged in the programme included miscarriages and injury to health of tens of thousands of people including sixteen deaths.[8]

However, despite being one of the loudest voices of censure, the BBC succumbed to Trafigura's legal challenge. In December 2009 they settled the case, apologised for the allegations and paid Trafigura £25,000 in damages. This is more an indication of the power the oil trader is able to wield relative to that of the BBC than evidence of Trafigura's innocence. Pressure from Trafigura and its legal team led by Carter-Ruck appears to have been too much for the broadcaster to bear. In this situation one can only speculate that the BBC's legal team made a cost-benefit analysis between the censuring of Trafigura and the potential costs of a libel claim by Trafigura against the BBC. The pressure applied by Trafigura was part of an orchestrated attempt to deny the past and cover up (or neutralise) the public record of the dumping event.

When asked about its recidivist history by journalists, Bell Pottinger, acting for Trafigura, reported that "Trafigura has always done its business in an ethical and transparent manner" (Leigh 2009b). But the reality appears to be that the actions of Trafigura are frequently labelled as deviant and very often opaque. Following the dumping, Trafigura instigated, as shall be seen, a cover-up operation which had both great successes and calamitous failures from the corporation's point of view. The next section reveals how Trafigura and its agents, including law firm Carter-Ruck and public relations consultants Bell Pottinger, constrained the activities of large sections of civil society through a wide-scale and systematic operation of all three forms of Cohen's (1993) denial that spanned a number of years. The section provides an overview of the tactics employed by Trafigura and reveals how overzealousness in covering up the dumping actually precipitated wide-scale censure by the British public.

On 6 of November 2006, Trafigura hired Peter Fraser (aka Lord Fraser) at the recommendation of Thomas Galbraith (aka Lord Strathclyde[9]), former Conservative leader in the House of Lords, UK, who was a director at Trafigura (and specifically at Galena Asset Management, a commodities hedge fund), to conduct an independent inquiry into the dumping incident. The report did not materialise before Fraser's death in 2013. The use by Trafigura of an 'independent' inquirer with strong links to the energy and commodities industry[10] and the subsequent extended delay and ultimate failure in publication of any final report can be seen as an attempt to literally deny the dumping by evading conclusions based on the available facts. In May 2007 *de Volkskrant* reported that the press officer of Trafigura, operating under the username 'Press Office T NL', three times attempted to alter the Dutch Wikipedia article about the *Probo Koala* "with intent to clear the company's name" (Trommelen 2007a). This is denial of the past with an attempt to remove details of the dumping from the public record. But Wikipedia has proven itself a site of resistance and fought back against the attempted airbrushing of the past, with administrators locking the user's account. The 'Press Office T NL' Wikipedia profile now contains the following 'warning' message: "if you use an account only for vandalism it can be blocked for an indefinite period of time".[11] Bell Pottinger claim to have "all sorts of dark arts" at their disposal, including teams that can manipulate Google results to "drown" out negative coverage of corporate human rights violations and "sort" negative Wikipedia coverage of clients and their activities (Newman and Wright 2011). This policy of altering the public record and public perception involves all three forms of Cohen's (1993) denial: records are erased or suppressed, conclusions (or 'negative coverage') are evaded and a different construction of events is proposed. In August 2009 *de Volkskrant* reported that Trafigura had filed a case against the Dutch government in an attempt to keep secret the report of the Netherlands Forensics Institute (NFI) on the dumping that had been handed over to Leigh Day (Trommelen 2007b). The use of the legal system to implement Trafigura's policy of denial is detailed in the following section.

On top of the lacklustre attempts by Fraser, Trafigura suppressed its own commissioned research into the cause of the deaths and illness reported in Abidjan. John Minton, of Trafigura's scientific consultants Minton, Treharne & Davies, reported initially on the serious toxic consequences of the dumping. After the Minton report was leaked by the *Guardian* (Leigh 2009a), Minton became engaged in the whitewash of his own research and released a statement denying its findings: "I had no information on the quantity, composition or concentration of the chemicals involved" (Minton 2009: 1). This, however, was a literal denial of the initial Minton report, which clearly stated at the outset that "the combined slops from these washing operations were reported as follows: 150m$^3$ NaOH, 370m$^3$ treated naphtha and free water and 24kg ARI-100 EXL catalyst" (Minton 2006a: 1). The report claimed that the waste was capable of causing the reported "severe human health effects" including death (Minton 2006a: 7). The suppression of the report, as we will now see, was just one attempt by Trafigura to silence its critics.

## British media silenced

Further to the activities of suppression applied to the leaked report, there were efforts to use the British legal system to limit the freedoms usually enjoyed by the mainstream media. In this section all three forms of Cohen's (1993) denial can be again observed in an analysis of the cover-up.

In September 2009 the *Guardian* newspaper leaked the internal emails which revealed that Trafigura was aware of the hazardous nature of the waste in advance of the dumping (Leigh 2009b). This was the first sign that civil society organisations were gaining traction in the struggle to censure Trafigura, and the denial and systematic attempts at concealment were beginning to be unravelled. The emails had been handed over to the *Guardian* by an anonymous London NGO[12] and highlighted the importance of the networks that the civil society actors are able to employ. Once in the hands of the media, the documents could potentially be used to censure the corporation much more effectively than had they remained with the NGO alone. The documents were further shared among other civil society and media organisations (such as Amnesty International, Al Jazeera and NRK),[13] and soon thereafter *Newsnight* reported again on the dumping based on these newly revealed documents. The report evoked the following response from Trafigura (through its legal team at Carter-Ruck): "Trafigura is concerned to note that the BBC is proposing to revisit these matters bearing in mind that they are, as you know, the subject of ongoing libel proceedings" (BBC 2009). They continued: "it is Trafigura's position that insofar as it is suggested that these individuals died as a result of hydrogen sulphide exposure, that hydrogen sulphide cannot have come from or been generated or caused by the *Probo Koala* slops" (BBC 2009). The continued denial of responsibility, even in the face of documentary evidence, is testament to the legal power that the corporation was confident in deploying, and on 12 December 2009 that confidence was given a further boost when the BBC deleted an online video of the *Newsnight* report as well as an associated BBC News online article. Angry bloggers, however, resisted the cover-up and responded by reposting the video on YouTube[14] (Eaton 2009).

By the end of 2009, national newspapers – a source of the public record – that had originally reported on Trafigura's role in the dumping started to alter that record with corrections and apologies, despite the wealth of available evidence outlining Trafigura's role. This resulted in a bolstering of the discourse of Trafigura's denial and the company having placed online copies of corrections and apologies from the *Times*, *Times Online* and the *Guardian* newspapers.[15] The *Times* (2009) correction, on Monday, 7ʰ September 2009, states that "the dumping was carried out illegally without Trafigura's knowledge by an independent local contractor. Trafigura have always disputed that the dumping caused, or could have caused, the deaths and serious injuries referred to in the article" and adds, "We are happy to put the record straight". The *Times Online* (2010) correction on Friday, 30 April 2010, states:

> We wish to make clear that the dumping was not carried out by Trafigura as the article may have suggested but by an independent local contractor without Trafigura's authority or knowledge. . . . Furthermore, in September 2009 lawyers for Ivorians who were suing Trafigura over injuries allegedly caused by the dumping acknowledged that at worst the waste

could only have caused flulike symptoms. . . . We apologise for these errors.

In May 2009 the following statement appeared in print and on the *Guardian* website:

> Our item headlined Success for the Guardian (26 April, page 2) erroneously linked the dumping of toxic waste in Ivory Coast from a vessel chartered by Trafigura with the deaths of a number of West Africans . . . We apologise for our error.
>
> (Guardian 2010)

And the cover-up extended to other national publications in the UK. The *Independent* initially reported that the dumping

> caused at least 100,000 residents from . . . Abidjan to flood into hospitals and clinics complaining of . . . nausea, breathlessness, headaches, skin reactions and a range of ear, nose, throat and pulmonary problems [and] miscarriages, still births and birth defects.
>
> (Independent 2009)

The article concluded that it was "one of the worst pollution incidents in decades" (Independent 2009). These were very strong censuring statements, but all have now been deleted from archives by the *Independent*.

The reasons behind these apologies, corrections, clarifications and deletions from the public record are obvious to some, and Monbiot argues:

> This could be one of the worst cases of corporate killing and injury since the Bhopal disaster, but much of the media wouldn't touch it with a bargepole. The reason isn't hard to divine: Trafigura has been throwing legal threats around like confetti.
>
> (Monbiot 2009)

The use of libel laws and aggressive lawyers has been a success for Trafigura in suppressing information about the dumping that may have an effect on public opinion, and this effect persists to the present. Caroline Lucas, the first Green Party member to be elected to the UK parliament, in her first speech to parliament, took the opportunity to raise the case and noted the continuing media 'blackout' on the dumping:

> Last year, hon. Members from both sides helped to shine a light on the actions of . . . Trafigura, and the shipping of hazardous waste to the Ivory Coast. There was particular concern that the media in this country were prevented from reporting the issues fully and fairly. That remains the case,

for new legal actions concerning Trafigura have been launched in the Dutch courts and are being reported widely in other countries but not here.

(Lucas 2010)

The event that allowed members of parliament to 'shine a light' on the dumping was in fact a tactical error by Trafigura, the kind of error on the part of state or corporate agents that Lasslett argues might "open up a horizon of opportunities for resistance movements" (Lasslett 2012a). Trafigura's decision to take out a super-injunction is an example of a 'fundamental miscalculation' that opened the way for civil society to censure the actions of Trafigura, on this occasion, not through the mainstream media but through the 'blogosphere'[16] (Rusbridger 2009).

## The super-injunction

On 12 October 2009, Trafigura's legal firm Carter-Ruck, in pursuit of its policy to cover up, applied to the court for an injunction to prevent the *Guardian* newspaper from reporting on a parliamentary question by Paul Farrelly[17] (see what follows; Leigh 2009c). The injunction further stipulated that the *Guardian* could not report on the question's existence. This extreme form of censorship has led such injunctions to be known as super-injunctions. Alan Rusbridger, the editor of the *Guardian*, expressed surprise at the fact that his newspaper might be in contempt of court for releasing the document: "we had never encountered a situation when we had been forbidden for reporting on parliament" (Rusbridger 2009).

The super-injunction was a turning point in the struggle over corporate censure and was ultimately unsuccessful as a tactic of denial. The Guido Fawkes political blog quickly identified Paul Farrelly's written question as likely to be linked to the super-injunction (Guido Fawkes 2009). The question was:

> To ask the Secretary of State for Justice, what assessment he has made of the effectiveness of legislation to protect (a) whistleblowers and (b) press freedom following the injunctions obtained in the High Court by (i) Barclays and Freshfields solicitors on 19 March 2009 on the publication of internal Barclays reports documenting alleged tax avoidance schemes and (ii) Trafigura and Carter-Ruck solicitors on 11 September 2009 on the publication of the Minton report on the alleged dumping of toxic waste in the Ivory Coast, commissioned by Trafigura.

In a letter to the Speaker of the House of the House of Commons, Alan Rusbridger stated:

> [Carter-Ruck] asserted that the Guardian would be in contempt of Court and sought an immediate undertaking that we would not publish. The

letter also stated that Carter-Ruck did not even accept that the publication by Parliament of Mr Farrelly's question placed the existence of the injunction in the public domain![18]

Rusbridger argued that the development was a regression of free speech versus censorship: "in some ways we're going backwards, I think after Thalidomide, after the Pentagon papers, we thought that the notion of prior constraint[19] was gone" (Rusbridger 2009).

At around noon on 13 October 2009, the day after the injunction was obtained, Trafigura (via Carter-Ruck) withdrew its claim that the *Guardian* reporting on the parliamentary debate revealing the injunction's existence would be contempt of court (Leigh 2009d). This climb-down was as a result of Farrelly's question having been released into the public domain by bloggers, who are not subject to the same restrictions as mainstream media (BBC 2011). The *Guardian* claimed that the super-injunction was neutralised by "a combination of legal sense and digital communications" (Busfield 2010). WikiLeaks had previously released the Minton report into the public domain, but the online response to the super-injunction significantly raised both the report's and Trafigura's profile. Social media, especially Twitter, provided an innovative technique to circumnavigate the challenge to exposing crime posed by the aggressive use of injunctions. Rusbridger recalls the flurry of activity: "The blogosphere just went berserk; I mean, I've never seen anything like it. Over the last sixteen hours, I've never seen this amount of activity on Twitter, of people really upset by it" (Rusbridger 2009). One tweet at the time read: "The Twitterverse is going mental for #trafigura" (Massie 2009), referring to the hashtag, '#trafigura'. The application for the super-injunction and the subsequent reaction was "a fantastic PR own goal" (Rusbridger 2009) for the company and raised their profile in the public eye overnight: "I think most people, yesterday wouldn't have heard of this company, Trafigura" (Rusbridger 2009). Matthiesson (2010) argues that the 'spectacular public relations fallout' from the Trafigura case (and another case involving a well-known soccer player) may force media lawyers to "reconsider whether super-injunctions are the most advisable method to protect their client's interests in the first place" (Matthiesson 2010: 153).

The reaction of the UK state to the super-injunction contrasts to apparent inaction in the previous years to Trafigura's aggressive use of libel laws to suppress journalistic reports. This may have been a direct result of the publicity and public outrage displayed online. Alternatively an apparent reason is that the injunction was not an attack on civil society – as the libel campaign had been – but an attack on parliament, an institution of the state. David Heath[20] argued in the House of Commons that

> [a] fundamental principle of this House is now being threatened by the legal proceedings for an injunction and the consequent proceedings for

contempt of court in respect of injuncted material. As you know, we have enjoyed in this House since 1688 the privilege of being able to speak freely.

(Hansard 2009)

Lord Judge[21] reiterated the fact, couching the injunctions in terms of the power struggle between the judiciary and parliament: "I should need some very powerful persuasion indeed that it would be constitutionally proper for a court to make an order to limit discussions in parliament" (Rogerson and Dean 2009). Within a matter of months, in April 2010, a judicial committee headed by Lord Neuberger was set up to examine super-injunctions and in May 2010 reported back that the law and judiciary function as they should (Neuberger 2010). Rusbridger argued that the use of the super-injunction was about cover-up activities:

This is really just about embarrassment, there's no great legal principle here. The company didn't want the world to know that they were clamping down on newspapers, it was embarrassing for them, but the courts shouldn't be so spineless as to agree to these super-injunctions.

(Rusbridger 2009)

Moore (2009) reported how Twitter users claimed that Trafigura's prompt withdrawal of the injunction was a victory for press liberty, and quotes a 'typical' tweet: "Hurrah for free speech and freedom of information . . . don't mess with the people" (quoted in Moore 2009). Another read, "The Twitterati and the Blogosphere have prevailed in the great Battle of Trafigura" (Massie 2009). Lord Neuberger, the most senior civil judge in England and Wales at the time, took a different view and claimed that these forms of online technology are "totally out of control" (BBC 2011). However, if the online community of civil society actors had been under the stronger control of the state, and under the same restrictions as the mainstream media, this injunction may not have come to light, and a chance to censure Trafigura may have been missed.

The struggle to label Trafigura's actions as deviant was only successful after elements of civil society capitalised on a miscalculation by the corporation. However, the censure focused on an attempt by the corporation to 'gag' the British press from reporting on parliament. The subject matter of the injunctions – the damning report on the dangers of the waste dumped in Abidjan – received considerably less attention.

## Civil society sanctions

In Ivory Coast there were no reported attempts by the domestic NGOs to seek sanctions against Trafigura through the courts. However, INGOs have made repeated attempts to engage the legal systems of Europe (specifically the Netherlands, France and the UK).

Greenpeace Nederland reported the dumping to the Dutch public prosecutor, who claimed to lack jurisdiction (Day 2010). Greenpeace Nederland thereafter filed a complaint,[22] as an interested party,[23] against Dutch prosecutors for failing to prosecute Trafigura, its CEO and Puma for their roles in the dumping. The charges sought included murder, gross maltreatment, manslaughter, grievous bodily harm, work- or profession-related criminal offences, forgery and membership in a criminal organisation[24] (Böhler 2009). On the criminal liability of Trafigura as subject of the criminal justice system, Greenpeace Nederland argued that "this legal person can and must be called to account for the offences" (Böhler 2009: 15). This statement tried to pre-empt an argument against the legal individual versus organisational problem.

The law association NGO, Sherpa, pressed for a criminal prosecution in France but was unsuccessful. According to Day, "The French authorities said, look, we've got no jurisdiction in the Ivory Coast. We cannot realistically send across examining magistrates . . . to Abidjan" (Day 2010). This failure to prosecute, for whatever reason, was a failure of the operationality of control on an institutional level, and as Welch maintains, "state-corporate crime persists because it is afforded impunity against prosecution" (2009: 352).

However, the Dutch public prosecutor pursued Trafigura for crimes[25] committed in Amsterdam port before the dumping, namely, failing to inform the Dutch authorities of the nature and origin of the waste and forgery of documents designed for that purpose and exporting hazardous waste.[26] In 2010 the company was convicted and fined €1 million by a Dutch judge and cleared of a forgery charge, whereas the captain of the *Probo Koala* was sentenced to a five-month (suspended) prison term for forgery.

Greenpeace Nederland also lodged a complaint with the Dutch advertising authority for advertisements released by Trafigura that suggested that the High Court in London had ruled that the toxic waste from the *Probo Koala* could not cause any fatal or otherwise serious health conditions. Greenpeace argued that "Trafigura attempted to falsely create the impression that a judgement had been made in favour of the company" (Greenpeace International 2010). The advertisements were an attempt by the corporation at implicatory denial and sought "to negotiate or impose a different construction of the event" (Cohen 1993: 110) by claiming that an agreement in the *Motto* case (see as follows) between the parties was in fact a finding of a British judge.

All of these cases took place in the Netherlands, and the consequences were the application of relatively minor sanctions to Trafigura for deviant behaviour. None, however, were concerned with the toxic waste dumping in Abidjan. A civil case in the UK looked more promising.

## *Motto and Others v Trafigura*

In October 2006 Leigh Day was contacted to provide legal assistance to victims of the dumping. Leigh Day says it were also approached directly by Chief

Motto, chief of Djibi village, who told the BBC that all 2,000 villagers became ill, and three people had died.[27]

Leigh Day originally took on twelve Ivorian clients, and by early 2007 they were forecasting that there would be between 3,000 and 5,000 claimants. The final figure in the case of *Motto & Ors v Trafigura*[28] of 29,614 claimants was, however, to dwarf those early predictions. By the time the claim form was filed, it was the largest collective action personal injury claim ever filed in England and Wales (Dunt 2009). In October 2008, Trafigura agreed to no longer defend its actions with regard to the dumping (Dunt 2009). Leigh Day called the decision a 'climb-down', and Martyn Day reported: "I am pleased that Trafigura have seen sense and accepted that the game is up. For the last two years they have tried to pull the wool over the eyes of the world, in terms of their actions". The extended campaign of implicatory denial described by Day is part of the overall cover-up already discussed, but Day's damning statement too has now been deleted from the Leigh Day website. An international media correspondent based in West Africa was told by Day that Trafigura conceded that they had a duty of care to the victims and had breached that duty and were likely to settle out of court in the spring of 2009.[29] Leigh Day explained: "In early September [2008] we served them a whole host of documents and with a dossier of requests regarding their defence, which I think were unanswerable ... They realised the game was up" (Dunt 2009). Day argues that Trafigura was "forced into taking that step in the face of overwhelming evidence against it" (Day 2008). In September 2009, Trafigura reached a settlement agreement which included payment to 30,000 victims and their families of about £1,000 each (Leigh 2009c; Moore 2009). The judge ordered that the £30 million settlement be held in trust by Leigh Day, "exclusively and solely for the claimants" (quoted in Verkaik 2009). Trafigura paid £30 million into a bank account in Abidjan on 23 September 2009, but an injunction granted by an Ivorian court in favour of victims' organisation CNVDT blocked distribution. This unexpected intervention meant that the distribution of compensation to victims was severely delayed and "even now it has not been completed."[30] As well as the problems with the injunction granted by the Ivorian judiciary, the case posed other serious difficulties. The cost of running such a case is prohibitive; Leigh Day served a bill of costs on Trafigura of £104,707,772.72, including an insurance premium of more than £9 million.[31] This level of legal costs would have been enough to compensate another 104,000 victims.

As an act of censure, the *Motto* case was generally unsuccessful and has in fact further bolstered Trafigura's denial of the toxic waste dumping. Given it was settled out of court and that settlement contained a confidentiality clause, documents held by the law firm after extensive investigations and Trafigura's defence have not become public record and could not be used for this book. Furthermore, the 'global' settlement "will mean that claims of more serious injuries caused by the waste – including miscarriages, still births and birth defects – will now not be tested" (Milmo 2009a). The author asked Martyn

Day about this settlement agreement in 2010, and his response is quoted in full for what it reveals about the capacity of a powerful corporation to silence critics even as it admits guilt:

*Thomas MacManus:*

When talking to victims they would say: "Why has 'Mr Martin' signed an agreement with Trafigura to say that Trafigura had nothing to do with it? Why would he get involved in such a conspiracy with the company?" How would you answer those questions?[32]

*Martin Day, partner at Leigh Day:*

I can't talk massively about it . . . due to the confidentiality agreements. But the primary issue here, and it's a great difficulty when you've got a . . . big group claim. Acting for 30,000 people when we entered into negotiations with Trafigura, part of what they wanted was confidentiality. And we then had to work out, well was this a decent deal for them taking everything on board and we had to feel in the end it was. We went out to Abidjan in September 2009 and we managed to meet with 25,000 of our clients in two weeks. We gave them all the opportunity to say 'yes' or 'no' to the agreement knowing of the confidentiality, knowing of the position. Every single one, bar none, signed the deal: that they wanted to have the money in their pocket rather than some of the concerns that have now been raised. It's difficult. I hate confidentiality agreements. I think in the end it's important that society learns from what has happened and that everything is open book, everything is transparent but where a defendant comes to you as a lawyer and says look we are offering you 'X' but a part of the deal is that it's confidential, you have to put that deal to the client, you can't say well sorry, we don't like the deal, we're not going to agree to it.

. . .

As I say for me, if we had this situation in the [United] States [of America] you can't actually sign something in these sorts of deals as you can in the UK and I would feel much more easy if the Law Society was to ban, for example, that you cannot. Again one of the parts of the deal is we can't continue acting for anybody else in the Ivory Coast, that was part of the deal we had to sign. In the States that's simply not allowed, as a part of any deal. I think that would be a massively useful thing if the Law Society was to say, as a solicitor you simply can't enter that deal. Well, that would be great because it would then cut off the area that is such a major part of what happened and I think it's a retrograde step for our society because it means that we don't learn all the lessons of what has happened.

The agreement contained the following phrase: "the claimants now acknowledge that the fumes could, at worst, have caused only a range of short term relatively low level flu-like symptoms and anxiety" (*Motto & Ors v Trafigura*[33]). Here, from an implicatory denial point of view, we are presented with a 'denial of responsibility' and a "different construction of the event from what might appear the case" (Cohen 1993: 110). Furthermore, the agreement precludes Leigh Day from representing any more clients on the issue. Both are factors that block future compensation claims by the victims in Abidjan that were not party to this case.

As a legal sanction the case is therefore also a failure: Trafigura can still claim to be without liability for the dumping. The settlement was part of the larger scheme of denial and ensured that the actions of Trafigura would not be considered by a law court in this case, with all the media attention that entails (Dunt 2009).

## Conclusion

This chapter analysed the reaction of international civil society actors to the dumping and sought to assess the capacity of these actors to label the corporation as criminal and to sanction the state-corporate crime that took place in Abidjan. The chapter examined two events: the first, the attempt by mainstream British media to censure Trafigura for the dumping, and the second, a 30,000-claimant personal injury case filed against the corporation in London. Both were major attempts at censure or sanction, and the analysis reveals a power struggle between the corporation (engaged in denial) and civil society organisations attempting to expose, censure and sanction corporate wrongdoing through the arenas of law and media.

The evidence is clear. Trafigura employed all three forms of Cohen's denial – 'denial of the past', 'literal denial', and 'implicatory denial' in its cover-up of its role in the toxic dumping. The 2007 attempt by Trafigura to alter the Dutch Wikipedia article about the *Probo Koala* and the 2009 case against the Dutch government to suppress an NFI report on the dumping are clear attempts to erase the dumping from the public record. When the record could not be suppressed, the corporation resorted to aggressively initiating libel legal threats through a British law firm including the 2009 libel action against *Newsnight*, which was settled for £25,000 along with an apology to Trafigura. The corporation even tried to suppress its own commissioned research using a super-injunction. It employed public relations firms like Bell Pottinger, whose 'dark arts' tactics are designed to reinvent and re-present damaged reputations. Bell Pottinger in this role insisted that the 2009 UN report (UNHRC 2009) was "inaccurate" (Independent 2010). The discourse presented by Trafigura follows what Cohen calls 'a complete spiral of denial':

> First you try 'it didn't happen'. There was no massacre, no one was tortured. But then the media, human rights organisations and victims show that it does happen: here are the graves; we have the photos; look at the

autopsy reports. So you have to say that what happened was not what it looks to be but really something else.

(Cohen 1993: 102)

Thereafter, the audience is subjected to the next stage of the spiral: "if it did happen, 'it' is something else" (Cohen 1993: 103). The final stage of the spiral of denial is 'justification'. When Eric de Turckheim, a Trafigura director, was interviewed by Jeremy Paxman on the BBC's *Newsnight* programme on 16 August 2007,[34] he claimed that "this [waste] material was not dangerous for human being [sic]; smelly, but not dangerous". Trafigura later argued that the dumping was carried out illegally and without its knowledge by an independent local contractor (Milmo 2009b), thereby denying the company's responsibility but suggesting that even 'if' the waste were dangerous, it was not in fact dumped by Trafigura. De Turckheim's 2007 television appearance also revealed Trafigura's attempts at the 'justification' stage of Cohen's spiral model when he argued that "[t]he discharge of slops is a routine operation that is carried out worldwide, and Abidjan is a sophisticated port fully equipped to handle such waste" (BBC 2009c). This commercially orientated justification for the discharge of the waste in Ivory Coast conflicts with the report of the National Inquiry, which insists that the lack of port facilities available at Abidjan would have been discovered by minimal due diligence.[35]

Challenging Trafigura's strategy of denial were domestic and INGOs, independent journalists and other members of civil society (e.g., MIDH, APDH, Greenpeace, Amnesty International, the Guardian, etc.) all acting as a potentially powerful social audience. INGOs have the capacity to access international networks of civil society actors (including socially orientated law firms, journalists and other NGOs) which ultimately strengthens their capacity to label actions as deviant or criminal. Domestic Ivorian NGOs assumed the role of a social audience that could interpret the legality, criminality and human rights impact of the dumping. However, Ivorian NGOs failed to mount a comprehensive challenge to the crime. Suffering from a lack of institutional funding, resources and quality personnel, they were incapable of mounting a serious campaign of resistance. These weaknesses were compounded by a self-imposed isolationism which precluded working relationships with sympathetic elements of the state and other NGOs. By contrast, INGOs are generally well funded and resourced and attract high-quality personnel. Furthermore, they display a capacity to form networks with other civil society actors across national boundaries and enjoy access to the sanctioning mechanisms of the state and most importantly various domestic legal systems. International civil society organisations, especially Greenpeace (which initially became concerned with this case because of the resultant environmental damage), were successful in publishing reports and mounting legal cases in the Netherlands as part of their censuring campaigns against the corporation. However, as this chapter has demonstrated, even after a network of civil society actors formed a strategic, issue-based alliance and launched a coordinated campaign in the UK to label the corporation's actions as deviant, the 'barriers of denial' that are provided by the current configuration of the UK legal system are formidable.

## Notes

1 Interview, International NGO Programme leader London, April 2011 (anonymous).
2 The report of the National Commission of Inquiry on the Toxic Waste in the District of Abidjan, page 48.
3 The Daniel Pearl Awards are presented by the International Consortium of Investigative Journalists, a project of the Center for Public Integrity in Washington, DC.
4 See www.journalism.co.uk/news/trafigura-investigators-honoured-with-daniel-pearl-award/s2/a538421/.
5 European Parliament resolution on the export of toxic waste to Africa, Official Journal 313 E, 20/12/2006 P. 0432–0434.
6 Available at search.who.int/search?q=trafigura&ie=utf8&site=default_collection&client=_en&proxystylesheet=_en, accessed October 2010.
7 Email correspondence between the author and a scientist at the International Programme on Chemical Safety, Evidence & Policy on Environmental Health (EPE), WHO, Geneva, from October to December 2011, has been frustratingly unsuccessful in determining reasons for the lack of a report – but one explanation offered was as follows: "it so happens, more for staff resource reasons than anything else, that we didn't compile and publish a final report on the WHO mission to Cote d'Ivoire at the time" (email from a scientist at the International Programme on Chemical Safety, EPE, WHO, Geneva on 8 December 2011).
8 Claim No. HQ 09X02050; Trafigura Limited (Claimant) and British Broadcasting Corporation (Defendant); Defence (of 11/09/2009) against claim issued on 15 May 2009 in the High Court of Justice, Queens Bench Division, drafted by Andrew Caldecott QC and Jane Phillips, and signed by Stephen Mitchell, head of Multimedia Programmes at the BBC (available at http://wikileaks.org/file/bbc-trafigura.pdf or mirror.wikileaks.info/leak/bbc-trafigura.pdf, accessed 16/02/2010), page 2.
9 Also known (at Companies House UK) as Lord Thomas Dunlop Galloway De Roy De Blicquy Galbraith Strathclyde, Thomas Strathclyde, Lord Thomas Galbraith Strathclyde, Lord Thomas Galloway Dunlop Du Roy De Blicquy Galbraith, Thomas Galloway Dunlop Du Roy De Blicquy Galbraith and Lord Thomas Dunlop Galloway De Roy De Blicquy Galbraith Strathclyde.
10 Peter Fraser claimed to be on the payroll of JKX Oil and Gas plc, Alkane Energy plc, International Petroleum Exchange, London Metal Exchange and Total Exploration UK Ltd, and see lordfraser.com/interests.html, accessed May 2012.
11 Available at http://nl.wikipedia.org/wiki/Sjabloon:Waarschuwing-Engels (accessed October 2010).
12 Interview, London, April 2011 (anonymous).
13 Ibid.
14 See https://youtu.be/x04vIFmsJec.
15 Available at www.trafigura.com/PDF/Major-corrections-and-apologies.pdf, accessed June 2012.
16 The term is here taken to refer to a loose community of independent, Internet-based commentators, bloggers and micro-bloggers and includes the concepts of the 'Twitterverse' or the 'Twitterati'.
17 Labour, UK Member of Parliament for Newcastle-under-Lyme.
18 Letter of Alan Rusbridger, editor of the *Guardian*, to John Bercow MP, available at www.scribd.com/doc/21187200/16-October-2009, accessed 16/02/2011.

19  Injunctions are the judicial form of prior restraint, the legal mechanism by which states attempt to prevent the publication of information.
20  Liberal Democrat, UK Member of Parliament for Somerton and Frome.
21  Then Lord Chief Justice.
22  Under Article 12 of the Dutch Code of Criminal Procedure.
23  Dutch law allows organisations with a direct interest in a case to lodge these types of complaints. Greenpeace evidenced their interest by reference to their Articles of Association.
24  Articles 287, 302, 307, 308, 309, 225 and 140 of the Dutch Penal Code (respectively).
25  The Economic Offences Act, the Environmental Management Act, the Environmentally Hazardous Substances Act, EEC Regulation No. 259/93 and the Dutch Penal Code (Böhler 2009).
26  Charges against Trafigura Beheer B.V., Amsterdam public prosecutor's office, no. 13/846003–06.
27  Claim No. HQ 09X02050; Trafigura Limited (Claimant) and British Broadcasting Corporation (Defendant); Defence (of 11/09/2009) against claim issued on 15 May 2009 in the High Court of Justice, Queens Bench Division, drafted by Andrew Caldecott QC and Jane Phillips, and signed by Stephen Mitchell, head of Multimedia Programmes at the BBC (available at http://wikileaks.org/file/bbc-trafigura.pdf or mirror.wikileaks.info/leak/bbc-trafigura.pdf, accessed 16/02/2010), page 2.
28  [2009] EWHC 1246 (QB) Case No: HQ06X03370.
29  Interview, Abidjan, September 2010.
30  [2009] EWHC 1246 (QB) Case No: HQ06X03370.
31  [2009] EWHC 1246 (QB) Case No: HQ06X03370.
32  Question asked by the author at Symposium on Business and Human Rights – University of Essex, 17 September 2010.
33  [2009] EWHC 1246 (QB) Case No: HQ06X03370.
34  Available online (YouTube) at www.youtube.com/watch?v=tQBS82kFQjE, accessed June 2012.
35  The report of the National Commission of Inquiry on the Toxic Waste in the District of Abidjan.

# Chapter 10

# Conclusion

The objective of this research was to understand the role of Ivory Coast civil society organisations in resisting, sanctioning and censuring perpetrators of state-corporate crime. These crimes, when committed on a large scale, have the potential to cause widespread social harms and violations of human rights. Corporate organisations and states are widely involved in carrying out these deviant acts in a collaborative way and often with a high degree of impunity. Welch (2009) argues that the persistence of state-corporate crime lies in its immunisation from prosecution. However, whereas few state-corporate crimes result in a criminal prosecution in the courts, Green and Ward (2004) propose that "the potential arises for civil society to impose informal sanctions (at the very least) on those agencies that are criminally responsible for so much human suffering and environmental degradation" (Green and Ward 2004: 51).

This book has documented the intersection of crimes perpetrated by three sectors of society (the state, the market and civil society) in the case of Trafigura's dumping of toxic waste in Abidjan, Ivory Coast, in August 2006. It is an exploration of the criminogenic relationship between the state and corporations, and the state and civil society. The evidence presented demonstrates that the role of the Ivorian state was instrumental in the dumping crime, the impunity afforded Trafigura and the subsequent 'criminalisation'[1] of a section of civil society. One of the most striking findings of the research for this book is that a criminal state can act as a nexus for crimes by all three sectors of society by facilitating crime by actors in both the market (state-corporate) and third (civil society) spheres of society.

Research undertaken in London and Abidjan revealed the impunity that was enjoyed by the Ivory Coast government (and its agencies) and Trafigura for this state-corporate crime. This impunity was underpinned by the power of the corporation and by failures of both domestic and international legal regimes as well as civil society organisations that might have been expected to have labelled and challenged the crimes.

This book set out to investigate the reasons for the apparent impunity afforded to Trafigura years after the dumping of toxic waste in Abidjan in August 2006. At the time UN Special Rapporteur on Toxic Waste, Okechukwu Ibeanu took the commonly held view that civil society was well placed to assist the Ivorian state with the consequence of the dumping: "I would like to call on the Government to include civil society and victim associations in the follow-up of this crisis" (Ibeanu 2008). To some extent this corresponds with Green and Ward's (2004) approach, namely, that civil society can play a significant role in applying censure and sanction to state-corporate crime. However, my research found that the same victims' organisations that Ibeanu was calling upon were in fact entrenched organised criminal actors facilitated by a criminal state. These victims' organisations were engaged in a process described in this book as 'commodifying victimhood' – specifically, charging victims of the dumping a fee in return for a promise of participation in some notional future legal compensation claim. In so doing these civil society organisations contributed in significant measure to the mechanisms of impunity which surrounded Trafigura's crime and to the victims' suffering.

This research originally aimed to survey human rights NGOs in Ivory Coast to determine the factors that may inform their reaction to large-scale corporate crime. The data gathered during fieldwork in Ivory Coast revealed that these organisations were severely limited by both internal and external factors by the disproportionate power of the corporate entity and by organisational crime perpetrated by groups masquerading as members of civil society. In addition, the economic and political environment in which the NGOs found themselves, a lack of intuitional funding, no access to skilled personnel and a criminal state precluded domestic NGOs from carrying out potential sanctions. A further surprising feature was the isolationist stance of the domestic NGOs. In addition Ivorian NGOs do not have a record of collectively resisting objectionable government[2] policies. However, and perhaps most significantly, mainstream Ivory Coast NGOs deliberately chose not to engage with the struggle of victims of the dumping to avoid an association with the government-backed victims' organisations who were taking advantage of the general impunity afforded to Trafigura and the Ivorian state.

Responsibility for impunity, however, did not rest with the Ivory Coast state alone nor with its apathetic and criminally organised sector of domestic civil society. It is also argued in this monograph that one of the primary reasons for a lack of censure by civil society of Trafigura in the UK was a fear of the corporation's legal and financial might (in the context of the UK's libel laws). As British political commentator George Monbiot noted, "The law of defamation . . . discourages people from investigating abuses of power" (Monbiot 2009). The Gramscian conception of 'struggle' was a common theme and was employed by various actors when referring to the battle for censure that raged in the UK in the face of a cover-up, which one commentator dubbed "the great Battle of Trafigura" (Massie 2009). But it was not simply Trafigura's financial and legal prowess that inhibited actions against the corporation. There were, at least perceptually, more sinister factors in play. When I proposed the idea of a private criminal prosecution in the UK against Trafigura for its role in the dumping, a senior executive at a well-known, influential international NGO replied, "I've dealt with that company. If you do that, I will look out for you floating in the Thames on my walk to work." It is therefore likely that Trafigura's aggressive reputation has had a cooling effect on academics and other commentators similar to that observed in relation to the UK press.

In the years that followed the dumping, limited academic literature has focused on the crime. Scientific articles of particular interest include Bohand et al.'s (2007) empirical study of the medical evidence, which argues – rather uncontroversially – that the export of industrial waste may result in public health consequences. Goode's (2010) presentation at the British Criminology Conference – titled "Is My Cousin a Mass Murderer?" – sought to gauge the reaction of family members of a Trafigura executive to the news that he was involved in the deaths of Ivoirians. The paper provides a useful insight into these types of crime on the individual level of analysis. White's (2008) *Toxic Cities: Globalizing the Problem of Waste* sought to raise the profile of the dumping but does not provide any detailed analysis of the factors contributing to the Ivorian disaster.

Legal academics have published on the super-injunction in the UK and the breach of environmental law that occurred in the Netherlands, using the dumping as a practical example. Matthiesson's media law analysis argues that super-injunction gagging orders are "unwieldy, draconian and disproportionate" (Matthiesson 2010: 153). Carney (2010) too examines the super-injunction, but his research is primarily a public law examination of parliamentary privilege. Legal critiques of the international waste control regime, and the Basel convention in particular, have been written by Eze (2008), Cox (2010) and Pratt (2010). And Sachs (2008) examines the limited possibilities for a tort remedy to crimes similar to the dumping. Dutch court cases concerning Trafigura's breach of environmental law at the Amsterdam port have received some attention from Verschuuren (2010) and Jesse and Verschuuren (2011). More ambitious is Manirabona's (2011) article (in French), which argues that these types of environmental crimes may be better conceptualised as international crime (and specifically crimes against humanity). Although immensely valuable, none of this literature focuses on the specific incidence of the dumping as crime.

Outside academia, two popular books have also been written. The first, published in French by Dussol and Nithart (2010), recalls the voyage of the *Probo Koala* and circumstances surrounding the dumping and is written in a distinctly journalistic manner. The book reads like a thriller novel and provides little academic analysis. The second, a Dutch-language publication by Vink (2011), proposed, contrary to the available evidence presented in this book, the theory that the dumping was not harmful, did not cause any deaths and any reported symptoms were psychosomatic.

Two other major publications by NGOs worth making reference to include Amnesty International & Greenpeace's (2012) report, *The Toxic Truth*:

> A three-year investigation by Amnesty International and Greenpeace has uncovered the central reason for the tragedy that unfolded in Abidjan: in the absence of effective law enforcement, one company acted to secure corporate profit without regard for the human and environmental costs. That company was Trafigura.
>
> (Amnesty International and Greenpeace 2012: 3)

To this list must be added the Paris-based association of NGOs, FIDH,[3] published report in April 2011 which outlines how this crime was dealt with by the domestic and international justice systems.

This book provides a criminological case study that can be added to a growing library of corporate crime and state-corporate crime scholarship. It contributes to the empirical literature on state and state-corporate crime and modestly develops our understanding of the means by which powerful entities are able to avoid censure and punishment.

One criticism which might be levelled at an approach focusing on sanctions and censure, rather than on the failure of a control regime (Kramer et al. 2002), is that it is primarily backward looking and does not seek to prevent crime. However, the impunity effectively granted to Trafigura through its cover-up campaign has permitted the corporation to walk away from its victims. There was no requirement for Trafigura to clean up the dump sites, provide health care for the victims or compensate the victims or families of the dead. Furthermore, the impunity from prosecution ensured that the corporation's criminal behaviour persisted. Trafigura's behaviour highlights both the effect of its continued impunity as well as the potential of civil society organisations to resist corporate power. After leaving Abidjan in August 2006, the *Probo Koala* sailed to Estonia. The ship was boarded by environmental officials upon arrival at Paldiski, and it passed inspection. On 25 September, Greenpeace activists blockaded the ship with an icebreaker and rubber rafts and issued demands to the Estonian authorities to immobilise the *Probo Koala*. The following day the *Probo Koala* unloaded waste that was found to contain the same substances that had been dumped in Ivory Coast the previous month (Helsingin Sanomat 2006). There were also preliminary reports of high levels of toxins found in blood samples taken from crew members (New Europe 2006), up to sixty times the normal level according to Dimas (Helsingin Sanomat 2006). The police impounded the ship and a criminal investigation was initiated. This incident is indicative of the systemic recidivist nature of the Trafigura corporation. A month after dumping in Ivory Coast with injurious effects, the corporation again attempted to deviantly offload toxic waste – concealing the true nature of the waste from an unsuspecting port authority. Estonia's minister of the environment (Villu

Reiljan) reported that he was "convinced that the ship tried to take advantage of the lack of experience of the new EU member state, and to leave its bilge and waste water, which contained toxic substances, in Paldiski" (Helsingin Sanomat 2006). EU Commissioner for the Environment Stavros Dimas visited the 'toxic crime scene' to give his "full support to the efforts of the Estonian authorities in their quest to prosecute the criminals who perpetrated this crime" (Dimas 2006). Dimas responded to Greenpeace's actions with this: "let me extend my thanks to Greenpeace which took a decisive step by preventing the departure of the Probo Koala" adding that this kind of activity "is exactly the kind of role we expect from civil society" (Dimas 2006).

But the findings presented here suggest that scholars of state crime should adopt a more cautionary approach to civil society's capacity to label, censure and sanction than that suggested by Green and Ward (2004). Moreover, in the case of this particular example of state-corporate crime, civil society as an agency of censure and sanction played a distinctly retrogressive role. Here, in fact, state crime facilitated organised crime's insertion into civil society through a process I have defined as 'the commodification of victimhood'. This ensured that impunity was virtually guaranteed for corporation and government. The implications of the findings of this book suggest new directions of research for criminology and in particular a more penetrating study of the concept of civil society.

I am not proposing that civil society should be abandoned as a mechanism for the sanction of corporate and state criminality, rather I argue for a more nuanced and more critical approach to civil society actors. As Grugel has argued: "NGOs are not 'perfect' organizations always on the side of poor or marginal groups; nor are they always effective instruments of change" (Grugel 2000: 103). Civil society organisations – whether in Ivory Coast, other African nations or elsewhere – can be an important challenge to the power wielded by large, powerful and potentially dangerous corporations (as well as the states they negotiate with). This will be especially true in the case of state-corporate crime, if as Day claims, "governments have, in the end, little power when it comes to the operations of multinationals primarily in the developing world" (Day 2010).

Further to the difficulties with relying on civil society, this book also revealed the problematic nature of applying sanctions to powerful corporations by way of the criminal and civil justice systems.

Despite the efforts of INGOs, the CPS refused to prosecute (Ball and Davies 2015), and Dutch and French authorities have had similar reservations. And whereas law firms akin to Leigh Day & Co may currently be one of the only ways to hold corporate criminals to account using law, they risk be branded as 'ambulance chasers'. Professional standards for lawyers usually outline prohibitions on the unsavoury practise of arriving at 'sites of disaster' to recruit clients. In the £105m *Motto* costs case, the judge stated that "Greenpeace International ...

asked Leigh Day to provide legal assistance to victims".[4] A senior Greenpeace Netherlands lawyer disputes this:

> No. Martyn Day issued a press release at some point in which he stated that he'd been asked by Greenpeace International to represent victims in this case. I had him correct this. I did discover a colleague had suggested to Martyn to look into the matter. But that's not the same.[5]

The benefits to the victims of a class action in the UK, sorely lacking in the Trafigura case, needs to be weighed against problems of insufficient due diligence on the part of the legal team and the requirements of legal ethics.

The situation in Ivory Coast today is a direct result of the impunity which Trafigura continues to enjoy. In November 2015 the Ivory Coast government announced that,after more than nine years, "all locations affected by the dumping of toxic waste have been cleaned" (quoted in Iob 2015). We still await verification of this claim.

Victims' organisations continue to register victims while charging membership fees, and according to RENADVIDET, about one-third of the 100,000 victims from the 2007 'settlement' and the majority of claimants in the 2009 *Motto* case have yet to receive any compensation (Iob 2015).

This book has attempted to shed some light onto the unfit nature of the world's multifarious legal systems when it comes to controlling corporate crime. In the UK particularly, the CPS needs to be held to account for its neglect in the Trafigura case. Despite the introduction of Defamation Act 2013, UK libel law is still in urgent need of review. The reformed defamation law changed criteria for a successful claim by requiring claimants to show actual (or probable) serious harm, which for a corporation is restricted to serious financial loss. I would suggest a further reform: reverse the burden of proof back to the plaintiff in defamation cases.

When seeking to help the victims of corporate crime, law firms seeking to engage civil justice systems must take a much more serious approach to due diligence in to avoid a hijacking of civil society by proliferating the commodification of victimhood.

Trafigura would like to continue enjoying its impunity and has stated:

> given over the last decade the Probo Koala incident has already been exhaustively investigated by authorities in the Ivory Coast, the UK and the Netherlands and settlements have been reached in a number of jurisdictions, it is time to move on.
>
> (Ball and Davies 2015)

I have no doubt the victims and the families of those killed will take a different view. The Trafigura case raises many issues, but the most pressing may be the sobering fact that corporate criminal impunity appears to be systematically imbued in the current form of global capitalist society.

## Notes

1 Here the term 'criminalisation' is not used in the traditional sense of describing the processes by which behaviours and individuals are transformed into crime and criminals through the application of labels but rather the process by which organised state crime insinuated itself in a realm of civil society and engaged in practises of theft and extortion behind a human rights veneer.
2 Interview, Abidjan, September 2010 (Club UA 2010).
3 See www.fidh.org/Cote-d-Ivoire-In-view-of-the-intensification-of, accessed November 2011.
4 Motto & Ors v Trafigura Ltd & Anor (Rev 3) [2011] EWCA Civ 1150 (12 October 2011), available at www.bailii.org/ew/cases/EWCA/Civ/2011/1150.html.
5 Personal email correspondence with the author.

# Victim card (issued by **FAVIDET**)

Front (redacted by Author):

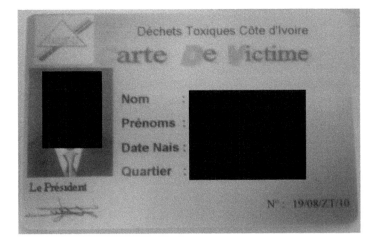

Reverse:

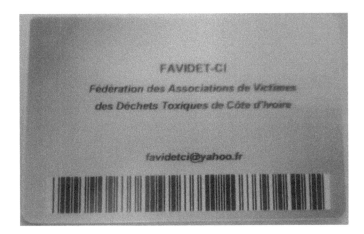

# Bibliography

Abdel-Salam, O. H. (1970) 'The Evolution of African Monetary Institutions', *The Journal of Modern African Studies*, 8(3), 339–362.

Adamoli, S., et al. (1998) *Organised Crime Around the World*, Publication Series No. 31, Helsinki: European Institute for Crime Prevention and Control.

Adamson, W. L. (1987) 'Gramsci and the Politics of Civil Society', *Praxis International*, 7(3–4), 320–339.

Adejunmobi, M. (2009) 'Urgent Tasks for African Scholars in the Humanities', *Transition, This Issue: Looking Ahead*, 80–93.

African Elections Database (2010) 'Elections in Côte d'Ivoire', *Africanelections.tripod.com* <http://africanelections.tripod.com/ci.html> (accessed July 2012).

Agence France-Presse (AFP) (2006) 'Corruption, Apathy Led to Ivory Coast Toxic Waste Scandal', 24 November 2006 <http://reliefweb.int/report/c%C3%B4te-divoire/corruption-apathy-led-ivory-coast-toxic-waste-scandal-report> (accessed November 2015).

Aka, J. C. (2010) 'Recevant les victimes des déchets toxiques, hier/Alassane Ouattara (candidat du Rhdp): "C'est le Dg du Port d'Abidjan qui a autorisé l'entrée du Probo Koala, il devrait être arrêté"', *Le Nouveau Réveil*, 25 Novembre 2010 <www.lenouveaureveil.com/a.asp?n=381068&p=2680> (accessed August 2010).

Alexander, A. S. (1963) 'The Ivory Coast Constitution: An Accelerator, Not a Brake', *The Journal of Modern African Studies*, 3, 293–311.

Allan, G. (2003) 'A Critique of Using Grounded Theory as a Research Method', *The Electronic Journal of Business Research Methods*, 2(1), 1–10.

Alvesalo, A. and Whyte, D. (2007) 'Eyes Wide Shut: The Police Investigation of Safety Crimes', *Crime, Law and Social Change*, 48, 57–72.

Ammann, D. (2009) *The King of Oil: The Secret Lives of Marc Rich*, New York: St. Martin's Press.

Amnesty International (1992) 'Document – Cote d'Ivoire: Silencing the Opposition – 77 Prisoners of Conscience Convicted', AFR 31/008/1992, 1 July 1992 <www.amnesty.org/en/library/asset/AFR31/008/1992/en/3a9e32c9-ed9c-11dd-9ad7-350fb2522bdb/afr310081992en.html>

Amnesty International (2004) 'Cote D'Ivoire: Fear for Safety/Death Threats', AFR 31/006/2004.

Amnesty International (2008) 'Blood at the Crossroads: Making the Case for a Global Arms Trade Treaty', ACT 30/015/2008.

Amnesty International and Greenpeace (2012) 'The Toxic Truth' <www.amnestyusa.org/sites/default/files/afr310022012eng.pdf>

Amoore, L. and Langley, P. (2004) 'Ambiguities of Global Civil Society', *Review of International Studies*, 30, 89–110.

Andersen, D. G. (1996) 'Bringing Civil Society to an Uncivilised Place: Citizenship Regimes in Russia's Artic Frontier', in Hann, C. and Dunn, E. (eds.), *Civil Society: Challenging Western Models*, London: Routledge.

Anheier, H. K. and Carlson, L. (undated) 'How to Measure Civil Society' <http://fathom.lse.ac.uk/features/122552/> (accessed November 2011).

Anheier, H. K. and Katz, H. (2004) 'Network Approaches to Global Civil Society', in Kaldor, M., et al. (eds.), *Global Civil Society*, London: Centre for the Study of Global Governance.

APA (2010) 'Compensation Begins for Victims of Toxic Waste in Cote d'Ivoire', 28 March 2010 <www.apaphoto.net/apa.php?page=print&id_article=121005>

Appelbaum, R. P. and Robinson, W. I. (eds.) (2004) *Critical Globalization Studies*, New York: Routledge.

Arnett, E. J. (1935) 'Economic Conditions in French West Africa', *Journal of the Royal African Society*, 34(137), 434–445.

Assi, Y. R. (2010) 'Enquête express/Recensement des victimes de déchets toxiques: Les arnaqueurs ont sévi', 1 Septembre 2010 <www.225business.com/news/44485/enquete-express-recensement-des-victimes-de-dechets-toxiques-les-arnaqueurs-ont-sevi> (accessed August 2010).

Associated Press (2008) Two guilty in Ivory Ocast toxic waste dumping, 23 Octovebr <http://www.nbcnews.com/id/27342632/ns/world_news-africa/t/two-guilty-ivory-coast-toxic-waste-dumping/> (accessed Novemebr 2017).

Aulette, J. R. and Michalowski, R. (1993) 'Fire in Hamlet: A Case Study of State-Corporate Crime', in Tunnell, K. D. (ed.), *Political Crime in Contemporary America: A Critical Approach*, London: Garland Publishing Incorporated.

Austin, G. (1987) 'The Emergence of Capitalist Relations in South Asante Cocoa-Farming', *The Journal of African History*, 28(2), 259–279.

Azam, J. (2001) 'The Redistributive State and Conflicts in Africa', *Journal of Peace Research*, 38(4), 429–444.

Azam, J. and Mesnard, A. (2003) 'Civil War and the Social Contract', *Public Choice*, 115(3/4), 455–475.

Babbie, E. (1998) *The Practice of Social Research*, London: Wadsworth.

Baker, G. (2002) 'Problems in the Theorisation of Global Civil Society', *Political Studies*, 50(5), 928–943.

Baker, J. (1977) 'Oil and African Development', *The Journal of Modern African Studies*, 15(2), 175–212.

Bakke, S. and Knudssøn, K. (2010) 'Historisk Vest Tank-dom', Norwegian Broadcasting Corporation, 26 March 2010 <www.nrk.no/nyheter/distrikt/hordaland/1.7057730> (accessed November 2011).

Balford, H. (2006) 'Trafigura Probe', *Jamaica Observer*, 19 November 2006 <www.jamaicaobserver.com/news/115508_Trafigura-probe#ixzz1G0dW6UJ> (accessed 28 May 2010).

Bantekas, I. and Nash, S. (2007) International Criminal Law. London: Cavendish Publishing.

Ball, J. and Davies, H. (2015) 'UK Authorities 'Lack Resources' to Investigate Trafigura Over Toxic Waste', *The Guardian*, 23 July 2015 <www.theguardian.com/world/2015/jul/23/ukauthoritieslackresourcestoinvestigatetrafiguraovertoxicwaste> (accessed 10 October 2015).

Balnaves, M. (2001) *Introduction to Quantitative Research Methods*, London: Sage.

Barnett, H. C. (1981) 'Corporate Capitalism, Corporate Crime', *Crime and Delinquency*, 27, 4–23.

Bartlett, B. R. (1990) 'Capitalism in Africa: A Survey', *The Journal of Developing Areas*, 24(3), 327–350.

Bassett, T. J. (1988a) 'The Development of Cotton in Northern Ivory Coast', *The Journal of African History*, 29(2), 267–284.

Bassett, T. J. (1988b) 'Development Theory and Reality: The World Bank in Northern Ivory Coast', *Review of African Political Economy*, 41, 45–59.

Bassett, T. J. (2005) 'Card-Carrying Hunters, Rural Poverty, and Wildlife Decline in Northern Côte d'Ivoire', *The Geographical Journal*, 171(1), 24–35.

BBC (2009a) 'Trafigura Statement Newsnight Enquiries', 16 September 2009 <http://news. bbc.co.uk/1/hi/programmes/newsnight/8260004.stm> (accessed 16 November 2011).

BBC (2009b) 'Ivorian Joy at Trafigura Ruling', 6 November 2009 <http://news.bbc. co.uk/1/hi/world/africa/8347513.stm> (accessed 16 February 2011).

BBC (2009c) 'Dirty Tricks and Toxic Waste in Ivory Coast: Censored Newsnight Story', 9 December 2009 <www.scribd.com/doc/24179873/Censored-Newsnight-Story-PDF> (accessed 16 February 2011).

BBC (2009d) 'Censored BBC Story Parts 1 and 2', *YouTube*, 15 December 2009 <www. youtube.com/watch?v=50PUNdaXjeg> and <www.youtube.com/watch?v=uIxAJ lppIZc>

BBC (2009e) 'BBC Trafigura Part1', *YouTube* user 1bigstink07 <www.youtube.com/watch ?v=ocwLgilzmV8&feature=player_embedded>

BBC (2011) 'Journalist's Twitter Posts Spark Prosecution Call', 22 May 2011 <www.bbc. co.uk/news/uk-13489775>

Bebbington, A. (2004) 'NGOs and Uneven Development: Geographies of Development Intervention', *Progress in Human Geography*, 28(6), 725–745.

Becker, H. S. (1963) *Outsiders: Studies in the Sociology of Deviance*, New York: Free Press.

Beckman, B. (1993) 'The Liberation of Civil Society: Neo-Liberal Ideology and Political Theory', *Review of African Political Economy*, 20(58), 20–33.

Bekker, K. (2004) 'Interest and Pressure Groups as Means for Citizen Participation', in Bekker, K. (ed.), *Citizen Participation in Local Government*, Pretoria: van Schaik.

Bellamy, R. (ed.) (1994) *Gramsci: Pre-Prison Writings*, Cambridge: University Press.

Berg, B. (2001) *Qualitative Research Methods for the Social Sciences* (4th edn), Needham Heights: Allyn & Bacon.

Berry, C. and Gabay, C. (2009) 'Transnational Political Action and "Global Civil Society" in Practice: The Case of Oxfam', *Global Networks*, 9(3), 339–358.

Bierwirth, C. (1997) 'The Initial Establishment of the Lebanese Community in Côte d'Ivoire', *The International Journal of African Historical Studies*, 30(2), 325–348.

Bienen, H. and van de Walle, N. (1991) *Of Time and Power: Leadership Duration in the Modern World*, Stanford: Stanford University Press.

Blair, H. (1997) 'Donors, Democratisation and Civil Society: Relating Theory to Practice', in Hulme, D. and Edwards, M. (eds.), *Too Close for Comfort? NGOs, States and Donors*, London: Macmillan.

Blas, J. and Sakoui, A. (2010) 'Publicity-Shy Trafigura Unveils Profit of Almost $1bn Last Year', *Financial Times*, 21 April 2010 <www.ft.com/cms/s/0/952d0358-4cdc-11df-9977-00144feab49a.html#axzz1fgGRtZ7u>

Blum, W. (2002) *Rogue State: A Guide to the World's Only Superpower*, London: Zed Books <http://arcticbeacon.com/books/William_Blum-Rogue_State(2002).pdf>

Blunt, E. (2001) 'Ivory Coast to Fight Child Trafficking', 14 June 2001 <http://news.bbc. co.uk/1/hi/world/africa/1389185.stm>

Bobbio, N. (1988), 'Gramsci and the Concept of Civil Society', in Keane, J. (ed) Civil Society and the State, New European Perspectives, London, New York: Verso.

Bogan, J. (2009) 'With Easy Oil Gone, Pemex Sobers Up', Forbes, 5 July 2009 <www.forbes.com/2009/05/07/pemex-petrobras-mexico-business-energy-oil.html>

Bohand, X. et al. (2007) 'Déchets Toxiques Déversés A Abidjan (Côte-d'Ivoire) et Conséquences Sanitaires', Médecine Tropicale, 67, 620.

Böhler (2009) 'Complaint Concerning Failure to Prosecute for an Offence', Greenpeace <www.greenpeaceweb.org/trafigura/trafigura_complaint.pdf> (accessed February 2011) (English translation of complaint in Dutch language).

Böhler (2010) 'Complaint Lodged by Greenpeace Nederland Concerning Failure to Prosecute for an Offence Under Article 12 of the Dutch Code of Criminal Procedure Made to the Court in the Hague by Franken Koppe Wijngaarden Lawyers (now Böhler)'.

Boone, C. (1993) 'Commerce in Cote D'Ivoire: Ivoirianisation Without Ivoirian Traders', The Journal of Modern African Studies, 31(1), 67–92.

Box, S. (1987) Recession, Crime and Punishment. London: The Macmillan Press.

Braithwaite, J. (1988) 'White-Collar Crime, Competition and Capitalism: Comment on Coleman', American Journal of Sociology, (94), 627–631.

Brewerton, P. M. and Millward, L. J. (2001) Organizational Research Methods, London: Sage.

Brown, J. (2009) 'Open Letter of Widney Brown', Amnesty International, AFR 31/003/2009 <www.leighday.co.uk/LeighDay/media/LeighDay/documents/Open-Letter-to-Ivory-Coast-Minister-of-Justice.pdf?ext=.pdf>

Brown, J. and Waters, I. (1993) 'Professional Police Research', Policing, 9.

Brydon, L. (2001) 'Slavery & Labour in West Africa', Review of African Political Economy, 28(87), 137–140.

Bryman, A. (1988) Quality and Quantity in Social Research, London: Routledge.

Bryman, A. (1989) Research Methods and Organization Studies, London: Routledge.

Bryman, A. (2001) Social Research Methods (2nd edn), Oxford: Oxford University Press.

Burgess, R. (ed.) (1982) Field Research: A Source Book and Field Manual, London: Allen & Unwin.

Busfield, S. (2010) From Trafigura to John Terry: Is the age of the superinjunction over?, The Guardian, 29 January, <https://www.theguardian.com/media/greenslade/2010/jan/29/superinjunction-john-terry-trafigura> (accessed November 2017).

Business and Human Rights Resource Centre 'Case Profile: Trafigura Lawsuits (re Côte d'Ivoire)' <http://businesshumanrights.org/Categories/Lawlawsuits/Lawsuitsregulatoryaction/LawsuitsSelectedcases/TrafiguralawsuitsreCtedIvoire>

Buttigieg, J. A. (1995) 'Gramsci on Civil Society', boundary 2, 22(3), 1–32 <www.jstor.org/stable/303721> (accessed May 2012).

Buttigieg, J. A. (2005) 'The Contemporary Discourse on Civil Society: A Gramscian Critique', boundary 2, 32(1).

Buttigieg, J. A. (2006) 'The Impoverishment of Civil Society', boundary 2, 33(3).

Camard, W. (2011) 'Resilient Côte d'Ivoire Gets $615 Million IMF Loan to Back Recovery', International Monetary Fund Survey Magazine <www.imf.org/external/pubs/ft/survey/so/2011/car110411a.htm> (accessed November 2015).

Cameron, R. G. and Stone, A. B. (1995) Serving the Public: A Guide for Practitioners and Students, Pretoria: van Schaik.

Campbell, B. (1974) 'Social Change and Class Formation in a French West African State', Canadian Journal of African Studies, 8(2), 285–306.

Campbell, B. (1975) 'Neocolonialism, Economic Dependence and Political Change: A Case Study of Cotton and Textile Production in the Ivory Coast 1960 to 1970', *Review of African Political Economy*, (2), 36–53.

Caney, S. and Jones, P. (eds.) (2001) *Brown in Human Rights and Global Diversity*, Illford, Essex: Frank Cass.

Cannon, C. (1996) 'NGOs and the State: A Case Study From Uganda', *Development in Practice*, 6(3), 262–269.

Carney, G. (2010) 'Another Judicial Skirmish With Parliamentary Privilege: Trafigura's Super Injunction Against the Guardian Newspaper', *Public Law Review*, 21(1), 5–9.

Carola, H. (2005) 'Big Oil Groups Implicated in Oil-for-Food Scandal', *Financial Times*, 28 October 2005 <www.ft.com/cms/s/0/1f250dd4-47de-11da-a949-00000e2511c8.html#axzz1G1ftOgOp> (accessed 8 March 2011).

Caruso-Cabrera, M. (2011) 'Mexican Oil Chief Expects 2011 Production Increase', *CNBC*, 20 January 2011 <www.cnbc.com/id/41181692/Mexican_Oil_Chief_Expects_2011_Production_Increase> (accessed 21 February 2011).

Chambers, S. (2002) 'A Critical Theory of Civil Society', in Chambers, S. and Kymlicka, W. (eds.), *Alternative Conceptions of Civil Society*, Woodstock: Princeton University Press.

Chambliss, W. J. (1989) 'State-Organized Crime', *American Society of Criminology, Criminology*, 27, 183–208.

Chandhoke, N. (2005) 'What the Hell Is "Civil Society?"', *Open Democracy*, 17 March <https://www.opendemocracy.net/democracy-open_politics/article_2375.jsp> (accessed November 2017)

Chanthavong, S. (2002) 'Chocolate and Slavery: Child Labor in Cote d'Ivoire', TED Case Studies Number 664 <www.american.edu/TED/chocolate-slave.htm> (accessed April 2011).

Chappell, D. A. (1989) 'The Nation as Frontier: Ethnicity and Clientelism in Ivorian History', *The International Journal of African Historical Studies*, 22(4), 671–696.

Cheikna, S. (2011a) 'Indemnisation des victimes des déchets toxiques: ake n'gbo se saisit du dossier', 13 February 2011 <www.fratmat.info/component/content/article/37-societe/7173-indemnisation-des-victimes-des-dechets-toxiques-ake-ngbo-se-saisit-du-dossier> (accessed August 2011).

Cheikna, S. (2011b) 'Manifestation des victimes des déchets toxiques – Les victimes reclament leur dédommagement avant l'élection présidentielle, Publié', 11 February 2011 <www.agendadesannonces.com/printarticle.php?id=27> (accessed August 2011).

Cheikna, S. (2011c) 'Victimes des déchets toxiques: Sit-in au Ministere de la Justice le 28 Juillet', 11 July 2011 <www.fratmat.info/component/content/article/37-societe/9098-victimes-des-dechets-toxiques-sit-in-devant-le-ministere-de-la-justice-le-28-juillet> (accessed August 2011).

The Chemical Engineer (TCE) Today (2009) <www.tcetoday.com>

Chenorkian, R. (1983) 'Ivory Coast Prehistory: recent developments', *African Archaeological Review*, 1(1), 127–142.

Clapham, C. (1970) 'The Context of African Political Thought', *The Journal of Modern African Studies*, 8(1), 1–13.

Clark, W. (2007) 'Philanthropic Imperialism: The National Endowment for Democracy', *International Endowment for Democracy*, 29 June.

Clarke, A. (1999) *Evaluation Research: An Introduction to Principles, Methods and Practice* London: SAGE.

Clinard, M. B. (1983) Corporate Ethics and Crime: The Role of Middle Management, Beverly Hills: Sage Publications.

Clinton, W. J. (2001) 'My Reasons for the Pardons', *New York Times*, 18 February 2001 <www.nytimes.com/2001/02/18/opinion/my-reasons-for-the-pardons.html?pagewanted=4&src=pm> (accessed March 2011).

Conklin, J. E. (1977) *"Illegal But Not Criminal": Business Crime in America*, London: Pearson Education.

Clozel, F. J. (1902) 'Land Tenure Among the Natives of the Ivory Coast', *Journal of the Royal African Society*, 1(4), 399–415.

Coffee, J. C. (1980) 'A non-Chicago view of the economics of criminal sanctions', *American Criminal Law Review*, 17(4), 419–476.

Cohen, S. (1993) 'Human Rights and Crimes of the State: The Culture of Denial', *Australian & New Zealand Journal of Criminology*, 26(9), 97–115.

Cohen, S. (2003) States of Denial. Cambridge: Polity.

Colás, A. (2002) *International Civil Society: Social Movements in World Politics*, Cambridge: Polity Press.

Colás, A. (2005) 'Global Civil Society: Analytical Category or Normative Concept?', in Baker, G. and Chandler, D. (eds.), *Global Civil Society: Contested Futures*, New York: Routledge.

Coleman, J. W. (1988) 'Competition and the Structure of Industrial Society: Reply to Braithwaite', *American Journal of Sociology*, (94), 632–636.

Colin, J. and Ayouz, M. (2006) 'The Development of a Land Market? Insights From Côte d'Ivoire', *Land Economics*, 82(3), 404–423.

Comaroff, J. L. and Comaroff, J. (eds.) (1999) *Civil Society and the Critical Imagination in Africa: Critical Perspectives*, Chicago: University of Chicago Press.

Commission of the European Communities (2001) *Towards a European Strategy to Prevent Organized Crime*, Brussels: European Commission and Europol.

Companies House (2010) <http://wck2.companieshouse.gov.uk/> (accessed 27 May 2010).

Coulibaly, L. (2008) 'Two Jailed for Ivory Coast Toxic Dumping', *Reuters*, 23 October 2008 <www.reuters.com/article/2008/10/23/us-ivorycoast-toxic-idUSTRE49M31D20081023> (accessed 4 March 2011).

Cox, R. (1993) Structural issues of global governance: implications for Europe. In S. Gill (ed.),

Gramsci, historical materialism, and international relations. Cambridge: Cambridge University Press.

Cox, G. (2010) 'The Trafigura Case and the System of Prior Informed Consent Under the Basel Convention – a Broken System?', *Law, Environment and Development Journal*, 6(3), 263–283.

Croall, H. (1989) 'Who is the White-Collar Criminal?', British Society of Criminology, 29(2), 157–174.

Crook, R. (1990) 'Politics, the Cocoa Crisis, and Administration in Cote d'Ivoire', *The Journal of Modern African Studies*, 28(4), 649–669 <www.jstor.org/stable/160925> (accessed 26 January 2011).

Curaçao Commercial Register (2011) 'Excerpt From the Commercial Register' (number 61251) <www.curacaochamber.an/info/registry/excerpt.asp?mode=edit&companyid=61175&establishmentnr=0&legalformid=51> (accessed 5 March 2011).

Davids, I. (2005) 'The Strategic Role of Development NGOs', in Davids, I., Theron, F. and Maphunye, K. J. (eds.), *Participatory Development in South Africa: A Development Management Perspective*, Pretoria: van Schaik.

Davis, A. (2008) 'Vitol Lays Out Role in Oil Market: Dutch-Swiss Firm Explains Hedge Fund and Tanker Trades to CFTC', *Wall Street Journal*, 24 December 2008 <http://online.wsj.com/article/SB123007073568831225.html?mod=todays_us_money_and_investing> (accessed 28 May 2010).

Day, M. (2009) *People and Power-Dumping Ground*, Interview, Aljazeera, broadcasted on 20 May 2009.

Day, M. (2010) 'Keynote Address to Symposium on Business and Human Rights', University of Essex, 17 September 2010.

Day, R. J. F. (2005) *Gramsci Is Dead: Anarchist Currents in the Newest Social Movements*, London/Toronto: Pluto Press/Between the Lines.

De Beer, F. and Swanepoel, H. (2005) *Community Development and Beyond: Issues, Structures and Procedures*, Pretoria: van Schaik.

de Vaus, D. A. (2001) *Research Design in Social Research*, London: Sage.

de Vaus, D. A. (2002) *Surveys in Social Research* (5th edn), London: Routledge.

Decalo, S. (1992) 'Master-Tactician Houphouet-Boigny: The Process, Prospects and Constraints of Democratization in Africa', *African Affairs*, 91(362), 7–35.

DeCarlo, S., Murphy, A. D. and Ray, J. J. (eds.) (2010) 'Special Report: America's Largest Private Companies', *Forbes*, 11 March 2010 <www.forbes.com/2010/11/01/largest-private-companies-business-private-companies-10-intro.html> (accessed September 2011).

Demirovic, A. (2000) 'NGOs and Social Movements: A Study in Contrasts', *Capitalism, Nature, Socialism*, 11, 4.

Denzin, N. K. and Lincoln, Y. S. (2005) *The Sage Handbook of Qualitative Research* (3rd edn), London: Sage.

Derrick, J. (1984) 'West Africa's Worst Year of Famine', *African Affairs*, 83(332), 281–299 (accessed January 2011).

DeSombre, E. R. (2008) 'Globalization, Competition, and Convergence: Shipping and the Race to the Middle', *Global Governance*, 14, 179–198.

Dimas, S. (2006) 'Estonia: Illegal Waste Shipment: Statement by Commissioner Dimas', *Europa Press Release*, SPEECH/06/543, 28 September 2006 <http://europa.eu/rapid/press ReleasesAction.do?reference=SPEECH/06/543&format=HTML&aged=0&language=EN&guiLanguage=en>

DiPaola, A. (2011) 'Aramco Cuts Crude Prices, Iraq Buys Gasoline: Persian Gulf Oil', *Bloomberg*, 10 January 2011 <www.bloomberg.com/news/2011-01-10/aramco-cuts-crude-prices-iraq-buys-gasoline-persian-gulf-oil.html>

*Dirty Cargo* (English version) (2008) Norsk Rikskringkasting, Norway, 19 June 2008 <http://www1.nrk.no/nett-tv/klipp/584618>

Dowell, K. (2010) 'Leigh Day Makes "Staggeringly High" Costs Order of £105m for Trafigura Role', *The Lawyer*, 17 May 2010 <www.thelawyer.com/leigh-day-makes-%E2%80%98staggeringly-high%E2%80%99-costs-order-of-%C2%A3105m-for-trafigura-role/1004428.article> (accessed January 2011).

Downes, D. and Rock, P. (2003) *Understanding Deviance*, Oxford: OUP.

Drumbl, M. A. (2003–2004) 'Toward a Criminology of International Crime', *Ohio State Journal on Dispute Resolution*, 19, 263.

Du Toit, D. and Van der Waldt, G. (1998) *Public Management – the Grassroots*, Kenwyn: Juta.

Duckett, A. (2009) 'Trafigura's Pemex Cadereyta Refinery Coker Gasoline Waste Story Breaks', *Petroleumworld.com*, 14 October 2009 <www.petroleumworld.com/story09101419.htm>

Due, J. M. (1969) 'Agricultural Development in the Ivory Coast and Ghana', *The Journal of Modern African Studies*, 7(4), 637–660.

Dumett, R. E. (1973) 'John Sarbah, the Elder, and African Mercantile Entrepreneurship in the Gold Coast in the Late Nineteenth Century', *The Journal of African History*, 14(4), 653–679.

Dunt, I. (2009) 'Feature: Laying Waste in the Ivory Coast. How the British Arm of an Oil Multinational Found Itself Embroiled in Accusations of Dumping Toxic Waste in the Ivory Coast', *Politics.co.uk*, 17 September 2009.

Duruigbo, E. (2001) 'Multinational Corporations and Compliance With International Regulations Relating to the Petroleum Industry', *Annual Survey of International and Comparative Law*, 7(1), Article 8.

Dussol, B. and Nithart, C. (2010) *Le cargo de la honte: l'effroyable odyssée du Probo Koala*, Paris: Stock.

Easterly, W. (2005) 'What Did Structural Adjustment Adjust? The Association of Policies and Growth With Repeated IMF and World Bank Adjustment Loans', *Journal of Development Economics*, 76(1), 1–22.

Eaton, G. (2009) 'Trafigura Story Disappears From BBC Website', *New Statesman*, The Staggers: The New Statesman Rolling Blog, 15 December 2009 <www.newstatesman.com/blogs/the-staggers/2009/12/newsnight-investigation-bbc>

Edwards, M. (2006) *Civil Society*, Cambridge: Polity Press.

Edwards, M. and Foley, M. W. (2001) 'Civil Society and Social Capital: A Primer in Bob Edwards', in Foley, M. W. and Diani, M. (eds.), *Beyond Tocqueville: Civil Society and the Social Capital Debate in Comparative Perspective*, New Hampshire: University press of New England (Tufts University).

Ellenbogen, M. (2004) 'Can the Tariff Act Combat Endemic Child Labor Abuses – the Case of Cote d'Ivoire?', *Texas Law Review*, 82(5), 1315–1348.

Erikson, K. T. (1962) 'Notes on the Sociology of Deviance', *Social Problems*, Spring 1962, 307–14 (Paper read at the 55th annual meetings of the American Sociological Association, New York <www.soc.umn.edu/~uggen/Erikson_SP_63.pdf> (accessed May 2012).

Ermann, D. M. and Lundman R. J. (1978) 'Deviant Acts by Complex Organizations: Deviance and Social Control at the Organizational Level of Analysis', *The Sociological Quarterly*, 19(1), 55–67.

Espeut, P. (2010) 'Samfie Politics and Bounce Back', *Jamaica Gleaner*, 21 May 2010 <www.jamaica-gleaner.com/gleaner/20100521/cleisure/cleisure3.html> (accessed 28 May 2010).

Eze, C. (2008) 'The Probo Koala Incident in Abijan Cote D'Ivoire: A Critique of the Basel Convention Compliance Mechanism', *Eighth International Conference on Environmental Compliance and Enforcement*, 351–361, Geneva: United Nations Environment Programme.

Fage, J. D. (1980) 'Slaves and Society in Western Africa', *The Journal of African History*, 21(3), 289–310.

Falk, R. (2000) *Predatory Globalisation*, Cambridge: Polity.

Farchy, J. and Blas, J. (2013) 'Trafigura adds Lord Strathclyde to Board', *Financial Times*, 14 April 2013 <www.ft.com/cms/s/0/20d123d2-a51b-11e2-8777-00144feabdc0.html#axzz2ZPfg1jyq>

Farge, E., Tan, F. and Hasan, S. (2012) 'Trafigura Shifts Trading Centre to Singapore', *Reuters*, 23 May 2012 <www.reuters.com/article/2012/05/23/trafigura-trading-move-idUSL5E8GN56P20120523>

Ferguson, A. (1782) *An Essay on the History of Civil Society* (5th edn), London: T. Cadell <http://oll.libertyfund.org/index.php?option=com_staticxt&staticfile=show.php%3Ftitle=1428&Itemid=27>

Ferguson, J. (1998) 'Transnational Topographies of Power: Beyond "the State" and "Civil Society"', in Ferguson, J. (ed.), *Global Shadows: Africa in the Neoliberal World Order*, Durham: Duke University Press.

Fielding, J. and Gilbert, N. (2000) *Understanding Social Statistics*, London: Sage.

Fischer, S. (1991) 'Growth, Macroeconomics, and Development', *NBER Macroeconomics Annual*, 6, 329–364.

Foley, M. W. and Edwards, B. (1996) 'The Paradox of Civil Society', *Journal of Democracy*, 7(3), 38–52.

Fontana, B. (1993) *Hegemony & Power: On the Relation Between Gramsci and Machiavelli*, Minneapolis: University of Minnesota Press.

Fontana, B. (2006) Liberty and Domination: Civil Society in Gramsci, boundary 2, 33(2), 51–74.

Forgacs, D. (ed.) (2000) *The Antonio Gramsci reader: Selected Writings 1916–1935*, Lawrence and Wishart: London.

*Fortune 500*, Issue date: 3 May 2010 <http://money.cnn.com/magazines/fortune/fortune500/2010/full_list/>

Francese, J. (2009) 'Introduction "Gramsci Now"', in Francese, J. (ed.), *Perspective on Gramsci: Politics, Culture and Social Theory*, Oxon: Routledge.

Frank, A. G. (1991) 'No Escape From the Laws of World Economics', *Review of African Political Economy*, 50, 21–32.

Fraser, P. (2010) 'Second Interim Report of the Probo Koala Inquiry' <www.trafigura.com/PDF/Probo%20Koala%20Inquiry,%20Rt.Hon.%20The%20Lord%20Fraser%20of%20Carmyllie%20PC%20QC%20March%202010.pdf> (accessed October 2010).

Friedrichs, D. O. and Schwartz, M. D. (eds.) (2007) 'Introduction: On Social Harm and a Twenty-First Century Criminology', *Crime, Law and Social Change*, 48(1–2), 1–7.

Garrity, M. (1972) 'The 1969 Franc Devaluation and the Ivory Coast Economy', *The Journal of Modern African Studies*, 10(4), 627–633.

Gayama, P. (1993) 'Africa's Marginalisation: A Perception, Not a Process', in Adedeji, A. (ed.), *Africa Within the World: Beyond Dispossession and Dependence*, London: Zed Books.

Giddens, A. (1984) The constitution of society: outline of a theory of structuration. Cambridge: Polity.

Gilbert, N. (ed.) (2001) *Researching Social Life* (2nd edn), London: Sage.

Gill, J. and Johnson, P. (1997) *Research Methods for Managers*, London: Paul Chapman.

Gleditsch, K. S. and Beardsley, K. (2004) 'Nosy Neighbors: Third-Party Actors in Central American Conflicts', *The Journal of Conflict Resolution*, 48(3), 379–402.

Global Witness (2007) *Hot Chocolate: How Cocoa Fuelled the Conflict in Cote D'Ivoire*, Washington, DC: Author.

Golding, O. B. (2007) 'Statement by the Prime Minister: Investigations by Dutch Authorities Into Payments by Trafigura Beheer', 13 November 2007 <www.japarliament.gov.jm/attachments/028_statement-trafigura.pdf> (accessed 8 March 2011).

Gomm, R., Hammersley, M. and Foster, P. (2000) *Case Study Method: Key Issues, Key Texts*, London: Sage.

Gonto, E. D. (2010) Ivory Coast: The smoking rooms of Abidjan (pp22-28) in Fair Grants Investigations 2009–2010, Forum for African Investigative Reporters, Johannesburg, South Africa <avaiable at https://fairreporters.files.wordpress.com/2011/07/fair-small-grant-brochure-09-10-eng-proof-6.pdf> (accessed November 2017).

Goode, S.D. (2010) 'Is my Cousin a Mass Murderer?' The Case of the Oil-Trading Company Trafigura and Relatives' Perceptions of a 'Crime of the Powerful', in Papers from the British Criminology Conference, 10, 36–54.

Grabosky, P. N. (1989) *Wayward Governance: Illegality and Its Control in the Public Sector*, Canberra: Australian Institute of Criminology.

Gramsci, A. (1971) *Selections From the Prison Notebooks*, London: Lawrence and Wishart.

Gramsci, A. (1973) *Letters From Prison*, New York: Harper and Row.

Green, P. and Ward, T. (2000) 'State Crime, Human Rights, and the Limits of Criminology', *Social Justice*, 27(1), 101–115.

Green, P. and Ward, T. (2004) *State Crime: Governments, Violence and Corruption*, London: Pluto Press.

Green, P. and Ward, T. (2012) 'State Crime: A Dialectical View', in Maguire, M., Morgan, R. and Reiner, R. (eds.), *The Oxford Handbook of Criminology*, Oxford: OUP.

Greenpeace International (2006) *Toxic Waste in Abidjan: Greenpeace Evaluation*, Amsterdam: Author.

Greenpeace International (2010) 'Trafigura', 18 January 2010 <www.greenpeace.org/international/en/campaigns/toxics/trafigura/>

Greenpeace International (2011) 'Trafigura nouvelles accusations de corruption' <http://oceans.greenpeace.fr/trafigura-nouvelles-accusations-de-corruption?> (accessed 1 March 2011).

Greenstein, R. (2003) 'State, Civil Society and the Reconfiguration of Power in Post-Apartheid South Africa', Centre for Civil Society, *Research Report 8*, University of the Witwatersrand.

Griffiths, T. (2011) 'The War Is Over – But Ouattara's Struggle Has Barely Begun: Ivory Coast's New President New Faces Country Half Destroyed by Civil War and an Economy Starved of Investment', *The Guardian*, 11 April 2011 <www.guardian.co.uk/commentisfree/2011/apr/11/ivory-coast-gbagbo-ouattara-economic-crisis?intcmp=239> (accessed October 2011).

Gross, E. (1978) 'Organizations as Criminal Actors', in Wilson, P. R. and Braithwaite, J. (eds.), *Two Faces of Deviance: Crimes of the Powerless and Powerful*, Brisbane: University of Queensland Press.

Grugel, J. (2000) 'Romancing Civil Society: European NGOs in Latin America', *Journal of Interamerican Studies and World Affairs*, 42(2), 87–107.

Guardian, The (2006) 'From Traders to Tankers: Who Makes a Mint Out of $70-Barrel Oil', 29 April 2006 <www.guardian.co.uk/world/2006/apr/29/oil.business> (accessed 29 May 2010).

Guardian, The (2010) 'Corrections and Clarifications', 16 May 2010 <www.guardian.co.uk/theguardian/2010/may/06/corrections-clarifications> (accessed November 2011).

Guido Fawkes 2009. 'Guardian Gagged from Reporting Parliament', Guido Fawkes (blog), 12 October 2009, available at [http://order-order.com/2009/10/12/guardian-gagged-from-reporting-parliament/], accessed January 2013.

Hagan, F. E. (1997) *Research Methods in Criminal Justice and Criminology*, Boston: Allyn & Bacon.

Hakim, C. (1992) *Secondary Analysis in Social Research*, London: Allen & Unwin.

Hanretta, S. (2008) 'To Never Shed Blood: Yacouba Sylla, Felix Houphouet-Boigny and Islamic Modernization in Cote D'Ivoire', *Journal of African History*, 49, 281–304.

Hansard (2009) Parliamentary business, Publications and Records, Commons Debates, Daily Hansard, 13 October<https://publications.parliament.uk/pa/cm200809/cmhansrd/cm091013/debtext/91013-0004.htm> accessed November 2011.

Haraguchi, T. (1994) 'Structural Adjustment and Agriculture in Cote d'Ivoire', Institute of Developing Economies, Africa Research Series No. 6, 79–94 <www.ide.go.jp/English/Publish/Download/Ars/pdf/06_03.pdf> (accessed March 2012).

Harbeson, J. W., Chazan, N. and Rothchild, D. (eds.) (1994) *Civil Society and the State in Africa*, London: Lynne Rienner Publishers.

Harding, C. (2007) *Criminal Enterprise: Individuals, Organisations and Criminal Responsibility*, Cullompton: Willan.

Hargreaves, J. D. (1960) 'Towards a History of the Partition of Africa', *The Journal of African History*, 1(1), 97–109.

Harjono, M. (2009) 'Greenpeace Demands Further Prosecution of Trafigura Director Following Probo Koala Lethal Waste Dump', Greenpeace, 17 September 2009 <www.greenpeace.nl/press/releases/greenpeace-wil-verdere-vervolg/> or <www.endseurope.com/docs/90917a.doc> (accessed October 2011).

Harsch, E. (1993) 'Accumulators and Democrats: Challenging State Corruption in Africa', *The Journal of Modern African Studies*, 31(1), 31–48.

Harvey, P. (1998) 'Rehabilitation in Complex Political Emergencies: Is Rebuilding Civil Society the Answer?', *Disasters*, 22(3), 200–217.

Hearna, J. (2001) 'The "Uses and Abuses" of Civil Society in Africa', *Review of African Political Economy*, 28(87), 43–53.

Hecht, R. (1983) 'The Ivory Coast Economic "Miracle": What Benefits for Peasant Farmers?', *The Journal of Modern African Studies*, 21(1), 25–53.

Hegel, G. W. F. (2001) *Philosophy of Right*, originally published in 1821, translated by Dyde, S. W. (1896), Ontario: Batoche Books.

Heinricha, V. F. (2005) 'Studying Civil Society Across the World: Exploring the Thorny Issues of Conceptualization and Measurement', *Journal of Civil Society*, 1(3), 211–228.

Helsingin Sanomat (2006) 'EU Commissioner Dimas Denounces Actions of Tanker Probo Koala', 9 September 2006 <www.hs.fi/english/article/EU+Commissioner+Dimas+denounces+actions+of+tanker+Probo+Koala/1135221966774> (accessed 5 March 2011).

Henry, S. (2006) 'Crime', in McGlaughlin, E. and Muncie, J. (eds.), *The Sage Dictionary of Criminology* (2nd edn), London: Sage.

Hess, P. (2004) 'Iraqi Paper Publishes List of Oil Bribes', *United Press International*, 29 January 2004 <www.upi.com/Business_News/Security-Industry/2004/01/29/Iraqi-paper-publishes-list-of-oil-bribes/UPI-56141075412387/> (accessed 1 March 2011).

Hesse-Biber, S. and Leavy, P. (eds.) (2004) *Approaches to Qualitative Research: A Reader on Theory and Practice*, Oxford: OUP.

Hillyard, P., Pantazis, C., Tombs, S. and Gordon, D. (eds.) (2004) *Beyond Criminology: Taking Harm Seriously*, London: Pluto Press.

Hillyard, P. and Tombs, S. (2007) 'From Crime to Social Harm?', *Crime, Law and Social Change*, 48, 9–25.

Hirshleifer, J., Glazer, A. and Hirshleifer, D. (2005) *Price theory and applications: decisions, markets, and information*. Cambridge: Cambridge University Press.

Hodd, M. (1987) 'Africa, the IMF and the World Bank', *African Affairs*, 86(344), 331–342 <www.jstor.org/stable/722746> (accessed 27 January 2011).

Hollingsworth, M. (2009) 'The McCann Files', *Evening Standard Magazine*, 28 August 2009 <www.mccannfiles.com/id275.html> (Note: This article has already been removed from the online version of ES magazine and replaced by the message: 'Content has been suppressed for editorial and/or legal reasons').

Holloway, R. (1999) 'Freeing the Citizen's Sector From Global Paradigms: And Trying to Get a Grip on the Moral High Ground', paper presented at *NGOs in a Global Future Conference*, 10–13 January, University of Birmingham and in Eade Reader <www.develop

mentinpractice.org/sites/developmentinpractice.org/files/Development,NGOs%20 and%20Civil%20Society.pdf>

Home Office (1995) *Young People and Crime*, Research Study 145, London: Her Majesty's Stationery Office.

Honohan, P. (1993) 'Financial Sector Failures in Western Africa', *The Journal of Modern African Studies*, 31(1), 49–65 <www.jstor.org/stable/161343> (accessed 26 January 2011).

Hooper, D. (2003) 'Comment: The Carter-Ruck Chill', *The Guardian*, 23 December 2003 <www.guardian.co.uk/media/2003/dec/23/pressandpublishing.comment> (accessed May 2010).

Howell, J., et al. (2006) 'The Backlash Against Civil Society in the Wake of the Long War on Terror', *Civil Society Working Paper Series*, 26, Centre for Civil Society, London School of Economics and Political Science, London, UK.

Howell, J. and Pearce, J. (2002) *Civil Society and Development: A Critical Exploration*, London: Lynne Rienner Publishers.

Huizinga, J. H. (1959) 'Unique Experiment in French Black Africa', *African Affairs*, 58(230), 25–33.

Hulme, D. and Edwards, M. (1992) 'Scaling Up NGO Impact on Development: Learning From Experience', *Development in Practice*, 2(2), 77–91.

Hulme, D. and Edwards, M. (eds.) (1997) *NGOs, States and Donors: Too Close for Comfort?* Basingstoke: Macmillan.

Hulshof Commission (2006) 'Confidential Report of Findings of the Investigation of Events Surrounding the Arrival, Stay and Departure of the Probo Koala in July 2006 in Amsterdam' <www.amsterdam.nl/publish/pages/21670/rapportcommissiehulshof.pdf> (accessed March 2011, Dutch language).

Human Rights Watch (2005) 'Country on a Precipice: The Precarious State of Human Rights and Civilian Protection in Côte d'Ivoire', 17(6)A <www.hrw.org/sites/default/files/reports/cdi0505.pdf> (accessed August 2011).

Human Rights Watch (2008) '"The Best School", Student Violence, Impunity, and the Crisis in Côte d'Ivoire' <www.hrw.org/sites/default/files/reports/cdi0508_1.pdf> (accessed August 2011).

Hydro Carbons Technology 'Cadereyta Refinery Reconfiguration, Mexico' <www.hydro carbons-technology.com/projects/cadereyta/> (accessed 26 February 2011).

Ibeanu, O. (2008) 'Retranscription du point de presse hebdomadaire de l'ONUCI', *Radio France Internationale*, 8 août 2008.

Ibeanu, O. (2009) 'Report of the Special Rapporteur on the Adverse Effects of the Movement and Dumping of Toxic and Dangerous Products and Wastes on the Enjoyment of Human Rights: Mission to Côte d'Ivoire (4 to 8 August 2008) and the Netherlands (26 to 28 November 2008)', A/HRC/12/26/Add.2, United Nations High Commission for Refugees, Human Rights Council <http://www2.ohchr.org/english/bodies/hrcouncil/docs/12session/A-HRC-12-26-Add2.pdf> (accessed January 2011).

IBP USA (2013) *Cote D'ivoire Labor Laws and Regulations Handbook: Strategic Information and Basic Laws*, Washington, DC: USA International Business Publications.

ILRF (2002) *The World Bank and IMF Policies in Côte d'Ivoire: Impact on Child Labor in the Cocoa Industry*, Washington, DC: International Labor Rights Fund.

IMF (1995) 'IMF Approves Second Annual Loan for Cote d'Ivoire Under the ESAF', *International Monetary Fund*, Press Release No. 95/30, 22 May 1995 <www.imf.org/external/np/sec/pr/1995/pr9530.htm> (accessed July 2012).

IMF (1996) 'IMF Approves Third Annual ESAF Loan for Côte d'Ivoire', *International Monetary Fund*, Press Release No. 96/31, 14 June 1996 <www.imf.org/external/np/sec/pr/1996/pr9631.htm> (accessed July 2012).

IMF (1997) 'Côte d'Ivoire – Enhanced Structural Adjustment Facility Policy Framework Paper, 1998–2001', Table 1 <www.imf.org/external/np/pfp/cote/cdtab.htm> (accessed July 2012).

IMF (1999) 'African Views on Heavily Indebted Poor Countries (HIPCs), Enhanced Structural Adjustment Facility (ESAF) and Poverty Alleviation', *African Finance Ministers Press Conference*, 24 September 1999 <www.imf.org/external/np/tr/1999/tr990924.htm> (accessed July 2012).

IMF (2000) 'IMF Concludes Article IV Consultation With Côte d'Ivoire', Public Information Notice No. 00/76 <www.imf.org/external/np/sec/pn/2000/pn0076.htm> (accessed July 2012).

IMF (2009) 'Côte D'Ivoire: Enhanced Initiative for Heavily Indebted Poor Countries', *IMF Country Report No. 09/33* <www.imf.org/external/pubs/ft/scr/2009/cr0933.pdf> (accessed January 2011).

Independent (2010) 'Trafigura: no link identified between toxic dumping incident and serious injuries', 22 February 2010 <http://www.independent.co.uk/news/world/africa/trafigura-no-link-identified-between-toxic-dumping-incident-and-serious-injuries-1904830.html> (accessed January 2013).

Independent Inquiry Committee (2005) 'Oil Transactions and Illicit Payments', *Report on the Manipulation of the Oil-for-Food Programme*, Ch. 2, 9–248, 27 October 2005 <www.iic-offp.org/story27oct05.htm> (accessed March 2011).

International Crisis Group (2004) 'Cote D'Ivoire: No Peace in Sight', *Africa Report N°82*.

International Society for Human Rights (2002) 'Slavery in West Africa' <www.ishr.org/sections-groups/wac/slavery 2002.htm> (accessed 2 August 2004).

International Institute of Tropical Agriculture (2002) 'Child Labor in the Cocoa Sector of West Africa: A Synthesis of Findings in Cameroon, Cote d'Ivoire, Ghana, and Nigeria', *Sustainable Tree Crops Program* <www.iita.org> (accessed 12 May 2003).

Iob, E. (2015) 'Ivory Coast Toxic Waste Victims Still Await Payments', *Voice of America*, 12 November 2015 <www.voanews.com/content/ivory-coast-toxic-waste-victims-still-await-payments/3056111.html> (accessed 23 November 2015).

IRIN (2005) 'Cote D'Ivoire: Crime and Corruption Flourish Amid Political Crisis', <www.irinnews.org/report.aspx?reportid=53682>

IRIN (2007) 'Youth in Crisis: Coming of Age in the 21st Century', <www.irinnews.org/pdf/in-depth/Youth-in-crisis-IRIN-In-Depth.pdf>

IRIN (2008) 'Cote D'Ivoire: Toxic Waste Criminal Investigations May Indict Higher-Ups', 2 October 2008 <www.irinnews.org/report.aspx?ReportId=80710> (accessed 1 March 2011).

Ismael, T. Y. (1971) 'The People's Republic of China and Africa', *The Journal of Modern African Studies*, 9(4), 507–529.

Jaggernath, S. (1995) 'NGOs and Development in South Africa', in Reddy, P. S. (ed.), *Perspectives on Local Government Management and Development in Africa*, Westville: Ruth Wallis.

James, R. (2001) *INGOs and Indigenous Social Movements*, Oxford: INTRAC.

Jenkins, A. and Braithwaite, J. (1993) 'Profits, Pressure and Corporate Lawbreaking', *Crime, Law and Social Change*, 20, 221–232.

Jerven, M. (2010) 'The Relativity of Poverty and Income: How Reliable Are African Economic Statistics?', *African Affairs*, 109/434, 77–96.

Jesse, K. D. and Verschuuren, J. M. (2011) 'Litigating Against International Business Corporations for Their Actions Abroad: Recent Environmental Cases From the Netherlands', *Tilburg Law School Research Paper No. 12/2011, IUCN Academy of Environmental Law eJournal*, 1 <http://ssrn.com/abstract=1773165>

Jones, A. and Johnson, M. (1980) 'Slaves From the Windward Coast Adam Jones and Marion Johnson', *The Journal of African History*, 21(1), 17–34.

Jones, M. and MacKean, L. (2009) 'Dirty Tricks and Toxic Waste in Ivory Coast', BBC <www.informationclearinghouse.info/article23715.htm> (accessed 23 February 2011).

Kaldor, M. (2003) *Global Civil Society: An Answer to War*, Cambridge: Polity.

Kaldor, M., et al. (2004) *Global Civil Society*, London: Centre for the Study of Global Governance.

Kauzlarich, D. and Kramer, R. C. (1998) *Crimes of the American Nuclear State: At Home and Abroad*, Boston: Northeastern University Press.

Kauzlarich, D., Mullins, C. and Matthews, R. (2003) 'A Complicity Continuum of State Crime', *Contemporary Justice Review*, 6(3), 241–254.

Keane, J. (2003) *Global Civil Society*, Cambridge: Cambridge University Press.

Keck, M. and Sikkink, K. (1998) *Activists Beyond Borders: Advocacy Networks in International Politics*, Ithaca: Cornell University Press.

King, R. D. and Wincup, E. (eds.) (2000) *Doing Research on Crime and Justice*, Oxford: Oxford University Press.

Knauer, S., Thielke, T. and Traufetter, G. (2006) 'Toxic-Waste Ship "Probo Koala": Profits for Europe, Industrial Slop for Africa', Part 2: The "Ivorian Chernobyl", *Der Spiegel*, 18 September 2006 <www.spiegel.de/international/spiegel/0,1518,437842-2,00.html>

Konan, A. S. (2012) 'Côte d'Ivoire: le scandale des déchets toxiques emporte le ministre Adama Bictogo', *Jeune Afrique*, 22 May 2012 <www.jeuneafrique.com/Article/ARTJAWEB 20120522192455/>

Kramer, R. C. (1990) 'From White-Collar to State-Corporate Crime', *Conference Paper*, North Central Sociological Association, Louisville, 22 March 1990.

Kramer, R. C. (1992) 'The Space Shuttle Challenger Explosion: A Case Study of State-Corporate Crime', in Schlegel, K. and Weisburd, D. (eds.), *White-Collar Crime Reconsidered*, Boston: North East University Press.

Kramer, R. C. and Michalowski, R. J. (2005) War, Aggression and State Crime: A Criminological Analysis of the Invasion and Occupation of Iraq, The British Journal of Criminology, 45(4), 446–469.

Kramer, R. C., Michalowski, R. J. and Kauzlarich, D. (2002) 'The Origins and Development of the Concept and Theory of State-Corporate Crime', *Crime & Delinquency*, 48(2), 263.

Lasslett, K. (2010a) 'Crime or Social Harm? A Dialectical Perspective', *Crime, Law and Social Change*, 54(1), 1–19.

Lasslett, K. (2010b) 'Scientific Method and the Crimes of the Powerful', *Critical Criminology*, 18(3), 211–228.

Lasslett, K. (2012) 'Power, Struggle and State Crime – Researching Through Resistance', *State Crime*, 1(1).

Lasslett, K. (2014) State crime on the margins of empire: Rio Tinto, the war on Bougainville and resistance to mining. London: Pluto Press.

Lauterpacht, H. (2011) *The Development of International Law by the International Court*, Cambridge: Cambridge University press.

Lawler, N. (1997) 'The Crossing of the Gyaman to the Cross of Lorraine: Wartime Politics in West Africa', *African Affairs*, 96(382), 53–71.

Lawrence, P. G. and Nezhad, S. (2009) 'Accountability, Transparency, and Government Co-Option: A Case Study of Four NGOs', *International NGO Journal*, 4(3), 76–83 <http://www.academicjournals.org/INGOJ>

Laxer, G. and Halperin, S. (2003) *Global Civil Society and Its Limits*, London: Palgrave.

Le Vine, V. T. (1986) 'The States of Formerly French West Africa', in Duignan, P. and Jackson, R. H. (eds.), *Politics and Government in African States*, Stanford: Hoover Institute Press.

Le Vine, V. T. (1997) 'The Fall and Rise of Constitutionalism in West Africa', *The Journal of Modern African Studies*, 35(2), 181–206.

Legassick, M. (1966) 'Firearms, Horses and Samorian Army Organization 1870–1898', *The Journal of African History*, 7(1), 95–115.

Leigh, D. (2009a) 'Inside Trafigura: Accusations, Sour Deals and Friends in High Places', *The Guardian*, 16 September 2009 <www.guardian.co.uk/world/2009/sep/16/inside-trafigura-pollution-conservatives> (accessed January 2011).

Leigh, D. (2009b) 'The Trafigura Files and How to Read Them', *The Guardian*, 16 September 2009 <www.guardian.co.uk/world/2009/sep/16/trafigura-email-files-read> (accessed January 2011).

Leigh, D. (2009c) 'Revealed: Trafigura-Comissioned Report Into Dumped Toxic Waste', *The Guardian*, 17 October 2009 <www.guardian.co.uk/world/2009/oct/17/trafigura-minton-report-revealed> (accessed March 2011).

Leigh, D. (2009d) 'How UK Oil Company Trafigura Tried to Cover Up African Pollution Disaster', *The Guardian*, 16 September 2009 <www.theguardian.com/world/2009/sep/16/trafigura-oil-ivory-coast> (accessed November 2015).

Leigh, D. (2010) 'Trafigura Returns to Court in Attempt to Suppress Lawsuit Documents: Oil Trader Wants to Prevent Public and Media From Reading Allegations Made in £6m Lawsuit Brought by Consultant', *The Guardian*, 7 January 2010 <www.guardian.co.uk/world/2010/jan/07/trafigura-lawsuit-court-documents> (accessed January 2011).

Leigh, D. and Evans, R. (2007) 'Firms Accused of Bribing Saddam to Be Investigated by Fraud Office', *The Guardian*, 14 February 2007 <www.guardian.co.uk/business/2007/feb/14/iraq.oilandpetrol> (accessed October 2011).

Leigh, D. and Evans, R. (2009) 'Lord Strathclyde Severs Links With Oil Trader Trafigura After Waste Scandal', *The Guardian*, 17 September 2009.

Leigh Day & Co (2008) 'British Oil Company in Retreat Over Its Defence of Ivory Coast Toxic Waste Claims', 24 October 2008 <www.leighday.co.uk> (accessed October 2008, now deleted).

Leigh Day & Co (2009) 'Ivorian claimants' compensation hangs in the balance', 18 December <https://www.leighday.co.uk/News/2009/December-2009/Ivorian-claimants-compensation-hangs-in-the-balan> (accessed November 2017).

Leigh Day & Co (2010) 'Agreement Gives Hope to Ivorian Toxic Waste Claimants', 14 February 2010 <www.leighday.co.uk/News/2010/February-2010/Agreement-gives-hope-to-Ivorian-toxic-waste-claima> (accessed January 2011).

Lemert, E. M. (1951) *Social Pathology: Systematic Approaches to the Study of Sociopathic Behaviour*, New York: McGraw-Hill.

Lenning, E. and Brightman, S. (2009) Oil, Rape and State Crime in Nigeria, Critical Criminology, 17(1), 35–48.

Levitas, R. and Guy, W. (eds.) (1996) *Interpreting Official Statistics*, London: Routledge.

Levy, D. L. and Egan, D. (2003) 'A Neo-Gramscian Approach to Corporate Political Strategy: Conflict and Accommodation in the Climate Change Negotiations', *Journal of Management Studies*, 40(4), 803–829.

Levy, M. (2002) 'Organized Crime and Terrorism', in Maguire, M., Morgan, R. and Reiner, R. (eds.), *The Oxford Handbook of Criminology* (3rd edn), Oxford: Oxford University Press.

Levy, M. (2007) 'Organized Crime and Terrorism', in Maguire, M., Morgan, R. and Reiner, R. (eds.), *The Oxford Handbook of Criminology* (4th edn), Oxford: Oxford University Press.

Lewis, D. (2001) 'Civil Society in Non-Western Contexts: Reflections on the "Usefulness" of a Concept', *Civil Society Working Paper Series*, 13, London: Centre for Civil Society, London School of Economics and Political Science <http://eprints.lse.ac.uk/29052/1/CSWP13_web.pdf?>

Liebenberg, S. (2000) 'Non-Governmental Organisations as Agents of Development', in De Beer, F. and Swanepoel, H. (eds.), *Introduction to Development Studies* (2nd edn), Cape Town: Oxford University Press.

Linklater, A. (1998) *The Transformation of Political Community*, Cambridge: Polity.

Lombard, L. N. (2006) 'A Constant Threat: Armed Groups in West Africa', in *The Small Arms Survey 2006: Unfinished Business*, Geneva: The Small Arms Survey.

Lorch, J. (2008) 'The (Re)-Emergence of Civil Society in Areas of State Weakness: The Case of Education in Burma/Myanmar', in Skidmore, M. and Wilson, T. (eds.), *Dictatorship, Disorder and Decline in Myanmar*, Canberra: ANU E Press.

Lowe, A. V. (1975) 'The Enforcement of Marine Pollution Regulations', *San Diego Law Review*, 12, 624.

Lucas, C. (2010) 'Maiden Speech in House of Commons', 28 May 2010 <www.theywork foryou.com/debates/?id=2010-05-27a.304.3&s=speaker:24910#g369.0>

Luckham, R. (1996) 'Democratic Control Over Military Establishments', in Luckham, R. and White, G. (eds.), *Democratization in the South: The Jagged Wave*, Manchester: Manchester University Press.

MacKenzie, D. (2006) 'Toxic Waste Mystery in Ivory Coast Deepens', *New Scientist*, 15 September 2006.

MacLean, L. M. (2004a) 'Empire of the Young: The Legacies of State Agricultural Policy on Local Capitalism and Social Support Networks in Ghana and Côte d'Ivoire', *Comparative Studies in Society and History*, 46(3), 469–496.

MacLean, L. M. (2004b) 'Mediating Ethnic Conflict at the Grassroots: The Role of Local Associational Life in Shaping Political Values in Côte d'Ivoire and Ghana', *The Journal of Modern African Studies*, 42(4), 589–617.

Madison, G. B. (1998) *The Political Economy of Civil Society and Human Rights*, London: Routledge.

Maharaj, B. and Jaggernath, S. (1996) 'NGOs, Civil Society and Development: The South African Experience', in Reddy, P. S. (ed.), *Readings in Local Government Management and Development: A South African Perspective*, Kenwyn: Juta.

Makumbe, J. M. (1998) 'Is There a Civil Society in Africa?' *International Affairs*, 74(2), 305–317.

Malhotra, K. (2000) 'NGOs Without Aid: Beyond the Global Soup Kitchen', *Third World Quarterly*, 21(4), 655–668.

Malkin, E. (2007) 'Mexico: Pemex Oil Field Declining', *New York Times*, 8 February 2007.

Manchuelle, F. (1989) 'Slavery, Emancipation and Labour Migration in West Africa: The Case of the Soninke', *The Journal of African History*, 30(1), 89–106.

Manirabona, A. (2011) 'L'affaire Trafigura: vers la répression de graves atteintes environnementales en tant que crimes contre l'humanité', *Journal of International Law and Comparative Law*, (4), 535–576.

Manning, G. (2006) 'Trafigura Probe: Dutch Government Launches Investigation Into $31 Million Transaction', *Jamaica Gleaner*, 19 November 2006 <www.jamaicagleaner.com/gleaner/20061119/lead/lead1.html> (accessed October 2011).

Manzo, K. (2005) 'Modern Slavery, Global Capitalism & Deproletarianisation in West Africa', *Review of African Political Economy*, 32(106), 521–534.

Marshall, C. and Rossman, G.B. (1999) *Designing Qualitative Research* (3rd edn), London: Sage.

Martin, G. (1995) 'Continuity and Change in Franco-African Relations', *The Journal of Modern African Studies*, 33(1), 1–20 <www.jstor.org/stable/161543> (accessed 26 January 2011).

Martinez, A. and Rodriguez, C. (2009) 'Mexico May Emulate Petrobras as It Plans New Oil Laws (Update3)', *Bloomberg*, 4 September 2009 <www.bloomberg.com/apps/news?pid=newsarchive&sid=aJ1Vw5HsdTLI>

Martinussen, J. and Pedersen, P. (2003) 'Role of NGOs in Development Cooperation', in *Aid: Understanding International Development Cooperation*, Chicago: Zed Press.

Mason, J. (2002) *Qualitative Researching* (2nd edn), London: Sage.

Mason, J. (2006) 'Mixing Methods in a Qualitatively Driven Way', *Qualitative Research*, 6(1), 9–25.

Massie, A. (2009) 'British Press Banned from Reporting Parliament: Seriously', *Spectator*, 13 October 2009 <www.spectator.co.uk/alexmassie/5417651/british-press-banned-from-reporting-parliament-seriously.thtml> (accessed August 2010).

Matthews, R. A. and Kauzlarich, D. (2000) 'The Crash of ValuJet Flight 592: A Case Study in State-Corporate Crime', *Sociological Focus*, 3(3), 281–297.

Matthews, R. A. and Kauzlarich, D. (2007) 'State Crimes and State Harms: A Tale of Two Definitional Frameworks', *Crime, Law and Social Change*, 48, 43–55.

Matthiesson, S. (2010) 'Who's Afraid of the Limelight? The Trafigura and Terry Super-Injunctions, and the Subsequent Fallout', *Journal of Media Law*, 2(2), 153–167.

May, T. (2001) *Social Research: Issues, Methods and Process* (3rd edn), Buckingham: Open University Press.

May, T. and Williams, M. (eds.) (1998) *Knowing the Social World*, Buckingham: Open University Press.

M'Badiala, C. (1996) 'Côte D'Ivoire', *International Review of Education/Internationale Zeitschrift fürErziehungswissenschaft/Revue Internationale de l'Education*, 42(1/3), 41–58.

McCulloch, J. and Pickering, S. (2005) Suppressing the Financing of Terrorism: Proliferating State Crime, Eroding Censure and Extending Neo-colonialism, British Journal of Criminology, 45(6), 470–486.

McElroy, D. (2009) 'Trafigura Targets Greenpeace Over Toxic Allegations', *The Telegraph*, 19 September 2009.

McIlwaine, C. (1998). Civil society and development geography. Progress in Human Geography, 22(3), 415–424.

McMullin, J. (2009) 'Organised Criminal Groups and Conflict: The Nature and Consequences of Interdependence', *Civil Wars*, 11(1), 75–102.

Mercer, C. (2002) 'NGOs, Civil Society and Democratization: A Critical Review of the Literature', *Progress in Development Studies*, 2(1), 5–22

Michalowski, R. J. (1985) *Order, Law and Crime*, New York: Random House.

Michalowski, R. J. and Kramer, R. C. (1987) 'The Space Between the Laws: The Problem of Corporate Crime in a Transnational Context', *Social Problems*, 34–53.

The Middle East Media Research Institute (2004) 'The Beneficiaries of Saddam's Oil Vouchers: The List of 270', *Inquiry & Analysis Series Report No. 160*, 29 January 2004 <www.memri.org/report/en/0/0/0/0/0/0/1050.htm>

Milmo, C. (2009a) 'British Trading Giant Agrees to Pay Millions to Victims Maimed and Scarred by Dumping of Polluted Sludge', *The Independent*, 17 September 2009.

Milmo, C. (2009b) 'Toxic Shame: Thousands Injured in African City', *The Independent* <www.independent.co.uk/news/world/africa/toxic-shame-thousands-injured-in-african-city-1788688.html> (accessed 17 September 2011).

Milmo, C. (2010) 'Trafigura Found Guilty of Toxic Waste Offence', *Independent*, 24 July 2010. <www.independent.co.uk/news/world/europe/trafigura-found-guilty-of-toxic-waste-offence-2034313.html>

Milmo, C. and Adetunji, J. (2009) 'The Company: The Shadowy History of a Slick Oil Giant', *The Independent*, 17 September 2009.

Minton, J. (2006a) *Minton Report*, London: Minton, Treharne & Davies Ltd.

Minton, J. (2006b) 'John Minton Public Statement' <www.trafigura.com/PDF/JohnMintonPublicStatement.pdf>

Minton, J. (2009) *RE: Caustic Tank Washings*, Abidjan: Ivory Coast.

Mohan, G. (2002) 'The Disappointments of Civil Society: The Politics of NGO Intervention in Northern Ghana', *Political Geography*, 21, 125–154.

Monbiot, G. (2009) 'Trafigura's Attempts to Gag the Media Prove That Libel Laws Should Be Repealed', *The Guardian*, 17 September 2009.

Monga, C. (1995) 'Civil Society and Democratisation in Francophone Africa', *The Journal of Modern African Studies*, 33, 359–379.

Moore, M. (2009) 'Trafigura and Carter-Ruck End Attempt to Gag Press Freedom After Twitter Uprising', *The Telegraph*, 13 October 2009.

Morais, J. (2010) 'Trafigura & Carter Ruck Versus Freedom of Speech', 16 March 2010 <http://joana-morais.blogspot.com/2010/03/video-below-presents-censored-by-super.html>

Morel, E. (1902) 'The French in Western and Central Africa', *Journal of the Royal African Society*, 1(2), 192–207.

Moser, C. and Kalton, G. (1993) *Survey Methods in Social Investigation*, London: Dartmouth.

Mozgovaya, N. (2009) '"Iran Official: U.S. Fuel Sanctions Won't Harm Us" U.S. House Okays Iran Fuel Sanctions; If Senate Passes Similar Bill, U.S. Could Impose Harshest Sanctions Yet', *Haaretz*, 16 December 2009 <www.haaretz.com/news/iran-official-u-s-fuel-sanctions-won-t-harm-us-1.2006>

MSNBC (2008) 'Two Guilty in Ivory Coast Toxic Waste Dumping', 23 October 2008 <www.msnbc.msn.com/id/27342632/> (accessed 16 February 2010).

Murdie, A. (2009) 'The Impact of Human Rights NGO Activity on Human Right Practices', *International NGO Journal*, 4(10), 421–440.

Nafziger, W. E. (1990) 'Review: African Capitalism, State Power, and Economic Development', *The Journal of Modern African Studies*, 28(1), 141–150.

Naidoo, K. (2003) 'Civil Society, Governance and Globalization', *World Bank Presidential Fellows Lecture*, Washington, DC, 10 February 2003 <www.civicus.org/new/media/WorldBankSpeech.doc>

National Endowment for Democracy (2011) <www.ned.org/about> (accessed August 2011).

National Endowment for Democracy, Annual Reports (2005–2010) <www.ned.org/publications/annual-reports/2005-annual-report/africa/description-of-2005-grants/c%C3%B4te-d%E2%80%98ivoire> <www.ned.org/publications/annual-reports/2006-annual-report/africa/description-of-2006-grants/c%C3%B4te-d%E2%80%98ivoire> <www.ned.org/publications/annual-reports/2007-annual-report/africa/description-of-2007-grants/c%C3%B4te-d%E2%80%98ivoire> <www.ned.org/publications/annual-reports/2008-annual-report/africa/description-of-2008-grants/c%C3%B4te-divoire> <www.ned.org/publications/annual-reports/2009-annual-report/africa/description-of-2009-grants/cote-d%E2%80%99ivoire> <www.ned.org/publications/annual-reports/2010-annual-report/africa/c%C3%B4te-d%E2%80%99ivoire>

Ndegwa, S. N. (1996) *The Two Faces of Civil Society: NGOs and Politics in Africa*, West Hartford: Kumarian Press.

Neuberger, D. E. (2011) Master of the Rolls Report of the Committee on Super-Injunctions: Super-Injunctions, Anonymised Injunctions and Open Justice, 20 November <http://www.judiciary.gov.uk/Resources/JCO/Documents/Reports/super-injunction-report-2005 2011.pdf>, accessed January 2013.

Neuman, W. L. (2002) *Social Research Methods: Qualitative and Quantitative Approaches* (5th edn), Needham Heights: Allyn & Bacon.

Newman, M. and Wright, O. (2011) Caught on camera: top lobbyists boasting how they influence the PM, Independent, 6 December <http://www.independent.co.uk/news/uk/politics/caught-on-camera-top-lobbyists-boasting-how-they-influence-the-pm-6272760.html> accessed November 2017.

New Europe (2006) 'EU Environmental Commissioner Surprises With Visit to Estonia', Issue 697, 30 September 2006 <www.neurope.eu/articles/EU-Environmental-commissioner-surprises-with-visit-to-Estonia-/65435.php> (accessed 5 March 2011).

Newburn, T. (2007) *Criminology*, Devon: Willan Publishing.

Newbury, C. W. (1960) 'The Formation of the Government General of French West Africa', *The Journal of African History*, 1(1), 111–128.

Newbury, C. W. (1972) 'Credit in Early Nineteenth Century West African Trade', *The Journal of African History*, 13(1), 81–95.

Newbury, C. W. and Kanya-Forstner, A. S. (1969) 'French Policy and the Origins of the Scramble for West Africa', *The Journal of African History*, 10(2), 253–276.

Nicolas, F. and Berman, E. G. (2005) 'Part II: Armed Groups and Small Arms in ECOWAS Member States, 1998–2004', in Nicolas, F. and Berman, E. G. (eds.), *Armed and Aimless: Armed Groups, Guns, and Human Security in the ECOWAS Region*, Geneva: Small Arms Survey, 223–383.

Norberto, B. (1987) 'Gramsci and the Conception of Civil Society', in Bellamy, R. and Norberto, B. (eds.), *Which Socialism?* Translated by R. Griffin, Minneapolis: University of Minnesota Press.

Nzimakwe, T. I. (2008) 'South Africa's NGOs and the Quest for Development', *International NGO Journal*, 3(5), 90–97.

O'Connor, M. (1972) 'Guinea and the Ivory Coast-Contrasts in Economic Development', *The Journal of Modern African Studies*, 10(3), 409–426.

OECD (2011) 'OECD Tax Database' <www.oecd.org/ctp/taxdatabase>

Office of the Contractor General, Jamaica Houses of Parliament, 'Special Report of Investigation Conducted into the Oil Lifting Contracts Between the Petroleum Corporation of Jamaica and Trafigura Beheer', 14 September 2010 <www.japarliament.gov.jm/index.php?option=com_content&view=article&id=496:office-of-the-contractor-genrai-investigation-petroleum-corporation-of-jamaica-pcj-and-trafigura-beheer&catid=7:general-reports&Itemid=22> (accessed 8 March 2011).

Ogbodo, S. G. (2009) 'Environmental Protection in Nigeria: Two Decades After the Koko Incident', *Annual Survey of International & Comparative Law*, 15(1) <http://digitalcommons.law.ggu.edu/annlsurvey/vol15/iss1/2>

Ogunlesi, T. (2009) 'Nigerian Company Linked to International Toxic Waste Scandal', *Next*, 18 September 2009 <http://234next.com/csp/cms/sites/Next/Home/5460738-146/story.csp>

O'Keefe, P. (1988) 'Toxic Terrorism', *Review of African Political Economy*, 42, 84–90.

Onstad, E., MacInnis, L. and Webb, Q. (2011) 'Glencore: The "Biggest Company You've Never Heard Of" Is About to Go Public', *Huffington Post*, 25 February 2011 <www.huffingtonpost.com/2011/02/25/glencore-the-biggest-comp_n_828101.html>.

Organisation Mondiale de la Santé (2006) 'Déversement de Déchets Toxiques en Côte d'Ivoire: Note d'Information aux Médias', 15 September 2006, Genève: OMS.

Orvis, S. (2001) 'Civil Society in Africa or African Civil Society?', *Journal of Asian and African Studies*, 36(1), 17–38.

Packenham, T. (2003) *The Scramble for Africa: White Man's Conquest of the Dark Continent From 1876 to 1912*, New York: Perennial.

Paris Club (2011) 'List of the Debt Treatments', *Parisclub.org* <www.clubdeparis.org/sec tions/pays/cote-d-ivoire/viewLanguage/en> (accessed July 2012).

Parker, C. (2006) 'The "Compliance" Trap: The Moral Message in Responsive Regulatory Enforcement', *Law & Society Review*, 40(3), 591–622.

Parker, C. (2007) 'Meta-Regulation: Legal Accountability for Corporate Social Responsibility', in McBarnet, D., Voiculescu, A. and Campbell, T. (eds.), *The New Corporate Accountability: Corporate Social Responsibility and the Law*, Cambridge: Cambridge University Press.

Payne, R. (1980) 'Flags of Convenience and Oil Pollution: A Threat to National Security', *Houston Journal of International Law*, 3, 67, 69.

Pearce, F. and Tombs, S. (2001) 'Crime, Corporations and the "New" World Order', in Potter, G. (ed.), *Controversies in White-Collar Crime*, Cincinnati: Anderson.

Pearce, J. (2000) 'Development, NGOs and Civil Society', in Eade, D. (ed.), *Development in Practice*, Williamsburg: Kumarian Press.

Pelczynski, A. Z. (1984) 'The Significance of Hegel's Separation of the State and Civil Society', in Pelczynski, A. Z. (ed.), *The State and Civil Society*, Cambridge: University Press.

Pemex (2011) <www.pemex.com/index.cfm?action=content&sectionID=123&catID=11682>

Petras, J. (1997) 'Imperialism and NGOs in Latin America', *Monthly Review*, 49(7), 10–27.

Petras, J. and Veltmeyer, H. (2001) 'NGOs in the Service of Imperialism', in *Globalisation Unmasked: Imperialism in the 21st Century*, London: Zed Books.

Pidd, H., et al. (2011) 'The Rise of Glencore, the Biggest Company You've Never Heard of: Special Report: £37bn Flotation to Make Commodities Company – and the "Extremely Private" People Behind It – Very Public', *The Guardian*, 19 May 2011 <www.guardian. co.uk/business/2011/may/19/rise-of-glencore-commodities-company>

Plummer, K. (2000) *Documents of Life 2: An Invitation to Critical Humanism*, London: Sage.

PMI (2007) <www.pmi.com.mx/onepage/public/pmi_english.jsp> (accessed 21 February 2011).

Port of Brownsville (2011) 'About the Port' <www.portofbrownsville.com/index.php?option= com_content&task=view&id=12&Itemid=27> (accessed 3 March 2011).

Pratt, L. (2010) 'Decreasing Dirty Dumping? A Reevaluation of Toxic Waste Colonialism and the Global Management of Transboundary Hazardous Waste', *William & Mary Environmental Law & Policy Review*, 581–623.

Punch, K. F. (1998) *Introduction to Social Research: Quantitative and Qualitative Approaches*, London: Sage.

Punch, M. (1996) *Dirty Business: Exploring Corporate Misconduct: Analyses and Cases*, London: Sage Publications.

Punch, M. (2000) 'Suite Violence: Why Managers Murder and Corporations Kill', *Crime, Law and Social Change*, 33, 243–280.

Putnam, R. D. (1993) *Making Democracy Work*, Princeton: Princeton University Press.

Putnam, R. D. (2000) *Bowling Alone: The Collapse and Revival of American Community*, New York: Simon and Schuster.

Quinney, R. (1970) *The Social Reality of Crime* (4th edn), Boston: Little, Brown.

Quinney, R. (1980) *Class, State, & Crime*, London: Longman.

Randeria, S. (2007) 'The State of Globalization: Legal Plurality, Overlapping Sovereignties and Ambiguous Alliances Between Civil Society and the Cunning State in India', *Theory Culture and Society*, 24(1), 1–33.

Rapley, J. (1995) 'Côte d'Ivoire After Houphouet-Boigny', *Review of African Political Economy*, 22(63), 119–121.

Rapport de la Commision Nationale d'Enquete sur les Dechets Toxiques dans le District d'Abidjan <www.dechetstoxiques.gouv.ci/pdf/Rapport%20D%E9chets%20Toxiques%2021 nov2006%20d%E9finitif.pdf>

Reality of Aid (2006) 'An Independent Review of Poverty Reduction and Development Assistance' <www.realityofaid.org/roa-reports/index/secid/363/An-Independent-Review-of-Poverty-Reduction-and-Development-Assistance>

Reno, W. (1997) 'African Weak States and Commercial Alliances', *African Affairs*, 96(383), 165–185.

Reporters Without Borders (2006) 'Court imposes heavy fine on three journalists for insulting president', 18th September 2006 <https://rsf.org/en/news/court-imposes-heavy-fine-three-journalists-insulting-president> (accessed November 2017)

Reuters (2010) 'Trafigura Denies Paying for Toxic Waste Testimonies', 18 May 2010 <http://af.reuters.com/article/topNews/idAFJOE64H0DT20100518>

Review of African Political Economy (2006) 'Nestle Taken to Court', *State, Class & Civil Society in Africa*, 33(107), 161–162.

Ridler, N. B. (1985) 'Comparative Advantage as a Development Model: The Ivory Coast', *The Journal of Modern African Studies*, 23(3), 407–417.

Ridler, N. B. (1993) 'Fixed Exchange Rates and Structural Adjustment Programmes: Cote D'Ivoire', *The Journal of Modern African Studies*, 31(2), 301–308 <www.jstor.org/stable/161006> (accessed 26 January 2011).

Ritchie, J. and Lewis, J. (eds.) (2003) *Qualitative Research Practice: A Guide for Social Science Students and Researchers*, London: Sage.

Robinson, K. E. (1951) 'French West Africa', *African Affairs*, 50(199), 123–132.

Robinson, M. (1995) 'Strengthening Civil Society in Africa: The Role of Foreign Political Aid', *IDS Bulletin*, 26(2), 70–80.

Robson, C. (2002) *Real World Research: A Resource for Social Scientists and Practitioner-Researchers* (2nd edn), Oxford: Blackwell.

Rodriguez, C. M. (2010) 'Mexico May Extend Oil Output Declines for 7th Year', *Bloomberg*, 8 December 2010 <www.bloomberg.com/news/2010-12-08/mexico-may-extend-oil-output-declines-for-7th-year-update1-.html> (accessed October 2011).

Rogerson, P. and Dean, J. (2009) 'News: "Super-Injunctions" Under Fire', *Law Society Gazette*, 40(2), 22 October 2009 <www.lawgazette.co.uk/news/super-injunctions-come-under-fire-senior-judge> (accessed January 2010).

Rose, D. (2006) 'Partying on State Funds' – Bruce Golding Accuses Jamaican Government of Using Oil Money to Finance Conference', *Jamaica Gleaner*, 4 October 2006.

Ross, J. I. (ed.) (1995) *Controlling State Crime: Toward an Integrated Structural Model*, New York: Garland.

Ross, J. I. (1998) 'Situating the Academic Study of Controlling State Crime', *Crime, Law and Social Change*, 29(4), 331–340.

Rowlands, B (2005) 'Grounded in Practice: Using Interpretive Research to Build Theory', *The Electronic Journal of Business Research Methodology*, 3(1), 81–92.

Rusbridger, A. (2009) 'As a Way of Handling PR It Was a Fantastic Own Goal', *The Guardian*, 13 October 2009 <http://audio.theguardian.tv/audio/kip/standalone/media/1255451 656710/6263/gdn.new.091014.pm.rusbridger.mp3> (accessed January 2010).

Sachs, N. (2008) 'Beyond the Liability Wall: Strengthening Tort Remedies in International Environmental Law', *UCLA Law Review*, 55, 837–903.

San Juan Jr, E. (2009) 'Antonio Gramsci's Theory of the 'National-Popular' as a Strategy for Socialist Revolution', in Francese, J. (ed.), *Perspective on Gramsci: Politics, Culture and Social Theory*, Oxon: Routledge.

Sands, J. (2007) 'Organized Crime and Illicit Activities in Spain: Causes and Facilitating Factors', *Mediterranean Politics*, 12(2), 211–230.

Schachter, R. (1961) 'Single-Party Systems in West Africa', *The American Political Science Review*, 55(2), 294–307.

Schak, D. C. and Hudson, W. (eds.) (2003) *Civil Society in Asia*, Burlington: Ashgate Publishing Ltd.

Schecter, D. (1991) *Gramsci and the Theory of Industrial Democracy*, Avebury: Aldershot.

Schwartz, F. J. and Pharr, S. J. (eds.) (2003) *The State of Civil Society in Japan*, New York: Cambridge University Press.

Schwendinger, H. and Schwendinger, J. (1970) 'Defenders of Order or Guardians of Human Rights', *Issues in Criminology*, 5, 123–157.

Seale, C. (1999) *The Quality of Qualitative Research*, London: Sage.

Seale, C. (ed.) (2004) *Researching Society and Culture* (2nd edn), London: Sage.

Segal, A. (1964) 'Africa Newly Divided?', *The Journal of Modern African Studies*, 2(1), 73–90.

Sellin, T. (1938) *Culture, Conflict and Crime*, New York: Social Science Research Council.

Sesan, G. (2006) 'Social Enterprise in Africa: An Emerging Concept in an Emerging Economy', *International NGO Journal*, 1(1), 4–8.

Seyni, B. (2001) 'Cote d'Ivoire: Mystery Still Shrouds Yopougon Mass Grave', *Panafrican News Agency (Dakar)*, 5 January 2001 <http://allafrica.com/stories/200101050273.html> (accessed October 2009).

Sharma, A. and Gupta, A. (eds.) (2006) *The Anthropology of the State: A Reader*, Australia: Blackwell Publishing.

Shastri, R. K. (2008) 'A Strategic Action Plan for Managing Non Government With Special Reference of India Definition of NGOs', *International NGO Journal*, 3(3), 74–76.

Shaw, M. (2002) 'Globality and Historical Sociology: State, Revolution and War Revisited', in Hodben, S. and Hobson, J. (eds.), *Historical Sociology of International Relations*, Cambridge: Cambridge University Press.

Shaw, T. M. and Grieve, M. J. (1978) 'The Political Economy of Resources: Africa's Future in the Global Environment', *The Journal of Modern African Studies*, 16(1), 1–32.

Shearing, C. and Wood, J. (2003) 'Nodal Governance, Democracy, and the New "Denizens"', *Journal of Law and Society*, 30(3), 400–419 <www.jstor.org/stable/1410537> (accessed April 2012).

Silverman, D. (1999) *Doing Qualitative Research: A Practical Handbook*, London: Sage.

Silverman, D. (2001) *Interpreting Qualitative Data*, London: Sage.

Silverman, D. (ed.) (2004) *Qualitative Research: Theory, Method and Practice* (2nd edn), London: SAGE.

Simbi, M. and Thom, G. (2000) '"Implementation by Proxy": The Next Step in Power Relationships Between Northern and Southern NGOs?', in Lewis, D. and Wallace, T. (eds.), *New Roles and Relevance: Development NGOs and the Challenge of Change*, Bloomfield: Kumarian Press.

Skurnik, W. A. E. (1967) 'France and Fragmentation in West Africa: 1945–1960', *The Journal of African History*, 8(2), 317–333 <www.jstor.org/stable/179486> (accessed January 2011).

Small Arms Survey (2006) Unfinished Business. Oxford: OUP.

Sogge, D. (1997) *Mozambique: Perspectives on Aid and the Civic Sector*, Netherlands: Gemeenschappelijk Overleg Medefinanciering.

Spiegel (2006) 'Photo Gallery: Toxic Waste for Ivory Coast' <www.spiegel.de/fotostrecke/fotostrecke-16268.html> (accessed 29 May 2010).

Stephenson, C. (2005) 'Non Governmental Organizations', in Burgess, G. and Burgess, H. (eds.), *Beyond Intractability*, Conflict Research Consortium, Boulder: University of Colorado <www.beyondintractability.org/essay/role_ngo> (accessed 19 February 2008).

Stewart, P. D. S. (1997) 'What Is Development?', in Kotze, D. A. (ed.), *Development Administration and Management: A Holistic Approach*, Pretoria: van Schaik.

Stewart, P. D. S. (1999) 'Development at the Dawn of the Twenty-First Century', in Wessels, J. S. and Pauw, J. C. (eds.), *Reflective Public Administration: Views From the South*, Cape Town: Oxford University Press.

Sutherland, E. H. (1940) White-collar Criminality, Sociological Review, 5(1), 1–12.

Sykes, G. M. (1978) *Criminology*, New York: Harcourt Brace Jovanovich.

Sykes, G. and Matza, D. (1957) Techniques of neutralization: A theory of delinquency. American Sociological Review 22(6), 664–670.

Symon, G. and Cassell, C. (eds.) (1998) *Qualitative Methods and Analysis in Organizational Research*, London: Sage.

Tan, J. (2010) 'Europe Crisis Sparks Risk Aversion: Trafigura', *Reuters*, 24 May 2010 <www.reuters.com/article/idUSTRE64N0QQ20100524>

Tandon, R. (1991) 'Civil Society, the State and Roles of NGOs', Institute for Development Research, *IDR Reports*, 8(3).

Tandon, R. and Mohanty, R. (eds.) (2003) *Does Civil Society Matter? Governance in Contemporary India*, New Delhi: Sage Publications India.

Tape, A. (2010). 'Pollution toxique à Abidjan: la mort guette les abidjanais depuis 2006. Des malades se comptent par milliers'. Amanien.info, 6 September. Available online at www.amanien.info/actualite-984-pollution-toxique-a-abidjan-la-mort-guette-les-abidjanais-depuis-2006.-des-malades-se-comptent-par-milliers.html?PHPSESSID=fa44339bf927e4e51c01886ebdf6f012 (accessed September 2013).

Taylor, C. (1990) 'Modes of Civil Society', *Public Culture*, 3, 95–118.

Temin, J. (2003) 'Considering the Role of the BBC in African Conflict', *Review of African Political Economy*, 30(98), 654–660.

Theron, F. and Wetmore, S. (2005) 'Appropriate Social Development Research: A New Paradigm to Explore', in Davids, I., Theron, F. and Maphunye, K. J. (eds.), *Participatory Development in South Africa: A Development Management Perspective*, Pretoria: van Schaik.

Tickner, V. (1977) 'International: Local Capital: The Ivory Coast Sugar Industry', *Review of African Political Economy*, (8), Capitalism in Africa, 119–121.

Tiembre, I., et al. (2009) 'Aspects e´ pide´ miologiques et cliniques de l'intoxication par les de´ chets toxiques dans le district d'Abidjan', *Cahiers Santé*, 19(4), 189–194.

Tigana, K. J. (2010) 'Association of Victims of Toxic Waste – Mrs. Hortense Guidan Lobo Takes Power', *The Mandate*, 9 February 2010.

*Times, The* 2009. 'Trafigura – Correction', 4 September 2009, available at [http://www.thetimes.co.uk/tto/environment/article2144616.ece], accessed January 2013.

*Times Live* (2011) 'Trafigura Appeal Opens', 14 November 2011, www.timeslive.co.za/scitech/2011/11/14/trafigura-appeal-opens.

*Times Online* (2010) 'Trafigura – Correction', 30 April 2010 <www.timesonline.co.uk/tol/news/world/africa/article7111946.ece> (accessed November 2011).

Todaro, M. and Smith, S. (2006) *Economic Development* (10th edn), Addison Wesley, Harlow: Pearson Education Limited.

Tombs, S. (2004) 'The "Causes" of Corporate Crime', *Criminal Justice Matters*, 55(1), 34–35.

Tombs, S. and Hillyard, P. (2004) 'Beyond Criminology', in Hillyard, P., et al. (eds.), *Beyond Criminology: Taking Harms Seriously*, London: Pluto Press.

Tombs, S. and Whyte, D. (2002) 'Unmasking the Crimes of the Powerful', *Critical Criminology*, 11, 217–236.

Tombs, S. and Whyte, D. (2003a) 'Introduction: Corporations Beyond the Law? Regulation, Risk and Corporate Crime in a Globalised Era', *Risk Management: Special Issue: Regulation, Risk and Corporate Crime in a 'Globalised' Era*, 5(2), 9–16.

Tombs, S. and Whyte, D. (eds.) (2003b) *Unmasking the Crimes of the Powerful: Scrutinizing States and Corporations*, New York: Peter Lang.

Tombs, S. and Whyte, D. (2006) 'White-Collar Crime and Corporate Crime', in McGlaughlin, E. and Muncie, J. (eds.), *The Sage Dictionary of Criminology* (2nd edn), London: SAGE.

Tombs, S. and Whyte, D. (2007) *Safety Crimes*, Devon: Willan Publishing.

Toungara, J. M. (1990) 'Houphouet-Boigny: The Apotheosis of Cote d'Ivoire's Nana Houphouet-Boigny', *The Journal of Modern African Studies*, 28(1), 23–54. <www.jstor.org/stable/160900> (accessed January 2011).

*Trafigura* (2006) 'Trafigura Tests Contradict Media Speculation', 24 September 2006 <www.trafigura.com/trafigura_news/probo_koala_updates/press_statement_24092006.aspx> (accessed November 2011).

*Trafigura* (2010) <www.trafigura.com/about_us/key_facts.aspx> (accessed 28 May 2010).

Trafigura (2013) 'Lord Thomas Strathclyde Joins the Supervisory Board of Trafigura', *trafigura.com*, 15 April 2013 <www.trafigura.com/media-centre/latestnews/new-supervisory-board-member/?lang=NL#.UegPVNLVA8M>

Trafigura London (2009) 'Trafigura Director Pierre Lorinet Is Interviewed About Recent Legal Developments in the UK', *YouTube*, 16 October 2009 <www.youtube.com/watch#!v=51kQPGAEqOM&feature=related>

Trafigura (undated) 'Claude Dauphin Obituary: A Tribute From Trafigura', *trafigura.com* <www.trafigura.com/claude-dauphin-obituary>

Trentmann, F. (ed.) (2003) *Paradoxes of Civil Society: New Perspectives on Modern German and British History* (2nd edn), Oxford: Berghahn Books.

Trommelen, J. (2007a) ' "*Rederij gifschip was handen in onschuld*" Tot drie keer toe is het lemma over het gifschip Probo Koala veranderd', *Tevergeefs*, 18 May 2007 <www.volkskrant.nl/vk/nl/2844/Archief/archief/article/detail/856701/2007/05/18/Rederij-gifschip-wast-handen-in-onschuld.dhtml> (accessed November 2011).

Trommelen, J. (2007b) 'Trafigura: OM moet rapport geheimhouden' <www.volkskrant.nl/vk/nl/2686/Binnenland/article/detail/352672/2009/08/24/Trafigura-OM-moet-rapport-geheimhouden.dhtml>

Tuathail, Ó., et al. (2006) *The Geopolitics Reader*, Routledge.

Ungar, M. (2003) 'Qualitative Contributions to Resilience Research', *Qualitative Social Work*, 2(1), 85–102.

United Nations (2006) *Côte d'Ivoire – Urban Hazard Waste Dumping*, New York: UN Disaster Assessment and Coordination.

United Nations (2010) 'Merchant Fleet by Flag of Registration and by Type of Ship, Annual, 1980–2011', *Conference on Trade and Development*, 16 December 2010.

United Nations (2011) *World Population Prospects: The 2010 Revision*, New York: UN Department of Economic and Social Affairs, Population Division <http://data.un.org/Data.aspx?d=PopDiv&f=variableID%3A47> (accessed March 2011).

United Nations Environment Programme (2006) 'Liability for Côte D'Ivoire Hazardous Waste Clean-Up', *Environment Programme News Release*, 24 November 2006 <www.unep. org/Documents.Multilingual/Default.asp?> (accessed January 2011).

United Nations Environment Programme (2009) 'International Maritime Organization, Secretariat of the Basel Convention and the Government of Côte d'Ivoire', *Evaluation Report Assessment of the Port of Abidjan*, Geneva: UNEP.

United Nations Human Rights Council (2009) 'General Assembly, Report of the Special Rapporteur on the Adverse Effects of the Movement and Dumping of Toxic and Dangerous Products and Wastes on the Enjoyment of Human Rights, Okechukwu Ibeanu, Mission to Côte d'Ivoire (4 to 8 August 2008) and the Netherlands (26 to 28 November 2008)', A/HRC/12/26/Add.2 (3 September 2008).

United Nations Office on Drugs and Crime (2005) *Transnational Organised Crime in the West African Region*, New York: Author.

United Nations Office on Drugs and Crime (2009) *Transnational Trafficking and the Rule of Law in West Africa: A Threat Assessment*, Vienna: Author <www.unodc.org/documents/nigeria// publications/Assessments-research-programmes/West_Africa_Report_2009.pdf>

United States of America, Central Intelligence Agency Factbook (2011) *Africa: Cote d'Ivoire, The World Factbook 2011*, Washington, DC: Central Intelligence Agency <www.cia.gov/ library/publications/the-world-factbook/geos/iv.html> (accessed January 2011).United States of America, Department of Justice (2001) 'Pardon Grants January 2001', 20 January 2001 <www.justice.gov/opa/pardonchartlst.htm>

United States of America, Departmnet of State (US DoS) (2008) International Narcotics Control Strategy Report, Bureau of International Narcotics and Law Enforcement Affairs, March 2008 <https://www.state.gov/j/inl/rls/nrcrpt/2008/vol2/html/100807. htm> (accessed Novemebr 2017).

United States of America, Departmnet of State (US DoS) (2001) US Bilateral Relations Fact Sheets/Background Notes, Cote d'Ivoire Background Note, Cote d'Ivoire. Washington, DC: US Departmnet of State

United States of America, Departmnet of State (US DoS) (2006) US Bilateral Relations Fact Sheets/Background Notes, Cote d'Ivoire Background Note. Washington, DC: US Departmnet of State

United States of America, Departmnet of State (US DoS) (2010) US Bilateral Relations Fact Sheets/Background Notes, Cote d'Ivoire Background Note, Cote d'Ivoire (11/01). Washington, DC: US Departmnet of State <https://2009-2017.state.gov/outofdate/ bgn/cotedivoire/25641.htm> (accessed November 2017)

United States of America, Energy Information Administration (2008) 'Gross Heat Content of Petroleum Production, All Countries, 1980–2006 for the International Energy Annual 2006', 23 October 2008 <www.eia.gov/pub/international/iealf/tablec3.xls>

Urry, J. (1981) The Anatomy of capitalist societies: The economy, civil society and the state. London: Macmillan.

Vakil, A. C. (1997) 'Confronting the Classification Problem: Toward a Taxonomy of NGOs', *World Development*, 25(12), 2057–2070.

Van Rooy, A. (1998) *Civil Society and the Aid Industry*, London: Earthscan.

Van Wingerde, K. (2015) 'The Limits of Environmental Regulation in a Globalized Economy: Lessons From the Probo Koala Case', in van Erp, J., Huisman, W. and Vande, G. (eds.), *The Routledge Handbook of White-Collar and Corporate Crime in Europe*, London: Routledge.

Verkaik, R. (2009) 'Court Freezes Trafigura Compensation Lawyers Concerned That African Ruling Could Deprive Toxic Waste Victims of £30m', *Independent*, 5 November 2009 <www.independent.co.uk/news/world/africa/court-freezes-trafigura-compensation-1814793.html> (accessed 14 February 2011).

Verschuuren, J. M. (2010) 'Overcoming the Limitations of Environmental Law in a Globalised World', *Tilburg Law School Research Paper No. 020/2010* <http://ssrn.com/abstract= 1582857>

Verschuuren, J. M. and Kuchta, S. (2011) 'The New Faces of Victimhood, Victims of Environmental Pollution in the Slipstream of Globalization', *Studies in Global Justice*, 8(2), 127–156.

Vink, J. (2011) *Het Gifschip: Verslag van een journalistiek schandaal*, Amsterdam: Uitgeverij Prometheus.

Vogt, W. P. (1998) *Dictionary of Statistics and Methodology*, London: Sage.

Voice of America (2006) 'Ivory Coast Government Panel Releases Toxic Waste Findings', 23 November 2006 <www.voanews.com/english/news/a-13-2006-11-23-voa22.html> (accessed October 2011).

Walker, C. and Whyte, D. (2005) 'Contracting Out War? Private Military Companies, Law and Regulation in the United Kingdom', *International and Comparative Law Quarterly*, 54, 651–690.

Walklate, S. (2011) *Criminology: The Basics* (2nd edn), Oxon: Routledge.

Wannenburg, G. (2005) 'Organised Crime in West Africa', *African Security Review*, 14(4) <www.iss.co.za/pubs/ASR/14No4/F1.htm> (accessed October 2011).

Ward, T. (2004) 'State Harms', in Hillyard, P. et al. (eds.), *Beyond Criminology: Taking Harm Seriously*, London: Pluto Press.

Ward, T. and Green, P. (2000) 'Legitimacy, Civil Society, and State Crime', *Social Justice*, 27(4), 76–93.

Waters, I. and Brown, K. (2000) 'Police Complaints and the Complainants' Experience', *British Journal of Criminology*, 40.

Watson, J. H. A. (1963) 'French-Speaking Africa Since Independence', *African Affairs*, 62(248), 211–222.

Welch, A. W. (1982) 'The National Archives of the Ivory Coast', *History in Africa*, 9, 377–380.

Welch, M. (2009) Fragmented power and state-corporate killings: a critique of blackwater in Iraq, Crime, Law and Social Change, 51(3–4), 351–364.

Wengraf, T. (2001) *Qualitative Research Interviewing*, London: Sage.

West, D. J. (1969) *Present Conduct and Future Delinquency*, London: Heinemann.

Whaites, A. (1998a) 'Let's Get Civil Society Straight: NGOs, the State, and Political Theory', in Eade, D. (ed.), *Development in Practice*, Williamsburg: Kumarian Press.

Whaites, A. (1998b) 'Viewpoint NGOs, Civil Society and the State: Avoiding Theoretical Extremes in Real World Issues', *Development in Practice*, 8(3), 343–349.

White, G. (1996) 'Civil Society, Democratisation and Development', in Luckham, R. and White, G. (eds.), *Democratization in the South: The Jagged Wave*, Manchester: Manchester University Press.

White, R. (2008) 'Toxic Cities: Globalizing the Problem of Waste', *Social Justice*, 35(3), 107–119.

White, R. (2008) *Crimes Against Nature: Environmental Criminology and Ecological Justice*, Devon: Willan Publishing.

Whyte, D. (2003) 'Lethal Regulation: State-Corporate Crime and the United Kingdom Government's New Mercenaries', *Journal of Law and Society*, 30(4), 575–600.

Whyte, W. F. (1955) *Street Corner Society*, Chicago: University of Chicago Press.

Wild, F. (2010) 'Ivory Coast Oil Refinery Will Shut This Month on Lower Profits', *Bloomberg*, 11 January 2010. <www.bloomberg.com/apps/news?pid=newsarchive&sid=aTyVzr GC3CVk>

Williams, R. (1985) *Keywords: A Vocabulary of Culture and Society*, New York: OUP.

Woodiwiss, M. (2001) *Organized Crime and American Power*, Toronto: University of Toronto Press.

Woods, D. (1988) 'State Action and Class Interests in the Ivory Coast', *African Studies Review*, 31(1), 93–116 <www.jstor.org/stable/524585> (accessed 26 January 2011).

Woods, D. (1999) 'The Politics of Organising the Countryside: Rural Cooperatives in Côte d'Ivoire', *The Journal of Modern African Studies*, 37(3), 489–506.

Woods, D. (2003) 'The Tragedy of the Cocoa Pod: Rent-Seeking, Land and Ethnic Conflict in Ivory Coast', *Journal of Modern African Studies*, 41(4), 641–655.

World Bank (1981a) *World Development Report*, Washington, DC: World Bank.

World Bank (1981b) 'Ivory Coast: Structural Adjustment Loan Project', Vol. 1, *President's Report*, Washington, DC: Work Bank.

World Bank (1989) 'Involving NGOs in Bank-Supported Activities', Operational Directive 14.70, Washington, DC: Author.

World Bank (1994) *World Development Report*, New York: Oxford University Press.

World Bank (1995) 'Cote d'Ivoire Private Sector Assessment', *Report No. 14112*.

World Bank (2010) 'Defining Civil Society' <http://web.worldbank.org/WBSITE/EXTER NAL/TOPICS/CSO/0,,contentMDK:20101499~menuPK:244752~pagePK:220503~piPK:220 476~theSitePK:228717,00.html>

World Health Organisation (2006) 'Chemical dump in Côte d'Ivoire', 15 September 2006 <www.who.int/mediacentre/news/notes/2006/np26/en/index.html> (accessed October 2011).

Wu, X. (2005) 'Corporate Governance and Corruption: A Cross-Country Analysis', *Governance: An International Journal of Policy, Administration, and Institutions*, 18(2), 151–170.

Yanacopulosi, H. (2005) 'The Strategies That Bind: NGO Coalitions and Their Influence', *Global Networks*, 5, 1.

Yelly, T. (2010) 'Déchets toxiques - Le procès débute le 1er juin aux Pays-Bas'. *L'expression*, 20 May <news.abidjan.net/h/364733.html> (accessed September 2013).

Yin, R. (1994) *Case Study Research: Design and Methods* (2nd edn), Beverly Hills: Sage Publishing.

Young, R. A. (1991) 'Privatisation in Africa', *Review of African Political Economy*, 51, 50–62. <www.jstor.org/stable/4006050> (accessed 23 January 2011).

Zolberg, A. R. (1966) *Creating Political Order: The Party-States of West Africa*, Chicago: Rand McNally.

Zolberg, A. R. (1967) 'Patterns of National Integration', *The Journal of Modern African Studies*, 5(4), 449–467 <www.jstor.org/stable/158752> (accessed 26 January 2011).

# Index

For Product Safety Concerns and Information please contact our EU
representative GPSR@taylorandfrancis.com
Taylor & Francis Verlag GmbH, Kaufingerstraße 24, 80331 München, Germany

www.ingramcontent.com/pod-product-compliance
Ingram Content Group UK Ltd.
Pitfield, Milton Keynes, MK11 3LW, UK
UKHW020951180425
457613UK00019B/631

* 9 7 8 0 3 6 7 4 8 2 1 0 7 *